RIVENDELL

Editor:

Sebastian Matthews

Assistant Editors:
Monica Fauble, Ryan Walsh

Additional Editorial Staff:
Jonathan Carr, Rose McLarney

Website Design:
Morgan Davis

Editorial Advisory Board:
Richard Chess, Marie Harris, A. Van Jordan, Dana Levin,
m loncar, Barry Sanders, Richard Tillinghast, Ann Turkle, Chase Twichell

Printer: Thomson-Shore Press, Dexter, MI

Cover Photograph: Charter Weeks

Rivendell Logo: Bill Matthews

Subscription Rate:
$14 (1 yr / 2 issues); $25 (2 yr / 4 issues).

Send All Queries and Correspondence to:
Rivendell
P.O. Box 9594
Asheville, NC 28815
www.greenmanwalking.com

© Rivendell Journal

ISBN 0-9718003-1-6

PS
541
PS8
2003

RIVENDELL would like to thank its Charter Members
and Friends for their generous support.

SPECIAL THANKS TO: BOB ARNOLD, DEBORAH & JIM BOGEN, DAVID BUDBILL, RICHARD CHESS, GARY CLARK, ELLEN CLIMO & MARC LIPSON, JEFF CRAMER AT THE THOREAU SOCIETY, WYN COOPER, MARIE HARRIS, LAURA HERRMANN, JIM KOLLER, WESLEY MCNAIR, JACKSON WHEELER, AND THE WARREN WILSON COLLEGE PRESS.

This issue is dedicated to the memory of:
Esther Buffler, Kenneth Koch, and Catherine Young

Rivendell

North of Boston

Editor's Note

When I talk about RIVENDELL, people often shake their heads and say, "That must be a labor of love!" I want to say, "What isn't?" But I smile and tell them how much fun we're having. It *is* hard work, but the kind that repays our efforts ten-fold.

Hands down the best part of the job has been the correspondence. I thought this might be the case going in, for I have always loved sending and receiving mail. But there's something special about the connections I've made compiling each issue. By exchanging letters with so many other writers and artists, I am deepening my own understanding of the creative process. Or maybe it's RIVENDELL's special emphasis on place. Whatever the reason, I end up feeling like I am in close touch with a region.

The writers in this issue are a particular, dare I say peculiar, bunch. Many are editors of small presses, independent bookstore owners, handset press operators, farmers, carpenters. Some don't use email, or own a computer—and are proud of it. The one thing they all do, and do well, however, is write letters. It's exciting to come upon their letters in the mailbox.

There's something thrilling in reading one of Donald Hall's type-written pages or poring slowly over Kate Barnes' calligraphic lettering. Twice, I have received brittle overseas envelopes from Cid Corman that fold out into a page of hand-written poetry. There is the elegant handwriting of Wesley McNair, small and neat on its note-sized paper, or the even smaller writing of naturalist David Carroll. I came to cherish the few letters that arrived from Ted Enslin; they were friendly but prickly, challenging me on my half-formed ideas about place while whole-heartedly supporting my endeavors.

It's just plain fun to receive packages stuffed with poems, essays, photos and ads. I never know what to expect. One envelope came bearing maps of Maine, another a cartoon illustrating a contributor's poem. On one summery weekday, a large package arrived full of original charcoal sketches drawn in the late sixties.

Email gets a bum rap, at times deservedly so. But email has been integral to putting together these first two issues. In fact, emails, phone calls, and letters have all blended together in our daily goings-on. Often I'll check my email in the morning to find one of Bob Arnold's pleasant, talky, smart emails, or news from Peter Money along with a new section of his epic poem, "The Mountain." Or I'll find one of David Budbill's generous responses to my many queries regarding his interview, each email accompanied by one of his poems at the bottom of the screen.

After my morning coffee, I drive over to RIVENDELL's box at the local post office. My dog insists on coming along, and we go out walking on the nearby trails behind the old insane asylum where Fitzgerald brought Zelda. I read the poems as I ramble. The woodpiles and crows, old diners and back roads I read about could easily have come out of the Appalachian hills. It is on these walks that I come upon the poems of Elizabeth Tibbets, John Hyland, and Jim Schley—all new voices recommended to me by other New England writers. And on these walks that old friendships are re-ignited and new ones kindled. Indeed, it's been a romantic, almost nostalgic time, bringing me back to own childhood years in New England.

When I get back to my desk, I write letters or drop a contributor an email. Later in the day, after dinner, I might receive a call from Albert Dole with questions about the review he's working on, or I may call up Walter Clark and jot down his new edits on the canoe journal. (The canoe journal—with the four-way communication between fellow editor Ryan Walsh, Sam Manhart, Walter and myself—is a prime example of this beautiful weaving together of phone calls, emails, and postal routes.)

And this network of correspondence seems fitting, too, for these writers and the world they live in. It is just in this way that writers in northern New England manage to stay in touch. Earlier this year, Hayden Carruth celebrated his eightieth birthday. A series of readings were organized in his honor, and a plethora of tributes on the internet and in journals including a wonderful anthology of poems from Bob Arnold's Longhouse archives. Talk of the birthday event must have filled up the phone lines, email, and postboxes. The news traveled at various speeds and was, no doubt, welcome wherever it arrived.

Editing this journal, I have been constantly taken aback by the generosity of the authors I come in contact with. They allow me to reprint their work. They offer donations. They connect other writers and editors and booksellers by bringing copies of RIVENDELL to readings or putting our postcards in letters to friends. And now, here is our collection of "news" from Frost's land, "North of Boston."

SEBASTIAN MATTHEWS
ASHEVILLE, NC

photo by Nick DeFriez

"I always write from behind a persona. . . .Like an actor, I'm always hiding behind someone. I feel that freedom to say what I want to say from behind and inside a character who is not necessarily or totally me. So I write from back there behind the persona."

DAVID BUDBILL

BACK THERE:
AN INTERVIEW WITH DAVID BUDBILL

David Budbill was born in Cleveland, Ohio, in 1940. He moved to rural Vermont in 1969 and has lived there with his wife and children ever since. Budbill is the author of five books of poems, eight plays, a novel, a collection of short stories, a picture book for children and dozens of essays, introductions, speeches, book reviews and the libretto for an opera. He has been an occasional commentator on National Public Radio's "All Things Considered." In September 1999, Copper Canyon Press published his latest book of poems, *Moment to Moment: Poems of a Mountain Recluse.* Garrison Keillor has read frequently from *Moment to Moment* on his National Public Radio program "The Writer's Almanac." In 1999, Chelsea Green Publishing Co. released a revised, expanded and updated version of his collected poems, *Judevine*, first published in 1989. Budbill received a National Endowment for the Arts Play Writing Fellowship in 1991, a Guggenheim Fellowship in Poetry in 1981 and The Dorothy Canfield Fisher Award for Fiction in 1978.

David and I met during the 26th session of the New England Literature Program, on the southern tip of Lake Winnepesaukee at Camp Kabeyun in New Hampshire. It was early summer, 2001, and both Budbill and I were visitors to the program. The ice had only been off the lake for a few weeks, and we'd just come from a Robert Frost class I had co-taught with Sam Manhart. Budbill had been sitting in along with the poet, and NELP's co-founder, Walter Clark. During the informal class, which met in a small grove of trees at one of the points on the lakeshore property, several students got caught up in exploring the hidden meaning of Frost's nature references; Budbill made a comment about taking Frost literally: when he points out a bird, it's really a bird.

This interview was conducted in NELP Director Jackie Livesay's cabin. Jackie prepared tea and then generously left us her space. Budbill was to give a reading that night and put on a 12-bar blues class the following day. Our conversation began with talk of *Judevine*, Budbill's book-length epic poem that is often taught at NELP.

SEBASTIAN MATTHEWS

11

SM: When did *Judevine* first come out?

DB: The big book? It came out in the fall of 1989.

SM: When did you start writing it?

DB: *The Chain Saw Dance*, which was the very first of the little chap-books that started this whole series, came out in 1977. But I started writing it almost immediately after I went to work on a Christmas tree farm and met, started working with, a man who became Antoine. And that would have been the fall of 1969.

SM: Did you start writing the poem about him during that time, or did it take awhile?

DB: It took awhile. As soon as I started working with this guy in the woods, I saw that he was a linguist himself, a poet. His creative use of English was amazing, so I started taking notes on the things he said and the way he said them. I had a pickup truck, and I had my timecard on the visor over the steering wheel and I'd write down on the back of my timecard things like, "Shit a goddamn," or "Freeze like a turd."
       By the way, the guy who sang the Antoine part in the opera last fall, [*A Fleeting Animal: An Opera from Judevine*] was a French-Canadian from Montreal. He was driving down the road one day and suddenly realized that what he thought was Antoine's complete non sequitur "Freeze like a turd" was in fact a real French Canadian idiom, which translates "freeze like a turd."
       I'd write Antoine's sayings down on the back of my timecard. Some of the images and crazy phrases Antoine comes up with I made up myself, others are really what he'd say, like "Oh, I'd rather pick bluebird shit off the White Cliffs of Dover than..." you know, do whatever the next job was we had to do. I'd write down his phrases and way of speaking. That's how it started.

SM: Was there a time when you realized, "Oh, wait a second, I'm writing not just about Antoine but have got this larger work on my hands?"

DB: When *The Chain Saw Dance* came out, in 1977, I tried to organize the poems so that they told a story of the people who lived up in the hills in Judevine; and then when *From Down to the Village* came out, in 1981, it pretty much told a story about the village people rather than the hill people; and in *Why I Came to Judevine*, 1987, I tried to make a story out of that too. As the books went along I was trying to make each little book tell a story. So that narrative impulse was always there. It's there in everything I do.

But, I did not know, absolutely did not know, until I started   putting the big book together that what I had been doing for twenty years was writing an epic poem, a poetic novel. This event, occurrence, whatever, is to me one of the great illustrations of how a writer has to obey. [Laughs.] You really have to let your instincts take over because your inner self—the muse, whatever you want to call it—has an agenda for you that you may not, probably don't, know about, but that you absolutely must follow. This is what happened with *Judevine*. I was writing a 320-page poetic novel, an epic poem, and I didn't know that, had no idea, until twenty years after I started doing it. It's not until 1989 that I realized I'd been writing this big, long poem for the past twenty years.

SM: When you gathered *Judevine* together did you write poems to fill in gaps?

DB: I didn't do that consciously with the book, but, you see, what happened was, in about 1980, halfway through the process, the play started developing too. The first staged reading of some of the Judevine poems in a professional theatre was in 1980 at McCarter Theatre in Princeton, New Jersey. Then in 1984 McCarter did a fully mounted play with a two week run called *Judevine: A Vermont Anthology*. So at this point the play starts developing, as plays do, and I realize, geez, I need to have some kind of character for this situation that has arisen, or because of something that happens on stage, an improvisation from an actor for example, I realize "Oh, man, I gotta do this!"

So the play begins developing down one track, while the book of poems is developing down another track, and they start influencing each other. I write a poem that goes in the play; something happens in the play that goes in the book of poems. After awhile, these tracks start crossing, and the play and the book begin developing together. Back and forth like that. Sometimes one is ahead of the other, but they're both going down separate tracks that cross in many places.

An actor improvises something in rehearsal and it gives me an idea and I realize "Oh, man, I can do this!" One of the great things about working with really good actors, real pros, is that they give you so much to work with: they give you ideas, new directions to go in. In some ways, they understand your characters better than you do.

I remember when I was at McCarter I'd rewrite a scene after the run had begun and come in with a new speech or something and say, "Let's do it this way tonight." The actors loved that—those particular actors did—and they'd learn the new piece and try it out that way. I had this laboratory for my stuff every night. And that kind of experimenting with the Judevine material on stage happened all over the place as the play developed in Florida, California, Boston...

SM: What was your position? Were you the writer/director?

DB: No, I was always only the writer. These were mostly Equity theaters, not entirely but mostly. That's one thing you've got to learn in working in the theater, the difference between the writer, director, actor and so forth; you've got to learn about those separate territories. You've got to get permission to step into somebody else's territory. I didn't ever try to direct. I did talk to the director about ideas, all the time I did that, but I was busy thinking about what I could do with the script, the development of the script. It was amazing to me how the play influenced the book. And that's still going on. I keep thinking I'm done, finally done with *Judevine*, and then something happens and I discover I'm not.

SM: Were you writing poems that ended up in *Moment to Moment* interspersed within those twenty years?

DB: Yeah. I can't remember clearly, but one thing that has happened to me since *Moment to Moment* came out is people ask me, "When did you start doing these poems?" and I say, "Well, in 1983." Then I discover that it was 1975, no, 1970. Then I realized that I have on my shelves D.T. Suzuki's *Essentials of Zen Buddhism*, and another one called *A Taoist Notebook* by Edward Herbert and the date I first read them is 1963 while I was living in New York City. I'm still reading both those books, by the way.

What I am saying is: I kept discovering that I was working on this material a lot longer ago than I ever thought. This is another one of those inner-life, semi-conscious life examples, like writing the big Judevine book. The bulk of the *Moment to Moment* poems probably came in the 80s and 90s. But I was reading voraciously in ancient Chinese poetry—especially ancient Chinese, some Japanese, but mostly Chinese—all the time I was writing *Judevine*.

SM: When you wrote a poem that came out of your reading of Buddhist texts, did it just go off to the side in a box or did it end up in the *Judevine* box for awhile?

DB: I think they were sorted out. That's a good question. I really can't answer it. My papers are at The University of Vermont now, and somebody might be able to discover by looking at those things chronologically what the answer to that is. But I think I was keeping them kind of separate because they seemed separate works.

SM: *Judevine* and *Moment to Moment* feel like different worlds, almost parallel worlds. One is concerned with people, with social life, town life, and the other seems more about the private life of the narrator.

DB: Yeah, they are parallel, well, they are different in some regard too. And there are hints in *Judevine* about what will come next: like there is the poem "The Buddhas of Judevine" that talks about the Buddhas of Polonaruwa and quotes the *Bhagavad Gita*. And there are allusions: Tommy Stames likes ancient Chinese poetry, and he writes in that style, and he's got his little place up in the mountains, his hermitage sort of, and so on and so forth. So there are all these little hints and indications in *Judevine* about what's coming next.

SM: In *Judevine*, did you have a conscious credo for the narrator or his place in the town? How much did you want him to become a character?

DB: Well, I don't know that it was so much conscious as just inevitable. I'm going to tell you a little story. I was giving a reading in Jamestown, New York, years ago. I was reading from *Judevine*, and afterward a woman came up and she said, "Well, you know all the other characters in *Judevine* are all really interesting, but the person I'm interested in is David. What's he like?" And I thought, "Damn! I finally did it. Someone doesn't think David's me."

Someone thought David was a character in the book, and not necessarily me. And I was delighted by that. I think David is—as all poets are to some degree—an eternal outsider. He's always hovering at the edge of the community. He wants to be part of the community but he can't be. And also one of the reasons he can't be is because he doesn't want to be. There's something in David, the narrator, that just keeps him apart. And I think it's one of the reasons David is so interested in the cripples of the world: because he knows he's a cripple too.

In a way there is some kind of inevitable inability to connect because it is hard to be a part of something and watch it too. And, as the writer, he's watching, observing. He's noting down what Alice Twiss is like, or how Alice Twiss relates to Sam Hines. The writer is perpetually the outsider.

SM: Both you and the narrator, David, come from Ohio. In *Judevine*, we see you come and start working with Antoine. Do you think that outsider position changes? In New England you are an outsider for a long time; you can live there twenty years and you're still not considered from that area. Did the role change for you and for the narrator over time?

DB: I don't know for sure whether the role changed, but my attitude toward the role changed. When I first came, as a person coming from Ohio, via New York City and rural Pennsylvania, I really wanted to be a part of the community. And David the narrator did too. Both of us wanted to be a part of that place. By the end of the book, I think David, the narrator, and David, the writer, don't care about that so much anymore. I think that's what happened to me personally. I am just not hung up on that the way I was thirty years ago. I feel comfortable here in my outsider kind of way. I like this place. It's my home.

One of the reasons for this is that when I went to work in the woods in Vermont—coming from my working class background in Cleveland—I suddenly realized that the people I was working with in the woods were just rural versions of my relatives. Hell, I was going to work every day with my lunch pail, just like all my relatives did in the 1940s in Cleveland. These Vermonters weren't going off to Picker X-Ray or Tinnerman Speednut, to the factories and steel mills in Cleveland, the way my relatives did. They were going off to the woods. But they were still working-class people, they were still uneducated, they were still amazingly like my relatives. And even though I was in a physically radically different place—this northern New

England semi-wilderness and not on the streets of Cleveland—I had re-entered the strata of society from which I had come, and that gave it an important, profound, meaning for me.

And the role of David, the narrator, also changes from the beginning to the end of *Judevine*, because by the end David, the narrator, is a sadder and wiser person. At the beginning he is naive and wide-eyed with wonder to be in this new and strange place. By the end, he's been beaten up by life, just like his characters. He's twenty years older, and therefore sadder and wiser, sobered by what life does to people.

SM: Tell me more about the role of class in your work. Are you aware of it when you write?

DB: When *Judevine*, the play, was playing out in Wisconsin a number of years ago I did an interview with one of the Milwaukee papers and the reporter said, "You write about class. American playwrights don't write about class. English playwrights do. Americans don't." I thought that was an interesting and important observation. American playwrights really don't write about class, I mean white American playwrights. There are exceptions, of course, Clifford Odets, for one. And of course black and Latino playwrights write about class all the time, but, since this is such a racist society, we expect them to, assume they will. But there are very few white playwrights who have any real and controlling class consciousness. I have that consciousness. I've always had it. And I'm proud of having it.

I come out of the working class. When my grandmother, my father's mother, was a young woman growing up in Cleveland at the end of the 19th century, she was John D. Rockefeller's washerwoman. Even when she was in her 90s I can remember her face flushing with rage when she told how Rockefeller would pass out nickels to the poor on the streets of Cleveland.

My father, who was a streetcar driver when I was a baby, said to me again and again, "Stick up for the Little Guy, Bud." My father had an   intense class consciousness and I'm glad, proud, to carry that on. I'm always aware of class when I write, which is why I so often write about invisible people, the downtrodden, the put upon and the forgotten.

Because of all of that, I've always been somewhat embarrassed about being a writer, an artist. I don't like the elite and elitist air that so often casts itself over artists and the arts. It's obvious that many people involve themselves with the arts in order to distinguish themselves from the common people out of which I come and with whom I still fiercely identify. I hate pretense. I want to be clear. I want to make art that the common people can understand, use, find moving and meaningful and enjoy.

SM: In *Judevine* there's a big poem, not too far in, titled "Why I Came to Judevine." In any sense: where do you write from?

DB: Oh, boy. That's tough. I'd say I write from my imagination, but my imagination always needs a place to live, to be. So far this has been either this imaginary place called Judevine—the place I created called Judevine, which is terribly like where I actually live, in which David lives with all these other characters—or this other Judevine-like place out of which *Moment to Moment* comes. The Judevine-like place in *Moment to Moment* is much less populated with humans, because it's about a mountain recluse who lives on Judevine Mountain, which, as a matter of fact, is in Judevine.

　　　　I always write from behind a persona. I've got lots of personas in *Judevine*. In *Moment to Moment* there's just one, the mountain recluse whose name is Judevine Mountain. Like an actor, I'm always hiding behind some-one. I feel that freedom to say what I want to say from behind and inside a character who is not necessarily or totally me. So I write from back there behind the persona. That's one answer.

　　　　In *Judevine*, I was obviously writing from a place, a physical place, a region, and that was very important. The place out of which I am writing *Moment to Moment*—and I say "am writing" because I'm still working on that series of poems, just started really—is a real place too, but it is more of a spiritual place, a place in the soul somewhere. More ephemeral, less physi-cal. Although the physical location of the person in *Moment to Moment* is quite real, quite physically specific.

SM: To me *Judevine* feels like the town and the outskirts of the town, and one person's place in that town, David's, whereas *Moment to Moment* feels like home, or home-life, and then the outskirts of the land you walk on. The recluse walks a lot up in the mountains. Does that feel like a good analogy?

DB: I think that's exactly right. *Judevine* is social; it's got people in it; it's got all kinds of relationships. That's one of the reasons it works so well as a play, because there are all these relationships building up, being destroyed, accumulating, being assembled, then in some cases disassembled, and so forth. Whereas, *Moment to Moment* is about this person's inner life revealed in his outer activities and comments and thoughts.

SM: It's more apparent in *Moment to Moment* because of what you're reading, what the recluse reads, the book has so many references to the monastic life. But, in *Judevine*, is there a tradition that you are writing out of? You as a writer. Do you feel like there is a tradition of this kind of stuff going on?

DB: I am very conscious of the tradition I am writing out of. The epigraph for *Judevine* is a quote from the "Prelude" to Chaucer's *Canterbury Tales*; and in fact in early drafts of the big *Judevine* book the last poem was called "Budbill's Retractions," just like Chaucer's retractions. Saying, you know, "Anything good here is by the grace of God. And anything bad here is all my fault." So I was very consciously trying to write my own *Canterbury Tales*. The narrative poems about people and how they relate to each other is in a long-standing literary tradition in the English language beginning with Chaucer or maybe the Gawain poet.

      With *Moment to Moment* that tradition was even more obvious, I think, the tradition of the recluse poet. This is not so much a tradition in the United States as it is in Japan and especially in China. And it's been going on since forever, 1500 B.C.E. So I am very aware of that tradition, also, and very much aware of writing out of that tradition.

SM: In *Moment to Moment*, does Han Shan have the same relationship to his Cold Mountain poems as Chaucer does with *Judevine*?

DB: Yup. Maybe not just Han Shan, but Han Shan certainly is the pivotal figure of the recluse poet. Or Han Shan is at the beginning. Once you start really studying and reading about recluses in China, ancient and modern, you realize there have been and are thousands and thousands of them.

SM: So many of the *Moment to Moment* poems are of you out walking, looking at a crow, and thinking about things. The persona responds to outside events then writes a meditative, or raucous, poem about it. Frost does that so much throughout his poems, and they're probably personas as well. Is he a guide for you or do you feel like you have to, in a sense, turn away from him and get rid of his influence?

DB: Both. Frost definitely was a guide. And when he died in 1962, I had read everything he had ever written, and had been written about him; I was devoted to him. This was while I was still living in Ohio, long before I ever came to Vermont. I think coming to Vermont requires of writers a kind of divorce from Frost, if you're going to be yourself. I have a poem called "Killing the Ghost of Ripton" about getting rid of this guy, getting him out of my life. Hayden Carruth has the same kind of poem, a haiku. It goes:

> I live where Frost lived.
> So? It's a free country. Don't
> jump to conclusions.

        Everybody who moves to Vermont, poets I mean, have to come to some kind of break with Frost. At least this used to be true; I don't think it's so true anymore. The world has moved on. Frost's influence is on the wane. But he was definitely a big influence on me at one time.

SM: What are one or two of your favorites, still?

DB: Of Frost's? "A Servant to Servants." I love that poem. "Directive." Those are the two that pop into my mind. It's those dark, longer narrative poems, like "The Black Cottage," that really stick in my mind.

SM: Have you ever tried to write your own "Directive"? It's the kind of poem that seems to beg you to try to write a version of it.

DB: Yeah, well, as I may have mentioned, I finished a little novel this past winter called *Broken Wing*. I've been working on it, off and on, for eight years. There's a kind of a prologue in poetry where you go up into the mountains to see this recluse who is the narrator of the story. The story ends with a bunch of twists and turns in the "plot," questions about what's real and what isn't. A friend who read it said, "You took all this directly from 'Directive.'" I was totally unconscious of doing that, but she was right. That poem is way down inside me somewhere. As it turned out, I cut out the last thirty pages of the story so all that "Directive" stuff at the end is gone. The story still begins the way it did originally, begins with the "Back out of all this now too much for us" motif.

SM: What's the novel about?

DB: *Broken Wing* is about a bird with a broken wing who has to stay in the north country for the winter because it can't fly, can't migrate, and about a man called The Man Who Lives Alone in the Mountains and the relationship that develops between the two of them and how involved the man gets in the bird's struggle for survival. The book is really a meditation on birds and life and death and handicap and music. It's pretty plot-less, and it's short. It's just one of those things. I love writing about birds. I always have. I don't know why.

SM: There are a lot of crows in *Moment to Moment*.

DB: Right, mostly ravens actually. There are a lot of ravens around where I live. They are incredibly intelligent, communicative birds. They never cease to amaze me with what they do. I see them every day. We talk to each other.

SM: Let me switch directions. I want to ask you about jazz. There is not a lot of mention of jazz in *Judevine*, or maybe none. There's a little mention of it in *Moment to Moment*, I think. But you work with jazz bassist William Parker—as a duet, in collaboration, sometimes in a quintet. How did that start? And where did your love for jazz come from? When did it first start to bleed into your writing?

DB: Well, I fell in love with jazz when I was about 12 years old in junior high school. I was 12 in 1952, and, for reasons I can't explain, when all my friends were listening to Elvis Presley, I was listening to Zoot Sims and Chet Baker and the other West Coast Cool players—all white players. Then I discovered East Coast Hot, which was, very nearly, all black players. Why I got obsessed with this music I don't know. But I remember very clearly sitting in my room getting stoned out of my mind listening to Gerry Mulligan's Tentet. Maybe it was the harmonies, the rhythm, the swing; I don't know what it was, but that stuff blew my mind. The more I listened, the more I wanted to listen. It took me away from my life. It was like traveling in outer space. I was playing trumpet at that time. My interest in jazz just grew and grew and it's never stopped growing. And even though in *Judevine* there is no obvious connection to Black American classical music, I know that that long, loping, kind of prosy line that those narrative poems are written in, is directly influenced by my lifetime of listening to jazz.

William Parker and I hooked up about fifteen years ago. I read an interview with him in a Canadian jazz magazine called *Coda* and I wrote him a fan letter. I had never heard any of his music. And he wrote back, then I started sending him books and he started sending me records, and we got to be friends. We started working together about eight years ago. We did a quartet gig in New York. And then I had the chance when the *Moment to Moment* poems came out to develop this duet thing with my reading the poems and William doing music on lots of different instruments, not just upright bass.

Since then we've toured together with that show which is called *Zen Mountains-Zen Streets*. Boxholder Records brought out a double CD of a live performance of *Zen Mountains* in 1999. Then a couple of years ago in New York we did my *The Fire of Compassion: A Found Poem for Black Music* with a quintet, with William on bass, Hamid Drake on drums, Roy Campbell on trumpet and Kidd Jordan on tenor saxophone. Recently, we've done some trio work. We keep doing lots of different kinds of things. I have always had an intense love for music, almost all kinds of music, but especially Black American classical music.

SM: You're calling it "Black American classical music." Do you like the term "jazz"? Is it too general?

DB: "Jazz" is fine, I guess. I don't know. I think of it as Black American classical music, because it is a musical form that black Americans invented. There are some white Americans who can play it, but there are very few, almost no, white Americans who truly contributed in any significant way to it. It's very hard to stand up and improvise and create something genuinely new. There just aren't any white players who have turned the world upside down the way Ellington or Coltrane or Ornette Coleman did. So I think of it as black music. I think it should be thought of as black music. And it's a unique musical form and attitude and it has a deep, rich history, even though it's just a little more than a hundred years old; therefore I think it should be called Black American classical music.

SM: Having done this performing with Parker in various forms, do you now read your poetry live without music differently? Do you find that you want to have music accompany you now? To be engaged in that kind of setting?

DB: When I did that interview for "All Things Considered" back in March of 2001, Lisa Simeone asked me something like that. I still enjoy going a cappella [laughs], but it's harder now, much harder. That's why I've started playing ringing bowls and gongs and a chicken shake and flutes and percussion with my readings. I've gotten much more interested in making music myself to go with the poems. I don't do that with the Judevine poems, because I can't quite figure out what would be appropriate. But working with William and all those other musicians over the years has really changed the way I present my poems. My readings are much more performances now.

SM: On *Zen Mountains-Zen Streets*, you have a version of one of my favorite poems from *Moment to Moment*, "Bugs in a Bowl." You go through it twice, or you repeat the last stanza or two. On the CD it's even called "Bugs in a Bowl and Out." You extend it for a long period. Do you do that in the readings now, too?

DB: It depends on the situation. Usually when I am by myself, I might repeat, for example, "over and over and over and over and over again and again and again," whereas in the print it just says "over and over" I might do something like that if I've got room and time to stretch out.

When you listen to black performance poets, Jayne Cortez for example, there's so much repetition. When you read Langston Hughes' poems, repetition is all over the place. This is the influence of song on poetry. All poetry was originally song and these poets are just closer to the source. *The Book of Songs*, that poetry collection that Confucius put together of poems written between 1000 and 600 B.C.E., all those poems were originally song lyrics, and the people sang them; they didn't say them.

In the 12-bar blues, for example, the second line is a repetition, often with slight variations, of the first. "I love you, Baby, but I hate to tell you so. I said, I love you, Baby, but I hate to tell you so." Repetition has always been a big part of song and therefore of poetry also.

But for most white poets, because they are thinking about the poem only as something on the page, in print, to be read, all these influences on the language from song, like repetition, have gotten a bad name. They're too unsophisticated or something. But if you come to poetry as an oral and an aural thing, something to be heard and maybe even sung, then repetition is part of the great tradition. In performance, with music, those repetitions become fabulously interesting. Whereas if you just write the same line down four times and read it there on the page, it's not so interesting. There's this emphasis on off-the-page and performance poetry—among   ancient poets, non-academic, non-white poets and current performance   poets. I've got at least one of my feet in that tradition. It's a different kind of poetic tradition. As I grow older, I want to cross-over more and more to that.

SM: I know that today, for instance, you will be doing a class on the 12-bar blues. A performance, really. Have you written any traditional blues poems?

DB: I have a whole little chapbook of traditional blues poems that I've never shown anybody. Most of them are really raunchy.

SM: That's the traditional part [laughing]!

DB: That's right! I've written lots of 12-bar blues in that triplet stanza. I've got a lot in that form, and lots of different variations on that form. As I've been saying, poetry is close to music anyway, it's always been. The idea of reading your poems or performing your poems with music isn't just black American; it's African and troubadour French and Chinese and Japanese and so on. The Chinese guys, and the Japanese guys, sit there with their kotos or whatever and play the koto and sing their poems. Go to the art museum and look at those paintings of the Chinese scholars sitting around, reciting their poems; there are musicians all over the place. The idea of a man or a woman standing behind a lectern and droning on off a piece of paper is a very recent, white and unfortunate innovation in the history of poetry.

SM: In *Moment to Moment* so many of the poems are about being an outsider, about being a recluse, of not being famous, of wanting to be famous!

DB: [Laughs]

SM: They are funny poems. And they are also bitter poems, too. Now you are not so unknown. *Moment to Moment* is selling lots of copies. That book is kind of a hit in a way. You're traveling a lot, reading a lot, your poems are on NPR. Have you found your relation to those poems changed now that you've got some recognition? What's it like for you to have it?

DB: It's a little awkward. I'm acutely aware of the irony in all this. First of all, I am delighted the book is a hit. It's in its third printing, and it's still selling very well. I'm tickled pink. This is why these personas I like to hide behind come in handy, because one of the things I often say is something like, "These are the poems of a mountain recluse whose name is Judevine Mountain. He named himself after the mountain he lives on, just as Han Shan named himself Cold Mountain after the mountain he lived on. I'm here tonight to represent him and his poems, because he would never come here to read to you people way down here in Washington, D.C." That way I get a little distance between myself and the author of the poems. This bit of trickery is in a long-standing tradition.

SM: I have heard you do that at readings. You say that to the audience sometimes.

DB: Sometimes I do, sometimes I don't. For a long time, when I first started publishing these poems I wanted them published under the name Judevine Mountain. And a couple of editors said, "Well, don't you want *your* name on them?" And I said, "No, I don't. I want to be separate from Judevine Mountain." My original idea was we'd copyright the book under Judevine Mountain's name. It was a whole ego thing, trying to step outside of the ego. Apparently, I couldn't do it. [Laughs.] I couldn't get that far away from my ego. And besides, there were serious copyright problems. And the publisher didn't want to do it that way, anyway, so that settled it.

But I am very aware that this so-called recluse is chasing all over the place reading these poems. I'm not worried. Like my friends in the theater say: "Just because you're famous today, doesn't mean you won't be in the unemployment line tomorrow." I think there will be plenty of opportunity in the future to sit on the mountain and complain about not having any attention.

This business of attention is a funny thing. I write poems about how lonely I am and how nobody ever comes to visit, and I write poems about being afraid people will start coming around all the time to bug me.

Damned if you do, damned if you don't.

SM: Do you think you are a writer who writes directly about race? You have talked a bit about black American music. I know you have an email magazine that seems to me to be a lot about race—very consciously so, very politically so. And you have written about living in Vermont, a very white state. Can you tell me a little bit about your relationship to that subject and how you deal with it?

DB: I'm glad you asked because writing about race is one of the most important things in my life and has been for a long time. Right now I write almost exclusively about the subject in essays, most of which are published in my cyberzine, *The Judevine Mountain Emailite*, which is available on my website at www.davidbudbill.com. I try to publish these essays elsewhere first. Sometimes I can; sometimes I can't. Some of them are too far out or radical or something, like the one I did on Amadou Diallo, to get on NPR, but a few of them have been commentaries on "All Things Considered."

I'm working toward a book about race called *Different as Black and White*, which will be a collection of these race essays, plus some interviews I've done over the years with black friends. Like, for example, a long interview with an old friend of mine—he's dead now—whose name was W.T.M. Johnson. Bill was the first black, pure research chemist hired by DuPont in 1949. Bill was an inventor, scientist, teacher and one of the most militant civil rights activists I've ever known. It's an incredibly interesting interview, done over four days. I did it on assignment for the magazine, *Double Take*, but they refused it.

I've always been interested in race relations in the United States; ever since I was a little kid. One of my NPR commentaries is about my childhood hero worship in the 1940s of baseball player Larry Doby who was the second black man in the white major leagues.

And I like reading black poets: Langston Hughes, Lucille Clifton, Raymond Paterson, Jean Toomer, Gwendolyn Brooks, others. And, Oh my God, Richard Wright's haiku are amazing.

I've been reading Paul Lawrence Dunbar lately, and about him also, about the history and popularity of his poetry, and how he wrote two distinctly different kinds of poetry—a dialect poetry and straight Victorian English verse—and the way white people were only interested in the dialect stuff. I'm interested in writing about the history of race relations in America, and also about race in my own personal life.

I've lived in Vermont, the whitest state in America, for over thirty years. That simple fact, Vermont's whiteness, created this enormous hole in my life. In order to fill that hole, to overcome the segregation of Vermont, I have had to adopt what I call my "Personal Affirmative Action Program."

SM: What do you mean by "Personal Affirmative Action Program"?

DB: This is a segregated country. America is segregated. I don't care what the law says. And if you want to live an integrated life, as a white person, if you want to have black folks in your life, you have to go out, you have to consciously and dedicatedly go out and establish relationships with black folks. You can't just sit around and hope that they are going to show up on your doorstep. They are not. Why would they? Not in the workplace, not where you live. Nowhere.

What I mean by a "Personal Affirmative Action Program" is a conscious and deliberate effort to go out and establish, or re-establish, or make contact with black folks. Not just because they are black, but because sometimes when you happen to bump into some black person who you think you might really like to get to know better, you have to reach out, you have to work at it, and not avoid or pass over that possible friendship that you might have in a natural way if you lived in a world that was really and truly integrated. But since this country is not truly and genuinely integrated, you have to make this artificial effort, to begin with at least. And it does seem artificial, but our lives are artificial. They are segregated. I don't know, I suppose you could say, "Well, bluebirds, they hang together, and then there are blackbirds, and so on." But, for me, personally, I want to live an integrated life, and in order to live that life, I have to deliberately go out and get it. You have to deliberately and consciously desegregate your life.   Another reason to do this is to fight the racism that is so much a part of our American culture.

SM: Do you think that this endeavor you speak of is essentially risk-taking?

DB: Yes. It is risk-taking. You might get rejected. You *will* get rejected. I can see some black folks reading this and saying, "Oh, shit, here come the honkies." James Cotton's got a blues lyric that goes:

> I don't like white,
> and white don't like me
> And we stay away from each other,
> that's the way it ought to be.

Well, lots of black folks feel that way. If I were black, I might. But there are lots of black folks who don't feel that way too. Some black folks hate white folks and some don't. Just like us. Yes, it's risk-taking. It's dangerous. But if you want to live an integrated life and fight racism, you've got to do it. Black folks who might be approaching you are taking enormous risks too. It goes both ways.

All this is difficult. You are not friends with every white person who shows up in your life so obviously you're not going to be friends with every black person you meet either.

Here's an example: William Parker and I are artistically on the same wave length, and we like each other, we like hanging out and we like working together. But if I hadn't made that initial contact, and if William hadn't responded in kind; and if we hadn't gone out of our personal ways to establish a friendship, we wouldn't have one. We would not have found out that we are friends. We would have never known how much we enjoy working together. That's all I am trying to say.

In order to have even the possibility of these kinds of friendships you have to do extra things. You've got to work harder. Because of the nature of the segregated, racist society we all live in, you have to get involved in what, at times, might seem like artificial constructs in order to get to the point where it is not artificial. It's necessary that we do this, because we don't know each other. We are strangers to each other. We've got to get to know each other.

SM: One last question. We talked a little about how Frost was an influence you had to, in a sense, move past. Are there any other influences, or forces, that you feel the need to circumnavigate?

DB: Rather than other individual figures I had to pass around, like Frost, I think for me it was white American and European poetry and those traditions that I had to pass around. Even today, most white American poets know almost nothing about any poetry other than white American and European poetry. They don't know black American poets or South American poets or African poets or Chinese ancient or modern poets or anything but the same white American and European poets.

So one of the connections between my intense interest in black American poetry and music and ancient Chinese poetry and religion is that they are both *non-white*. In other words the thing I've spent most of the last few decades doing is getting outside my own white American/European poetical and cultural traditions.

For instance, one of the connections between this discussion of race and say our talk of Frost is the quote from Moms Mabley I use in "Killing the Ghost of Ripton." Moms was a black comedian that almost no white people had ever heard of, but she was wildly famous among black Americans. I put her in that poem because I thought it was a kick to have one of the whitest poets in the history of American literature upside one of the blackest of comedians in America and one white readers of Frost would most likely never have heard of.

SM: Can you read that poem now?

DB: Sure. I wrote this poem a long time ago, in 1975 I think it was.

KILLING THE GHOST OF RIPTON

It was last fall sometime.
I couldn't stand it any longer.
The old fart had helped me waste five years.
I got in my car, drove down 100, through Granville Gulf,
past the falls and up over Middlebury Gap.
I found the ghostly bastard standing in a meadow
pontificating to no one.

When I saw him, actually saw him, I almost lost my nerve.
He was pitiful standing there alone not knowing all that's happened.
Christ! I loved the old guy! But I had to do it.
There is no point in feeding a ghost.
It's like Moms Mabley says, "People is dyin' today
what never died before."

29

So I shot him three times through the heart.
I shot him once with the modern American language,
but he didn't fall; he understood.
I shot him with a thousand deserted farms.
He grabbed his chest and staggered back.
I pumped him full of Vermont slaves
hanging around all winter
waiting for the summer rich to come.

The old guy crumbled where he stood.
I scooped him up and stuffed him down the well
at the Robert Frost Memorial Wayside
just down the road from Breadloaf.

He's down there still.
Don't go looking for him here.

SM: Thank you.

DB: Thank you!

Geof Hewitt

FOR HAYDEN

The tourist, happy to be alive in a place like Vermont,
turns to the local stuck here twelve months a year
and says, "Where do *you* go to get away?"
Then corrects himself with a quick addition:
"Of course anyone lucky enough to *live* here doesn't need to get away!"
And that's the end of friendship there,
the loss of universal feeling
to a lie, in this case a patronizing one
because the local knows
that s.o.b. can choose ·
and he's here only three days a year!

The tourist moves closer to the barbwire fence
for a better view of the farmer
astride his tractor with the side-bar cutter
and the grass is falling in waves parallel
to the last row that was felled
while the squared-off stand remaining
gets surrounded smaller and smaller.
The cutter doesn't jam and the tourist
thinks that's the farmer's life and I shared it
for ten minutes while he squared
his field and made hay.
Meanwhile, farmer thinking:
that poor bastard got some time off from the city
and best he can do is watch me drive.
Thank God nothing's going wrong.

And fingers a dincher from the floor of his pack
as the tourist turns
back to the waiting family and automobile,
a family that never chose to cease

bickering and exit the car, but instead to sweat
and call periodically for him to drive them on.
The farmer on his tractor cannot watch them at all times
cornering the field, he cannot look back as they disappear, his vision
is the stop-frame picture of their positions
every time his tractor is headed straight down the row
toward their parking spot,
each time the father, now grown familiar with his foot on a strand,
gazes at him in the foreground, the carful of family
parked in the shade, exasperated,
behind. He makes another square,
a little farther from them as he hays
toward dead center of the field.
When the tractor straightens to the row
that lets him see the tourists
they are gone.

They were too far off to see the field sparrow's well-hidden eggs
crumble under the cutter-bar, and they would never recognize
the all-day, redundant, useless scold
of the field sparrow and her mate whose nesting grounds
and potential family have been unbelievably erased
lined up in horizontal rows
like grease stains on an earthen plate.

They left too soon to hear the cutter-bar clank
against another grass-hidden object this time not eggs, but stone,
and the ripping free of iron and the engine's overheated coughing to a stop
in gritty, diesel-wafting heat.
The scold is darting at the farmer as he tries to
coax the wounded cutter back on the bar.
Only a square of grass remains to be mowed
and the tractor's engine is rough to restart in this heat.
He gooses and coughs it back into action,
jumps free and checks the motion of the bar.
It works and back he climbs, too high
to see the minute dangers of his work,
too far from the retreating tourist

rehearsing for Monday's coffee break
as he describes to wife and children
what they sat through and never saw
anything there to start with.

Geof Hewitt

MOVING THE WOODPILE

Moving the woodpile I do my serious thinking:
Should I forswear speech, is my ego finally shrinking?
Questions posed against the health of sane activity,
The woodpile was there and should be here

And moved twice again before burning.
No matter where I place reserves
It's always wrong once the fire starts:
Too close for safety, too close for mere

Aesthetics, not pretty not functional, inconvenient,
Pure dangerous. So many excuses
To go electric! A nuke two hundred miles away
Might not burn us out the way this woodblaze

Wants free of its cast iron cell
Across the kindling, scattered dust
Across the cement floor to the bigger pile
And then to walls and joists and finally the roof.

A college kid at the ski slopes told me
Of his mother's home: she hopes it burns.
Because, he said, the timbers have rotted to kindling.
If it's taken by heat before wind moves it on,

Insurance will pay for their dream house,
No fairer price nor place on earth.

Kate Barnes

A WET EVENING

A wet evening.
        The clouds
                look brushed in

over the hills
        by a black brush
                on soaked paper.

Rain must
        already be falling
                on the other side

of the horizon
        where hilltops
                with a narrow band

of paleness floating
        over the blue-black
                undulation

of their crests
        outline
                a recumbent, stone

goddess
        who fell asleep
                some time ago

between the sea
        and this little, running,
                freshwater river.

Kate Barnes

TRACKS

Snow fell late this year,
but now, at last, the world is white
wherever I look, white fields and hills
ringing the horizon.
It's a hungry time. Small birds
flock, and a great crowd of brown doves
dive at the seed I've tossed them
so eagerly that a patch of frozen grass
lies pecked out of all that whiteness;
and when I go with my broom handle
to knock ice off the wide stone
under the back door,
I notice deer tracks all around the house,
circling, crossing, interlacing
back and forth in every direction.

At night, I stand by the bedroom window
staring out into the cold moonlight
in vain. Beautiful visitors,
why do I never see you?—and they answer
that they are like dreams, they can only come here
after my eyelids close.

Kate Barnes

Wanting to See a Moose

When I am full
of some transporting emotion,
what I see is that ordinary things
are all extraordinary. But
it's like gathered dew
on a blade of grass, it falls off
or dries up, and I can't hang on
to the feeling. In no time
I'm back asking the fates
to let me see a moose
as I drive my car through the marsh — & not
attending to the gathering darkness
of evening, the cloudy light
that lingers, the reeds, the ducks,
the black, still water opening
so silently
beyond the causeway.

John Hyland

THE BARBERSHOP

When I moved up here
I got my hair cut
regularly, a change for me, at a
barbershop that smelled of the 50s
down on the corner.

Every time I went there,
the barber, in his sixties, grey,
asked me the same question.
"You got a job?"
"No," and the conversation
would end as quickly as the reply.

Then one day I went
in and placed myself in the chair
and got the question. "Maybe, I
have an interview this afternoon."
Conversation bloomed.
"Where you from?
Some weather, huh?
Why are all these kids shooting each other?"

Robert Dunn

EVIDENCE OF JOHNNY APPLESEED

from the report of the Society for
Printing, Publishing and
Circulating the writings
of Emanuel Swedenborg
Manchester, England
January 14, 1817

"There is in the western country a very
extraordinary missionary of the New
Jerusalem. A man has appeared who seems
to be almost independent of corporeal wants
and sufferings. He goes barefooted, can sleep
anywhere, in house or out of house, and lives
on the coarsest and most scanty fare. He
has actually thawed the ice with his bare feet."

Evidence of Johnny Appleseed

Name: John Chapman

"by occupation a gatherer & planter of appleseeds"

There's a monument (he isn't under it)
and stories of Johnny Appleseed in Arkansas
from people who haven't seen him
and rumors of his passing
through Oregon and Vermont
and a general
silence of history books, but then
any fool can start a war.

born September 26, 1774 and 1775
in Leominster, Springfield and Boston

      born in fact
      several times
      in any number of places

educated variously at Harvard
      or not

read in a book called "Heaven & its Wonders
& Hell by Emanuel Swedenborg" most of his life

left the pages everywhere

conversed with angels

and is not known to have eaten animals
      or people

died on March 15 and 18, 1845 or 1847
      frequently
      among friends

leaving
      one old horse
      an empty sack
      several far patches of ground
      containing young appletrees
      secured against surrealists
      and enough money to bury him
      somewhere

leaving a story and a dream
      trees that he planted
      and scions of trees

Imagine a map showing appletrees
      and on it a figure moving...

a small man to look at
with bright eyes and night-black hair
always in motion even when standing still
like a hummingbird

seen passing by roads & passing by rivers
with a timber wolf for company

sharing a cave with bears
                whose reputation
as grudging hosts is on the whole unjust

passing peacefully among People driven
                by drink and despair to murder
& peacefully among pioneers driven to murder
                by drink, despair and the Bible

carrying his peace with him, and his hope
                and a bag of appleseeds

and coming where there is no way to go
                becomes the way

becomes in time a man of steadfast wisdom
or a first class fool, which is
substantially the same thing

You can order young appletrees by mail
                to say nothing of Blue Pearmains
                and Cox's Orange Pippins
also the Heavenly Arcana
in thirty volumes, bound in green cloth

untouched by
                human hands, but when

you plant a seed
right hand and left hand are witnesses.

Elizabeth Tibbetts

In the Lingerie Store

They're enough to make anyone want
a restless body, flawless skin, and hint
of flowers between the legs, these films
the color of evening clouds and silk cups
with slivered bones, thin as a baby's ribs.
But in the dressing room, when I wrestle
out of heavy clothes, and stand, exposed
before the mirror, fear turns me around
to check for hidden cameras, because
my breasts that rode happily all day
now lie there sleepy and blue-veined
in the thin light, and refuse to fit these
frail contraptions.
                    Outside, it's dusk.
The sky is the deep-blue of a slip I admired;
a half moon reclines above roof tops.
Here, I can imagine again you watching
as I undress each night. Oh, and I remember
how once my engorged breasts felt like bombs,
tight and intricately mapped with veins,
the ducts swollen like juice sacs
inside an orange, how I could spray a stream
across the room, and how my infant son
flashed his eyes at me, bit down, and finally
sucked as though his life depended on it.

Baron Wormser

ROOM (1936)

Perhaps in another lifetime I lived in this room.
I was a Gentile not a Jew. I came to this island
To make my fortune. I wonder what happened to me.
I wonder what happened in this little, bare room.

In this life I stand at the window that looks out
On a brick wall advertising a soda drink.
Although many adults consume it, it is a child's drink—
Some colored, sugared water. I prefer black tea.

Although I stopped praying decades ago,
I am talking to God when I say all this.
I would pray if I could but it fills me
With a shameful agony. I can feel my wanting—

The desire to make the Almighty take me personally—
And it is an evil thing, the harp of ungratefulness.
I am, in fact, in purgatory—a sooty tenement,
A darkened hall, a closet that smells like old clothes.

I read the advertisements around me quite carefully,
The way an idiot would. In my own time
I am going to die. Such a solace to me!
Meanwhile my soul buzzes around like a housefly.

Meanwhile I walk about this little room
And lower and raise the Venetian blinds.
The huge bottle stares at me. It is as much
My friend as anything in this century.

Baron Wormser

HEBREW SCHOOL (1955)

You sat at a long table in the cement
Floor cellar of the two-story wooden shul—
A shingled, ramshackle structure with weirdly
Narrow windows, a sort of Yankee-millwright-
Byzantine—and half listened as the rabbi
Droned intently about the glorious miseries
Of what he liked to call with a proud flourish
Of possessiveness—"our people." Boring.

If you sucked Necco wafers very slowly
A whole hour would somehow go by.
You had no patience and rightly so.
Dark eyes, dark hair, olive smolder of skin,
Your ardor couldn't help but loathe
Such parroting—a language no one spoke,
Impossible names, the coy Tetragrammaton,
And the awe you were bound to fabricate.

God seemed more emptiness than presence,
A well run dry, a motto voiced too often,
And what did he have to do with women?
Were you going to bleed and swell in order
To make soup and praise men's grievous certitudes?

You sat in the small town where once
The factories thrummed with the energy
Of ceaseless looms, where the hands of children
And women and men flew like mechanical birds
And where echoes of their entrapment
Still lingered in the huge empty buildings.

The afternoon passed like a caravan in a sandstorm.
The little rabbi insisted, pleaded, orated,
His gait wobbly with millennial weight.
Soon, you would have a new body,
Soon, you would leave the pale singsong of childhood,
And you dreamt, as dusk fell and cars crept by,
Of that ancient, godless flowering.

Baron Wormser

DJ (1965)

I lay in bed at night and listened on my transistor radio.
Radio waves seemed an active miracle to me and still do:
I can't believe the silent air brims
With those chattering arrows.

I was listening to a Negro man: "Greetings, earthlings,
From the big hot boss with the big hot sauce.
The man with the permanent sun tan, the jock
With no hair, no worldly care,
Your soul leader, oooh-poppa-dee-der."

Jumping Jesus, I thought to my dizzy self,
How did a man become a word-motor?
As the Dynamic Daddy-O, Master Metaphor Mixer,
Unblinking Syntactic Flicker of African-American Schtick,
Trick and No-Trick, he was ultra-bardic.

I lay there softly mimicking him:
The clicking consonants, alto rises and bullfrog plummets,
The flicking feints and jabs of sex-teasing phrases,
The long vowels caressed—oooh!—until they seemed
Like vocal limousines.

It was genius to equal the bulwark-of-
Western-civilization novel beside my bed.
I listened until I felt drowsy and hoped I would dream
Of that glowing yet raspy voice, that lovely razor of elocution.

Jean Pedrick

TARMAC

After the rain in the night, the flannel grey
almost black of old churchgoing suits.
Puddles like mirrors dropped at random
pewter-bright. In spring dusted with pollen
the sun spots through the lacy trees
like yellow buttons. (Grey-and-yellow
the color of a dream, a sweep of new
willow; behind that curtain, a comely man.)
In heat, malleable, all colors of grey
beside themselves where the mail-truck
swerved to the box, away. Too hot to cross
the road for the letter barefoot. But after supper
always in the long light our long walk, all barefoot,
dad, mum, small boy, smaller boy, prancy dog;
at the rear the grey striped cat, beyond the wall
the large, black cat, rustle with ear-points, shadow
pretending not be on the walk. Stops, as at
the Stations, for a flat shoe-sole of dead frog,
for a torn chunk of tar embedded with diamonds,
for a most unruffled grouse with fourteen babies,
for a domed turtle on long-considered migration
to dig a womb in the sand. In October, painted leaves
like hart's blood splattered on our summer road.

Walter Clark

PUZZLED DUST

Proud, angry, puzzled dust,
if led to water you may drink,
if beauty winks at you, you wink
but cannot comprehend the thrust
that tickles in your threaded bone;

bone dropped aside to flake and rust,
return to elemental grist
while ghost goes where you cannot guess.
Some say it goes to study trust-
ing earth as if that were its home

and it, when ready, also might return.
In any case, by then you're gone.
Whatever sticks it might pick up again
are not your creamy meal and bone,
long since locked up in stubborn stone.

But who would ever ask the dust
to name the height of its desire,
"Lift or be lifted somewhat higher?"
The summonsed earth need not atone
for being but the ground of song.

Walter Clark

MARSDEN HARTLEY AT MOOSEHEAD LAKE

Bring no desire here,
only your chill heart
and edgy mind,
seeing three-toed spruce flakes
as spilled print,
loving the cap of ice
on its washed rock,
watching the low sun
pitch javelins over wave-helmets,
watching armies march,
needing nothing,
having come here
to an echoing house,
torn velvet in the parlor
and at night
emptied bottles under the bed,
cat's claw testing the door,
Pamola's distant commotion
taking the shape of war
in your would-be-mastering mind.

Marie Harris

Memory Awake

Waking in this gray-yellow portholed light, it takes a moment to conclude
that the sounds that roused me were not the echoes of my stomach's churning
but the morning ruminations of a harbor seal on yellow rockweed, and I am
rocking in the belly of a boat set rocking by the workings of a lobster boat
that chews its way from pot to pot—diesel fume and herring gull spume in
spray off its stern—unconcerned that I am disconcerted. Not just because
I've been rocked awake but because I had been dreaming again: the shipwreck
of the marriage and the sons adrift.

Marie Harris

MACKEREL SKY ELEGY

At anchor near the silky brown verge of a tidal mudflat, I do not seem to
pose a threat to the heron stalking the shallows. It is alert to my small
movements in the cockpit—I smooth a wind-lifted page, raise and
lower binoculars—yet it displays an almost studied lack of concern.

So too, as I tack past the green can in Falmouth Foreside's teeming harbor,
the osprey in its unkempt nest; mottled harbor seals on ledges drying in the
retreating tide; the solitary loon. Nothing startles. Even when I slip off
the boat at sunset and swim toward a raft of terns, there is no
consternation, no flight.

I sail into Harpswell Harbor. On the chart this piece of the Maine coast
looks like a mackerel sky: striated, mysterious. I have never been here, by
land or sea, yet I feel an inexplicable sadness.

Now I remember: At the funeral, men with cropped silver hair and flecked
beards told stories about that summer place. How they gave each other
nicknames and drank good wine and smoked fine cigars. Oh, how they laughed.

How they remembered you.

From this vantage, anchored in the very cove you and your friends must have
overlooked from a porch on warm foggy evenings long after you and I had
anything left to say to one another, I can almost see you, as if through a
screen. In profile. Cigarette in one hand, snifter in the other. Holding
forth. You seem at ease, even happy. Then suddenly, peripherally, you notice
me. Momentarily taken aback, the surface of your composure fractures like
moonlight on a windy bay. But you neither turn nor move away. You must sense
that I'm only here for this evening with no intention of startling. And I...

This must be why I have come. To say goodby.

Marie Harris

FOLLOWING SEA

Not that the chrome-blue, white-lipped waves don't overtake, it's that they
don't overwhelm. Hard to believe when you're out there, fighting the tiller,
watching out for the jibe.

One by one each swell builds behind the straining dinghy and, as if to move
on to the larger task, lifts it like a drifting plastic milk jug and passes
under, bearing down on this stern now, encouraged by a stiff southwest
breeze; it overtakes, shoves our little sailboat this way, that way, moves on.

My senses are all I know. Deafening wind in my ears. Mainsheet chafing palm.
Leg muscles tuned to this tango. I see the world is as it is, all at once:
storm petrels and shearwaters, pitching horizon, buoys, calligraphies of
clouds, compass, boats passing. You. What did you say? Turn toward me
so I can see your voice.

The very repetition of waves reduces fear to acceptance, then monotony. By
Portland Head swell has lost to tide and current, persists as a string of
watery nudges: the past, the past, the past, taking forever to catch up. And
move on.

Jim Koller

Four Poems

Winnemucca to Reno at sundown,
hills black, the last light reflected.
Suddenly it's another time. This trip
ended long ago, late night Sebastopol.
My daughter Deirdre is again a kid, &
Thomas Thomas wags his tail, still
bouncing in the bed of the pickup,
anxious to be on the ground again,
to eat & drink, weary standing
all this time. My head fills with smells
of damp shut up rooms, as I open those doors.

*

Two clouds
         in the near
dark — I looked
         for you, thinking
I'd lost you,
      but,
wanted it
       another way,
sang it
    so, &
you appeared,
walking,
      waved to me, & we
talked our roads
        together.

*

The big red-headed bird
up from the bog
on his morning search,
calls twice, flys east over me
as I sit, start another day
under green leaves
in the outhouse.

*

After days of rain
the sky is clear.
Almost full, the moon
hides in a giant oak
until I walk
some distance from the house.
Midnight, I hear
a dog barking.
He hears more
than I do.
Geese straggling north?
You too are looking
at the moon —
just out our kitchen door,
in what seems from here
another country.
After sixty years,
they say, one can start again.
I think I will
need some sleep first.

David Huddle

MYSELF IN RETROSPECT

Last night as I was making what I thought
was a funny dinnertable remark,
it happened again—I imagined Lindsey
and Molly recalling what I'd just said
years after my death: *Do you remember*
that time Dad . . . You'd think such an idea
would be disturbing, but not so. An odd
comfort came with it: *Even when I'm dead,*
we can still clown around at dinnertime.
I don't even mind how I enter this
dimension more and more often—live me
and dead me reading through the old contract,
going over the fine print to make sure
I understand the terms of my release.

David Huddle

DEATHLIGHT

Each morning I wake up, a boy again,
but at night I trudge to bed, an old man.
I'm fifty-nine. Obituaries speak
to me now as poems did in my twenties.
"Light takes the tree," words that once named the pure
fact of beauty, I've learned to read as *Death*
will turn all living matter into so
much energy. Finite wattage. Shazam!
Suddenly I'll be starlight rocketing
through space toward another galaxy.
An average car lasts about twelve years,
a butterfly lives two days—when you think
about it, the human apparatus
is sturdier than it looks. Suicides
get thwarted by the body's insistence
on one more day of sunlight, one more spoon
full of oatmeal, or maybe just the hope
of a daughter's smile as she walks toward
the old failing thing. Did I tell you that
as a boy I was so afraid of the dark
I used to bribe my brother to keep me
company when I went to the bathroom
at night? But I think I'm slowly building
affection. Up on the mountain, the path
to Johnson Pond leads down through deepening
layers of darkness. Then it opens onto
silvery water with cool air rising
to your skin like death giving you a peck
on the cheek, so gently reminding you
of your true destination that you think,
Oh this is not bad, this is kind of nice.
What the obituaries never say,

though, is what keeps me reading them—in fact,
it's their lies ("after a courageous
battle...," "peacefully passed...," etc.)
that seem to keep the secret I'm after:
At the exact moment, could you tell if
she fell to darkness or burst into light?
But that's not it either. Oh, I don't know
what I want to know.

Kristen Lindquist

At the Carnival

I guess he got kicked out of rehab,
because I saw my uncle
at the carnival downtown
with a new haircut and a new woman.
I went to ride the Ferris wheel,
to gain perspective
on my small soiled city.
And there was my uncle, lurking
on the edges with everyone else's
missing uncles and aunts and sisters,
my sister there too, perhaps, released
from the psych ward, fitting right in
among neon lights and rock music,
tattoos and green hair spray.
This is where we all come,
my relatives, and I,
wandering alone on a summer night.
And what am I here for?
Play a game, win a prize.
Win a plush alien with glowing eyes.
Don't ignore me, the barker insists
as I hurry past, but I have to,
afraid if I stop, I'll recognize him, too.

Kristen Lindquist

FULL MOON

From my window, one hand on the phone, I strain
to hear the argument playing out below in a parked car,

a loud fight punctuated by slammed doors, a revved engine,
the man pounding the dashboard, yelling, "I didn't do anything!"

while the woman shouts over and over, "Just shut up!"
A giggling troupe of girls emerges from the pool hall

that serves anyone. They toss a pack of cigarettes back and forth,
stray out of the dark alley toward the lights of Main Street,

while hurrying the other way, a lawyer who's been working late,
her briefcase bulging around mounds of paperwork,

heads now for her car, the last one left in all-day parking.
A collection of elderly restaurant-goers strolls purposefully

down the sidewalk, well-dressed, inaudible, unflinching
as they pass the arguers' car. I should be asleep.

It must be after eleven; the movie marquee's lights
have just shut off. Something large crashes out back

behind the building. There's no one in my bed.
When I lean out at just the right angle, I can see the ocean

scarred by moonlight, the glowing zero of the moon's face
poised above the window, looking in.

Elaine Sexton

Summer Vernacular

Rolling pin and meat grinder, wax paper wrap, Salada Iced Tea, the torn skin
on a lilac tree branch, Lourdes water in a jar, Sea Road, Hunter's Lane,
Aunt Mardie's cottage out back, the hook & eye lock on the door to the bath, burnt
orange pine needles, holes in screened windows, scapulas, sachets,
pancake make-up, charm bracelets, surfboards, beach sand on the kitchen floor,
the Mother of God in the front yard, the prickly bushes with thorns on the path,
bare feet, the back steps, the milkman, the mailman, a black Mercury Comet
and pink Sting Ray bike in the drive, the neighbor boy in the shed, the Big Scoop,
the waves, swimming in rainstorms, rip tides, sleep-overs, ice-blue bug zappers,
 sunburns, mosquito-spider-bee bites, salty skin, wet towels, frizzy hair, letters,
mold in the books, dusty drawers, army blankets, dad: "deceased" on a card,
mother's thimbles, Hummels, talk radio, Singer sewing machine, St. Jude's Thrift Shop
bargains, the Enhance Your Vocabulary One-Word-A-Day lessons, The World Book,
the neighbor's twins, Keenie, their old German shepherd put down, lawn mowing,
crabapples, hornets' nests, the dirt tread cut through grass under the rope swing.

photo by Eleanor Donahue Sexton

Peter Money

TEAKETTLES, THE MOON

Landed in Vermont, I find myself spreading ash
over the icy driveway on the plateau where the house
sits, something of an Alice Springs with trees all
around—tall, several dozen thick pine trees
 seem to brace the sky along the upward driveway
  & around the house at the ridge, the trees
      create a natural parthenon in the vein
       of Maxfield Parrish—& at night the snow lawn
       glimmers blue under the wide eye of the moon
      high above the chicken coop. Ash will help
      our footing.
          One pine, behind the coop, is the size
          of a silo. The chickens sleep near
          its stem.
           I wonder,
          what do chickens look like
          when they're asleep—
          teakettles?
The moon's a mystery to me & that's no mystery at all,
as it's a mystery to most—perhaps even to those
who've walked its surfaces—jumped, bounced,
—I'm an acolyte & the moon's my catechism;
 I become fixed, blank, my cells freeze under hot
 ice, the moon's glow, is this demagoguery?

The golden dog wags his tail.

We're far from Islam & yet I've been
thinking about Islam for several days: how
the masses want to massacre the author of a western
book, a fiction.

The moon is not worth killing for, but I
would be sorry to see it go.

James Sturm 2002

Peter Money

PLUME & CLIMB

Impossible to see
but we knew
what was *there*
was mountain,

is, under a fogged page
so given to being
absent,
allowing us to

live without it
& so we reconcile
our choices & remain
until the vision lifts

or until we intuit
the other
side, until the differences
do not matter.

Cid Corman

6 Poems from Japan

1.

When you remember
being born you will know what
it feels like to die.

2.

PROMENADE
Even so
even so

to feel the
earth walking

the sky the
sky all there

3.

It isnt the
having been but

the being that
gives this moment.

4.

And then there was this —
the end of it all
and the beginning.

5.

EVER
Dying all you will get
away with.

6.

NOW
Not many *kaki*
on the tree but a lot more
in the stream under.

Donald Hall

THE FLIES

A fly slept on the field of a green curtain.
I sat by my grandmother's side, and rubbed her head
as if I could comfort her. Ninety-seven years.
Her eyes stayed closed, her mouth open,
and she gasped in her blue nightgown—pale blue,
washed a thousand times. Now her face went white,
and her breath slowed until it seemed to stop;
she gasped again, and pink returned to her face.

Between the roof of her mouth and her tongue,
strands of spittle wavered as she breathed. A nurse
shook her head over my grandmother's sore mouth
and fetched a glass of water, a spoon, and a flyswatter.
My grandmother choked on a spoonful of water
and the nurse swatted the fly.

              In Connecticut suburbs
where I grew up, and in Ann Arbor, there were houses
with small leaded panes, where Formica shone
in the kitchens, and hardwood in closets under paired
leather boots. Carpet lay thick underfoot in bedrooms,
bright, clean, with no dust or hair in them. Florist's
flowers leaned from Waterford vases
for the Saturday dinner party. Even in houses like these,
the housefly wandered and paused—and I listened
for the buzz of its wings and its tiny feet, as it struggled
among cut flowers and bumped into leaded panes.

In the afternoon my mother took over
at my grandmother's side in the Peabody Home,
while I went back to the farm. I napped in the room
my mother and grandmother were born in.

At night we assembled beside her. Her shallow, rapid
breath rasped, and her eyes jerked, and the nurse
found no pulse, as her strength concentrated wholly
on half an inch of lung space, and she coughed faintly,
quick coughs, like fingertips on a ledge. Her daughters
stood by the bed—solemn in the slow evening,
in the shallows of after-supper—Caroline, Nan, and Lucy,
her eldest daughter, seventy-two, who held
her hand to help her die, as twenty years ago
she did the same for my father.
                                        Then her breath slowed
again, as it did all day. Pink vanished from cheeks
we had kissed so often, and nostrils quivered.
She breathed one more quick breath.
Her mouth twitched sharply, as if she spoke
a word we couldn't hear. Her face was fixed, white,
her eyes half closed, and the next breath
never came.

                      She lay in a casket covered with gray linen
at Chadwick's Funeral Parlor in New London,
on the ground floor under the I.O.O.F. Her fine hair
lay combed on the pillow. Her teeth in, her mouth
closed, she looked the way she used to look,
except that her face was tinted, tanned
as if she worked in the fields.

                            The air was so still
it had bars. I imagined a fly wandering in,
through these dark-curtained windows, to land
on my grandmother's nose.

                            At the Andover graveyard,
Astroturf covered the dirt next to the dug shaft.
By the hole, Mr. Jones said a prayer,
who preached at the South Danbury Church
when my grandmother still played the organ.
He raised his narrow voice, which gave itself over

to August and blue air, and told us that Kate
in heaven "will keep on growing...and growing...
and growing..." and he stopped abruptly,
as if the sky abandoned him, and chose to speak
elsewhere through someone else.

                              I walked by myself
in the barn where I spent summers
next to my grandfather. In the tie-up a chaff
of flies roiled in the leather air, as he milked
his Holsteins morning and night, his bald head
pressed sweating into their sides, fat female
Harlequins. Their black and white tails
swept back and forth, stirring the flies up. His voice
spoke pieces he learned for the Lyceum,
and I listened crouched on a three-legged stool
as his hands kept time *strp strp* with alternate streams
of hot milk, the sound softer as milk foamed
to the pail's top.
                         In the tie-up the spiders
feasted like Nero. Each April he broomed the webs out
and whitewashed the wood, but spiders and flies
came back, generation on generation—like the cattle,
mothers and daughters, for a hundred and fifty years,
until my grandfather's heart flapped in his chest.
One by one the slow Holsteins climbed the ramp
into a cattle truck.

                         In the kitchen with its bare
hardwood floor, my grandmother stood
by the clock's mirror to braid her hair every morning.
She looked out the window toward Kearsarge,
and said, "Mountain's pretty today,"
or, "Can't see the mountain too good today."
She fought the flies all summer. She shut
the screen door quickly, but flies gathered
on canisters, on the clockface, on the range
when the fire was out, on set-tubs, tables, chairs.
Flies buzzed on cooling lard, when my grandmother

made doughnuts. Flies lit on a drip of jam
before she could wipe it up. Flies whirled
over simmering beans, in the steam
of maple syrup. My grandmother fretted,
and took good aim with a flyswatter,
and hung strips of sticky paper behind the range,
where nobody would tangle her hair.
She gave me a penny for every ten I killed.
All day with my mesh flyswatter I patrolled
kitchen and dining room, living room,
even the dead air of the parlor. Though I killed
every fly in the house by bedtime,
when my grandmother washed the hardwood floor,
by morning their sons and cousins
assembled in the kitchen, like the woodchucks
my grandfather shot in the vegetable garden,
that doubled and returned; like the deer
that watched for a hundred and fifty years
from the brush on Ragged Mountain,
and when my grandfather died,
stalked down the mountainside to graze
among peas and beans.

                        We live in their house
with our books and pictures, gazing each morning
at blue Kearsarge. We live in the house left behind.
We sleep in the bed where they whispered together
at night. One morning I woke hearing a voice from sleep:
"The blow of the axe resides in the acorn."

I got out of bed and drank cold water in the dark
morning from the sink's dipper,
at the window under the leaning maple,
and a fly woke buzzing beside me,
and swept over set-tubs and range,
one of the hundred-thousandth generation.
                                    I planned
long ago I would live here, somebody's grandfather.

Julia Shipley

Heron, Gnomon

1.
But it lingered, I fled.
It stood still as a needle
touched to a phonograph,
while the water slipped through
its simple legs, watched me
pass thread-like through the opening day.

2.
"An Eskimo culture offers an angry person
release by walking the emotion out of his
or her system in a straight line across the landscape:
the point at which the anger is expressed
is marked with a stick, bearing witness to the strength
or length of the rage."

3.
Once I suddenly noticed
I had no shadow except
directly beneath me. I
straddled a black so opaque,
it was the hole and the earth
was an urn
into which I will fit
entirely.

Dana Levin

QUELQUECHOSE

You want to get in and then get out of the box.

form breakage form

—

I was in the fish shop, wondering why being experimental means
        not having a point—

            why experimentation in form is sufficient unto itself
                        (is it)

But I needed a new way to say things:
        sad tired I with its dulled violations, lyric with loss in its faculty den—

Others were just throwing a veil over suffering:
        glittery interesting I-don't-exist—

All over town, I marched around,
        ranting my jeremiad.

Thinking, What good is form if it doesn't *say anything*—

And by 'say' I meant wake somebody up.

Even here at the shores of Lake Champlain
        mothers were wrenching small arms out of sockets.

Not just the mothers. What were the fathers doing,
        wrenching small arms out of bedside caches—

How could I disappear into language when children were being called

'fuckers'——
                by their mothers——

who were being called 'cunts' by their boyfriends——

who were being called 'dickheads' behind their backs——

It wasn't that I was a liberal democrat, it was that
                bodies had been divested of their souls——

        like poems——

Trying to get in or out of the box.

And the scallops said, "Pas des idees mais dans les choses."

And I said, "I'll have the Captain's Special with wedges instead of fries."

And everywhere in the fish shop the argument raged, it's baroque proportions,
        the conflict between harmony and invention.

But then a brilliance——

The movement of her gloved hands as she laid the haddock out
        one by one——

The sheered transparency of her latexed fingers,
        in and out of the lit display case as if they were yes, fish——

Laying haddock out in a plastic tub on a bed of ice,
        her lank brown hair pulled back from her face with a band——

Yes it was true she had to do this for the market
        but there was such beauty in it——

        she was the idea called Tenderness——

she was a girl who stood under fluorescent lights making
        six bucks an hour——

and she looked up at me and held out a haddock with both her hands,
        saying it was the best of the morning's catch.

Susan Thomas

HEIFER GARDEN

1.

In the morning garden
I roll in the high wet grass
and drink from a pansy's fierce round face.
The little heifers trot up;
they stick their heads right through the fence
to see what I'm up to now.
They think I'm peculiar.
No wonder—I can barely explain
what I'm doing here
talking to lilacs
singing to tulips and steering clear
of the central image
old and sorrowful,
the enormous bleeding heart.

2.

Swift heifers in the goldenrod
move so fast we only see
their rapt faces
flicker in the August wind,
and the parting goldenrod.
Our gardens are in
the last stage of labor
popping babies so quick
we trip over weeds to catch them.
And the weeds! The shame of it!
We who picked rows clean
of gill and purslane feel witchgrass
growing every minute underfoot.
But there's no time now—
just harvest what you can
and panting, run back for the rest.

Neil Shepard

_____

EVERY MORNING

Garbage men idle in their garbage
truck in a pull-off spot with a dawn
view. I'm up with them watching
their sweet waste waft up and bring down
the crows, who call and circle as if
over a dying beast. I'm trying
to guess their aesthetic, silly
as it sounds, wherever the sweet
spot in their bodies is, the leisure
that causes them to stop here.
Is it the mountain view, the mown pasture,
or just a place to flick butts
from the cab and ogle at the jogger
on her dawn run, the slim retiree
whose manse nearby in what used to be
south pasture is covered now in flowers.
And what's her highest pleasure?
She's at it every morning by six,
turning the compost pit, manuring
the beds, bending and straightening
her back, out there every morning
in her bikini top and running shorts,
leathery, gray-haired, lively.
Days ago I startled the guy
who parks his pickup here beside
north pasture every morning —
after the garbagemen go —
enjoying, I imagine, the morning
his way, windows down, smoking,
reading the news, smoking, taking in
the view, then back to news.
Lately, he'd turn up his radio,

country music jangling and twangling
over the hay. I knocked on his cab
and told him straight: I don't like sound-
tracks with my nature, the birds
dubbed out, the wind a syncopation
between notes of a hillbilly bass line.
Well, the guy startled — he was young
and dark — deeply tanned, black shock
of hair, well-muscled, and violent
in his face, his gruff "Excuse me
for livin!" before he choked
the ignition, stomped the gas, and spun
his tires in a spray of gravel and dust.
I felt bad but I felt right, too.
I wasn't denying him his view
but was limiting his pleasure,
the old compromise between one nature
and another, between a human song
and the wind's. Now he's on my mind
again. I wrote down his license plate —
just in case — some endangered bird
preceding the identifying numbers
that showed, I guess, he was more than
the gunrack on the back of his cab
and for everything he shot
there was something he gave back.
Now he's gone and put a hole in this
early morning as yesterday
his father found him dead, down there
in what we call the Johnson slum, a self-
inflicted gun-wound to the head.
I didn't know him but for the picture
in the morning papers. He lived
and died in a dark apartment
shaded by a fire escape, but he liked
the open air, his father told the local
news, he liked every morning
rising early, to take the morning air.

Cynthia Huntington

J.V. BASEBALL, EARLY MAY, NEW HAMPSHIRE

In the late green afternoon *muggy*
wet puffs of breeze whiff up from the grass,
forming invisible beads of rain on bare skin.
In the warm air, the field ringed with trees,
steams like a great terrarium. *Pollen*
makes me cough. The left fielder catches

the last sun in his eyes; he squints
and reaches; the ball falls out of space
beyond the outstretched glove. *"Out there*
in the boondocks, you just drive and drive..."
Not minding the boondocks.

Across the burgeoning field, a man
with dark glasses stares past us through the world:
clad in light raiments, a shirt and trousers,
a body released from ancient times.
Spirit, come closer, we need you—here

among the picnic tables and folding chairs,
released from your reverie, awakened
after aeons, risen in a body, dark and mortal.
You could say we are halfway there.
Hours go by, a strike, a call.

Is the count two or three? Groans and cheers,
watching the arc of a ball, the runner's trajectory.
Sucking out the half of an orange...
Is anyone alive out there?
These last hours of daylight
in which a great horned owl is sleeping,

at the edge of the woods, wrapped in leaves,
his keen ears buffeted by cries;
the hair on the back of our wrists grows
soft and grey, and the grass holds shadows
inside a net that covers the world.

Sacrifice your body, dive for home.
Darkness will end the game soon.
Lights come on on the hill
that seemed only woods before.
Little time left, only clouds turning,
the net spread loose, waving slack.

In a sweet, calm voice a woman said *the rain*
will come tonight—her voice heard
in the distance like part of a melody.
Whatever she said was like a blessing
though we were not always able to make out the words.
Sitting downwind of the trashcans,

now beginning to reek. *Come home*
on your stomach. And dusk flows out
of the trees, as we count
the balls and strikes. *Is it three? No, it's two.*
Bottom of the sixth. Everyone in his place,

as we count forward, coming back
around again, and you want too much
for the pattern to yield, break open,
for everything that is held in place
to shatter and fly outward,

the tension let go. Sacrifice fly.
Crying: *Way to be alive,* and:
Andy, it's worth a two-pound lobster
if you make this hit, or: *When will you*
stop trying to plan every second of my life?
Silence after the girl speaks angrily to her mother.

The players in shadow now.
Oxygen is rising from the cool grass. Cold
of the chain link fence, loosening connections. *I*
looked back at you but you were looking away.
You did not hold me in your gaze
as I moved to the edge of the grass, below the trees.

Below the trees the scent of bone and dried blood;
where the owl feasted, a few feathers.
A man with dark glasses, an ordinary man,
a stranger, is crossing from one world to the next
as he walks across the field and is taken up
into the trees' shadows. *I looked back*

at you, but you were already turning away.
Can you see me here, at the edge of the grass,
disappearing? Look for me
again...look... The boys wait, standing apart
from one another in a field; a car starts its engine.
No one is moving now; no one tells us when to move.

Michael Blaine

Monhegan I.

Behind her drops one hundred feet,
then deeper into the calmed ocean,
the speckled rock ledge, then nothing.

Earlier, the tour boat growls
rolls onward for hours, alien
people, art supplies, canvas bags

One black dog
patiently withstands
a hundred touches.

Distant island, stillness, us.
Pilgrims wait, anxious to disperse
to disappear within.

We study the veins and arteries,
point with stretched fingers
say, here we will follow.

Later, we will push ahead, focus only on our trail,
the weight of breeze and breath heavier now.

Christmas trees and rocks, she says.

David Giannini

FATHER VISITING, AT 83

He feels to walk
down
      stairs outside—
there's a
railing—
        something
to grip

descent. He
wants
      his son in front
down
      the steep rust
and steps
into the hands of his wife.

Bill Holshouser

FIREWEED'S PROGRESS

Fireweed climbs itself like a ladder toward autumn,
the ruin of the lupine has come again,
and I am shocked to learn once more that my life
is not perennial but anecdotal. Indian pipes appear
among fallen leaves and acorns, the corpse flowers.

Don't get poetic on me. I am not my son.
Any eyes he sees in the forget-me-not are different eyes,
the stories the touch-me-not tells me are mine.
From the ground, I see a tanager and think him beautiful.
What the tanager sees—don't we wish we knew?

Joseph Bruchac

LEGWASSO

1.

the big man stood,
lifted up his arms,
    scratched his nails
        on the trunk of the tree

i watched him, smiling,
wondering how
    i could measure
        his reach against mine

when i woke
it was hours later
    i was on the road
        along the narrows

and i remembered
    he was Bear

the scent of pine pitch
    on my fingers

2.

two white tail deer
heads lifted,
        listening
where the roads diverged
    their knoll
        a small green island

coats red with late summer
  horns still russet
    within velvet

no further from me
    than a breath
they stood
    eyes seeking mine

i do not know
    which of us sang
      for the wild then
      all around us

Legwasso means "He dreams" in Abenaki

Cleopatra Mathis

Envoy

The crows came back last night
in this, the black center of October,
the broken line the lush world draws

to the hungry days of December.
Already they'll eat anything, craned neck
and squawk at the rag of flesh,

their beaks in every winter morning,
shrieking, ripping the profits from the jay's
torn craw. They serve themselves.

I'm not the first to hate their flapping
claim to the season, lured to the window
by their raw, gut-filled, strutting

common pride. Oh they bring out in me
the loftiest of ideals, and see how I stumble,
falling back to the dog I gave away,

sour animal, who in the last moments
shook me with the wild sorrow
open in her comprehending face, pleading

clear as any speech: *don't leave me
with these strangers.* And I did,
I took that last look, and turned away.

Gary Clark

An Appearance in New Hampshire

After lunch I walked a street to the edge
of a little stream, where I chanced to see my father
sitting on a bench, enjoying the weather.
I hadn't seen him since the spring he'd died, and after
all this time he appeared more or less the same.
He hadn't even noticeably aged or thinned.
Driving back home that night across a high plateau
I came unglued, and at that moment
the sky spread wide and here came the season's first geese,
the same geese I'd seen in Oregon one time, wickedly
out of my mind, the same geese as which
my father still to this very day flies so high above
the milk trucks, oblivious to my plights.
Why? Because my plights are trivial and meaningless,
that's why, and he knows this, he knows how good my life actually is.
He is why my life is good, is why the church
is where we go to rummage for the perfect coat,
every day the same cold call of happiness:
get up, kiss the kids, go out into the world for oxygen
and don't stop sucking until the sadness you survive on bleeds back
into, through, and out of you until you're there
again, right here, home to everything you'll never know.
Stopping for a glass of wine, I sat all by myself
for the first time, it seemed, in many years.
I saw faces, cigarettes, skirts, pasta, floorboards, ice,
mirrors, pinballs, lollipops and much, much more.
Eventually I left and made it almost home.

Greg Joly

LOGGERHEAD

So I'm up to the old Moore lot
bullin out pine
from that blow down
we had back late May.
Gotta get those logs
out to mill before
the blue-stain sets in.
Now the mill is all
back-logged bout that time,
but I know Tommy C. the owner
personal & we got us an arrangement...
I can send a charge of logs
as long as it's under 10,000/week.
Got Ike Lowen hauling for me
& we keep a runnin tab
of footage as he loads up.
        Well now, one slip she comes back
from the mill scaled 2,000 ft short.
So I call Tommy & he says
he's got a new man scalin loads
& he'll talk to him. Fine by me.
Next slip comes back 2,500 ft short.
This time I ride the load down
with Ike. The old scaler Jenks is there.
He knows I don't come to the yard
for no ice cream social & just says,
"Earl, it weren't me.
 It's that new kid Bowie ya be wantin.'
& here comes the hot-shot round the truck
with his rule all set for scalin.
Old Jenks heads for the office.
I got my limbin axe with me

& I make like I'm dressin a log.
The kid puts out his hand.
Wants to shake.
Guess he figured that would make
everything triple A. So I grip him good,
twist that hand up against the log
& got my axe raised
when Tommy comes up puffin at a trot,
    "Hey Earl! What gives?"
I'm staring the kid in the face.
"Well Tommy, this runt spud's been scalin me short
 & I figure I own the hand's been cheatin me."
That's when I smelled the kid lose it.
        I let Tommy talk me down
into the yard-office to "work-things-out."
Fine by me. I'm not one to hold a grudge.
That load scaled out right smart.
Next one too.
                No problems after that.
Guess the kid's scalin' slab now.
Tommy even sent along a check
to cover what I was shorted.
Now That's
the proper way
to run a business.

Greg Joly

FIREDRILL

Man, ya shoulda seen Nat Heath
comin off Gilbert Hill full
tilt with 90 bales a straw
loaded in the backa Len Robyn's
new dump truck. Them new trucks got
the exhaust runnin thru the bed
& the heat torched those bales
& here's Nat cruisin 60 on the straight
with the bales flamin out the back.
He never even seen em smokin
til one of the town guys
jumped in the fire truck
& lit out afta him full bore.
Nat hears the siren goin &
finally sees the bales on fire,
so he swings into where Miller's choppin
his fed corn & dumps the whole thing
on the roll. That broke the pile open
to more oxygen & they damn near
got fried when all that corn went up.
That field burned so hot
it blistered the paint
on Miller's corn harvester
before he could get the hell
outta there. Well Sir, Nat's little
party kept the fire boys fully
involved well past supper
& the first card
at the Masonic Hall bingo.

Betsy Sholl

BASS LINE

for Milt Hinton

He needs a bigger body, bull fiddle
to make that thump, that deeper pulse, he needs

four fat inflexible strings made of gut
wrapped by steel so he can pluck each night

that tree and its strange fruit, its slumped shoulders,
and bulging eyes... As he fingers the neck,

as he frets, keeps the time, he can take
those naked feet hung like weights on a stopped clock.

If it's too much to say one sight winds up
a life and keeps it running, still

some things are burned into the eyes
like a maker's mark seared into walnut

belly or back, history always there,
no matter how the body is patched

and reglued, the gut and steel fine-tuned.
It's a deep groove in the brain,

whether you play on top or behind the beat,
walk the line or break out: to know a man can be

waiting for a train and because the crowd's
riled up get taken— If death unmakes him,

maybe music's a way of weeping,
of cradling the broken body,

its strained neck, its eyes that tried to jump
at what they saw, the sad hands, sad hands

that couldn't lift to brush a fly.
Night after night, rhythm wants to unwind

the wire cable from that tree, sway
the mob away from its drunken rush.

So if he humps that stiff body night
after night, if he slaps and slaps? It's to

accent the offbeat, strengthen the weak, swing
like somebody who knows, who knows what it is.

Betsy Sholl

_____

HERE

Wharves with their warehouses sagging
    on wooden slats, windows steamed up
        and beaded with rain—it's a wonder

weather doesn't wash them away. In time,
    they seem to say, you'll be gone too,
        your belongings left on a quay for the taking...

What's there to do, but stroll over cobbled streets,
    listing letters you owe, books, food, anything solid—
        cement stairs, bike chains, manhole covers,

anything to weigh yourself down. But later,
    sleeping, you'll run like rain downhill
        back to those ramshackle buildings

stacked like crates, windows pitted with salt,
    doors barely held on their hinges.
        You'll be there, on the slotted dock

with its barnacled pilings, its green
    weedy skirts that shimmy in slow time
        against wave wrack and slump: at home

in that floating world, as water unravels
    masts into rippling flags. You'll hear
        engine grind, halyard clank, and fog's

ghostly horn declaring water takes all
    in the end. Or is that the voice of some other
        shadowy self just wanting to see

how insubstantial we are, how loosely moored
to everything solid—and yet, here,
for a time, within this wash of oilslick

and cloud drift, this long-stemmed sea,
star-floating, gull-feathered, where all things
that have to end, begin.

Charles Simic

The Many Lauras

Alas, I burn and am not believed.
Petrarch

I loved three different Lauras
At one time or another.
They laughed at everything I said,
While I shed tears in secret.

Even in church they'd titter
At the memory of me,
Even in bed with someone else
They had smirks on their faces,

Or so I imagined, because I never
Saw them ever again.
It was a big city so I kept meeting
Their smiling ghosts.

Petrarch, you only loved one Laura
And wrote hundreds of poems to her.
I loved three but only wrote one,
And it's not even a good one.

Theodore Enslin

Being as it is   not numbered
cut down the dying tree
do not let it suffer your neglect.
To say it will come in leaf again
is to neglect its dying.

                    No more leaves.
No burr nor blossom after winter.
Not the leaf   there were too many others.
Being as it is   what it was remembered.
Look to a final seed   one left
in shade below its withering.
Cut down and leave it for memory
where it will rest.

                Cut down
this dying tree.

Feature:
Bob Arnold

photo by Susan Arnold

Bob Arnold's best poems are moments, intense milliseconds that fill the body. He fits himself into the natural world exactly enough; but the clear stream and the granite take light from the observation of a woman's tenderness....They are not John Milton and don't intend to be. I suppose they derive from W.C.W.'s plums in the refrigerator, cross-bred with Issa; the weight of realized and singular human experience keeps them from the merely literary.

Donald Hall

Jim Koller

ON BOB ARNOLD

The New England literary tradition includes the land. Maybe Thoreau started that. But it's a tradition kept up largely by gentlemen, walkers and sitters, who, though they are quite often acute in the observations they do make, can record nothing of the actual give and take with the land because for them there is none.

The hills a man works on get into his body rhythms, come out in his writing. The birds and animals that he notes while working are not an end unto themselves, but are rather integral parts of his days. When he builds with stone or clears away brush or drops trees he takes the place he lives into the flow of his life in a way that transcends any mere passage through that land. He knows his smashed fingers, his pulled muscles—the messages his brain receives are heightened.

Bob Arnold's literary tradition precedes New England. He writes out of his work and his life, which are totally intertwined with the land. His actual physical surroundings are more apparent to him than to most writing about the land they live on. Don't content yourself with reading him; get to know him.

Bob Arnold

TINY SUMMER BOOK

sink

Cooler nights and warm days. Hot working in the sun. We mowed
one place, lawns and a field today. Susan mows with a walkman on her
head listening to classical music or opera, imagine. I'm in a bandana
and headphones hearing my ears ring, mow dim under it all, a
propeller swathing down the field, trimming close the garden edges.
Swallows flying, bombing near me, for the insects flown up from the
fresh cut. I've to only watch for rocks, stumps (fruit trees I had
to cut down over 20 years, I recall each one) and cats. Maybe a
lumpy frog. Dreadful when one is sliced. We break for lunch mustard
and cheese sandwiches, lettuce, fruit and cookies at the backdrop of
two barns. Moss soft underneath us. In shade. Boots in the sun.
A pasture leaning high up hill in the distance where cows usually
settle at this hour. Near an old spring along the sugar bush.
From the farmhouse comes banging in the kitchen sink.

The acupuncturist today said we might have to give
up swimming in the river. Water too cold. In Chinese
medicine the ears prick up she said at the sound of
anything cold. How long have I swum like this? she asks.
All my life. Another Oh? look. And I don't want to imagine
not following each other down the road and then a skip
path through woods over collapsed stone foundation
walls of an old sawmill. The sawmill once went with the
house we live in. Everything is gone but the stone,
which now work as steps, where you pause always to look
for poison ivy. It's along the river. Where we swim,
sliding by the rock ledge I imagine a water wheel, a
sawyer stepping out to take a leak in the woods while watching
the river. A mound of saw-chips.

Because of bad knees for a month and told to stay
out of some work I build birdhouses with Carson all
week. Can stand at a table saw. Carson runs for tools,
unwinds the long cord so we can work in the sun.
By the third house after a few days he wants to see this
one painted. Strips off his shirt and in jeans barefoot
he goes at it. The birdhouse dries quickly when the day
is 95 degrees and by the evening we have two in a tree and
the largest one nailed to a post stuck into the pond.
We always notice lots of birds near the pond. We give them
this one. The next one we build will be painted yellow
and we will hang it on the side of our house. A house
on a house. The last one for the week will be built from old
boards, the better to disappear into an ash tree we have in mind.

Do you want to hear about making love? Does it
have to be such a revelation? This happened this
way: at midnight I went upstairs to bed, there was a bat
in the room and you were under a quilt very uncomfortable.
Neither of us had the energy to deal with the bat.
We opened a window and left the room.
Downstairs we pulled a foldout bed, gathered quilts
and curled up in them. I was already moved to you
seeing how you looked upstairs running from the bat.
Drawn we began to kiss immediately and you lay above
me and showed perfectly how it was you and me and the
open door river sound. Then later. Every sound.
The cat, it must have been daybreak by the windows, fully
in love with us two near our heads.

We met our friend Lyle at Robert Frost's gravesite in
Bennington, Vermont. It was an easy spot to find, first by
the signs and worn path but most anyone would know to look
for the pair of birch trees. Around these we met and over
Frost we talked, noticing on the marker most of his family
are buried there with him. There is a 200 year old sugar maple
tree that lunges up right there, too. Very Vermont. The full
course of sunshine that day made the hillish cemetery
pleasant as we wandered off from Frost, talking his poems and
then Robinson's and later Shelley's. Lyle was old enough in his
eighties to having memories of teaching Frost in school when
the poet was nearly an unknown. He is directing most of his
words to Carson and I know is on the edge of reciting something soon.

Just before the garden becomes very warm with morning
sun, above a bush of jerusalem artichokes, a spinnery of
bugs fly around and around one another. It doesn't seem to
make any sense but it draws my attention and always has.
There they are doing what they do, in the cool of shade,
in the early morning hours when it is best to work in the
garden. Bare feet brush against wet clumps of johnny jump
ups. Holding a hoe. Looking at bugs.

Chucky, our logger friend, stopped by the roadside
bookrack we have installed just this week loaded
up with 150 books and he is the first person to take
a look. None of the Vermont neighbors have stopped yet.
Chucky is right over the Massachusetts border
along this river we all live on. I met him 20 years ago
when he delivered poplar boards for a large job I was
doing and he spoke impressed that someone knew about
poplar and wanted that over fashionable pine. He was
a kid right out of high school then, drove truck for a
local sawmill. Another time he brought a full truck of
dimension lumber and didn't bat an eyelash when I said
we had to carry every stick over a foot bridge to a job
on a knoll. Of course he didn't have to, he didn't work
for me, but he stayed with me and did it. Neither of us
will ever forget. Now I buy some of my firewood from him
and tell others who buy from him too. He owns a log truck,
two skidders, eight chain saws, and a book about the Vietnam
War which he bought from us this morning.

Our nearest neighbor to the north, up river, is Herb,
and today while we are on bicycles he stops his truck on
the road and wants to talk for a moment. His window is rolled
all the way down on my side, big burly face and beard, and
the right eye was hit with a metal shaving and despite an
operation it will probably never work right. He wants to thank
me again for allowing permission to drop a few small trees that
border our land from his girlfriend's. His girlfriend is Bonnie
who sits in the passenger seat with her window opened a crack
maybe four feet from Susan on bicycle and Bonnie stares straight
ahead. Nothing to say. In the seven years she has lived here she
has said hello maybe three times, but today nothing. Herb is
going on how with the trees down he has been able to level the
ground and can park two tractors behind his shed. He's a pig
in shit when dealing with tractors and I love him for this.
Of course maple saplings and beech shouldn't stand in his way
of a thousand more hours of enjoyment. I met him just a week ago
when he called one night and asked if I might come over and look
at the trees with him. Carson and I bicycled over the next day,
took a look, talked tractors, firewood, last winter, more firewood
then Herb wanted to take us inside to see his cookstove
knowing now that was how we cooked. It's a good size trailer and
the cookstove is ornamental and polished. Old barn lanterns hang
from a fake beam. Herb moved in a year or so after Bonnie lost
her husband to cancer. Carson used to think he wasn't friendly.

Between Ives and Messiean you move and I move with you.
In one more stupid mall with cheap price CDs and three
hundred Sunday shoppers all with the same behavioral instincts,
what's to look at? The ceiling is more curious, all suspended
with some panels complete, some open straight up to the no man's
land of steel trusses and cheapness. I know when it rains it
rains in the book section, and wouldn't you know? A leak in
the roof still to be found. Before we leave with our fix of
CDs Carson wants to take me back into the book section to show
me where he sits each time we come right in front of a rack
of comic books and he often brings real books to this chair.
Now I know where to find him. I remind him this is the best
way to use this place—read for hours on a rainy day respectful
of the merchandise but don't buy a thing. How I move with you
is standing still, not even thinking of much; will it be a CD
Ives or Messiean juggling prices, and in green cotton dress
between racks you hesitate in its alphabetical organization,
tight waist and hips curve, a freshly and very fuckable look
between us.

From outside in the sun beginning body work on one of
our cars I heard the phone ring in the kitchen and ran for it.
I usually would forget this, let it ring and continue my work,
but Susan and Carson are away in town and something important
could be on the way. It is Carson. He is at the doctor's and
wants to tell me some results. He calls me "Dad" which
is funny because he always calls me "Kakes" but refers to me as
Dad or Daddy to everyone else. He has poison ivy, has had it
two weeks and the doctor that saw him two days ago ruling it
as fungus was wrong. Since then the foot swelled terribly and had
us worried. When we left the office we saw the doctor out in the
corridor, far down the hall, joking with nurses and slapping
his hands together after a mouthful of peanuts. The nurse who
saw the blistered foot before the doctor seemed smarter than
him but she was on the fungus track as well. Mistakes happen
all the time but these shits are living well off mistakes. If
a hardworking and exhausted bus driver makes a mistake,
you're going to get hurt. But Dr. Trumper saw it right away.
He is older with a white beard and Carson remembers
him since he was one years old it seems. This doctor always
bails him out. Carson's excitement on the phone is
breathless and giddy and I would never think to correct,
now at age 10, his pronouncing his doctor's name as
"Dr. Trumpet."

The writing on the page, any page, should be immediate
and fresh and entirely open, but changing, so on returning
to the page the reader finds something different, maybe a
whole different reading. Roland Kirk does this in his jazz
playing. Whether by instrument changes or combinations this
musician excelled as an orchestra. Just last night I sat in
childish capture listening to Roland Kirk play "Summertime"
on harmonica. What guts. Delving in crosswind directions
on each hole over the mouth organ. I couldn't talk to you for more
than five minutes before getting bored and confused and murky
about jazz. All the varieties, all the musicians, all the hype
and glory and style. But I know summertime, and I own and
play at least three harmonicas.

At 7:10 this morning the electricity for most of southern
Vermont and neighboring counties of Massachusetts was blown
out in a matter of minutes by what the power company termed
a "tornado" when we called up to inquire. I was still in bed
having been awake a few hours already in the night and the
gush of wind that blew into the room and over my body felt
splendid after a few nights in a row of 80s. Carson said
outside where he was the grass flattened. Susan was afraid of
the trees. The power would remain out for twelve hours. A long
time for a summer day that would peak at 100 degrees. We stayed
away from the refrigerator. Read books in the same room, hours
of silence and then right after noontime we all climbed down to
the river, low and coppery and despite the slow suds we each
lay down in the water with our clothes on. By that evening and
still no power we thought to take a drive, on the road down
river and a few more miles high off from the river where we
had a favorite road open to the sky in apple orchard country.
It was dark by now, large houses open to the stars lay under in
shuttered blackness. Cars were parked at home, people must be
around. And it was only when you looked closely you saw the
people, like forty years ago out on the porches and front stoops
and they knew they looked a little unlikely. Only one girl showed
the spirit by doing a cartwheel as we passed. I still can't quite
shake how we saw a very modern car pulled onto a front lawn with
the trunk opened for its conveniency light and how people stood
around there.

two

When we took Carson down to Sleepy Hollow in Concord,
Thoreau's grave was just as we had remembered—sort of a tooth poking up
from the ground, easy to trip over, but the same size as brother
John's and Sophia. There is a large masthead grave with THOREAU
boldly greeting the visitor who has climbed onto Author's Ridge, so
called for who is also buried there—the Alcotts, Hawthornes, Emersons.
Since a film has been released of Little Women, Louisa Alcott now
has flowers and leaves and mementos left at her tiny stone and even
cheap and small note pad paper have been left with messages at both her
and Thoreau's. Folded usually. One was blown or left open and bending
down for a look I could begin a thought, "Dear Louisa Alcott, I love
your book Little Women and the movie," and the rest of the message
lost in the crease. Under the thick pine woods and locust trees everything
is damp but hardly touched from a recent rain. The Thoreau and Alcott
families are alongside with you on the pathway, not at all segregated
as Hawthorne and Emerson folks, but how lovely and touching to finally
find 5 year old Waldo's gravestone so closely laid to papa Ralph Waldo
Emerson; a son who died leaving his father boyless, and this stone
situated as if like a boy hiding behind his father and peeking out
from around a pant leg. No mementos are left at either Hawthorne's or
Emerson's graves so catching an idea from Thoreau, Carson decides
to take fallen oak leaves and say something of his own for these two.

brownies

The book sales begin the same, usually on a Saturday
morning at either 8 o'clock or 9. We try to be there at least
an hour before hand, perhaps thinking ten steps ahead of someone
else could be ten better books in the hand. We are book dealers
but we act naturally as book lovers, book readers. Actually I can
no longer stomach the loud mouth at the front of the line, twin
boxes in his hands, ready to leap at the first door crack and
mounting to the "specials table" hoping to find gems. He is in
Vermont and comes from Florida, "just missed a set of Jack London
yesterday in New York State" he says loud enough for all to hear.
Trying to charm each womens league volunteer so he might
get closer to the stock, suddenly shutting up and offering to be of
some help. They have seen him a million times over. Inside he will
shove and perhaps argue, be gone within the hour to hustle another
library sale somewhere. A rocky van he leaves in. When the glut of
dealers are gone the little room of eight long tables owned of books
will air out nicely, helped by sunshiny tall windows. You have
your own stash of books but can now relax and touch the spines
walking slowly along each table. Pleasant with others and their two
paperbacks. These days it is a bestseller they want. For awhile there
was no smell but of old books. Now with less people and less books
comes the sweet bake sale aroma of brownies.

slept

Darby lives down river renting a house I built for friends
of ours 15 years ago. Darby has lived there now five years with her
companion Jim and they kayak the river and hike these hills. Darby
likes to hike with dogs, any dogs, and often a small pack can be
seen following her on the road along the river. It goes on day
by day. But one day one of the dogs went astray up into our place
and started digging at the chicken hut and we were already hit
hard once this year by another neighbor and his stupid dog.
Actually the owner is stupid, not the dog, remember that. But
this dog made quick and killed two chickens. Now here was another
dog at the chickens and we had no idea who it belonged to. It was
a gentle dog but blood crazy and it took some doing getting it far
from the bird hut and back down to the road and that was when Darby
showed up. Hot and bothered by now we showed no mercy letting her
know what we thought. Darby played dumb, grabbed the dog and left.
For a month afterwards she never waved, barely nodded a hello and
it was only a matter of time one of us would run into one another
and words would be again said. This time I was scything the roadside
one morning and saw Darby and waved and she nodded but I guess
others would say she scowled. I cried aloud it was "ridiculous"
perhaps coming louder because of the sweep of the tool and before
I knew it Darby was at my face demanding what it was I said.
I repeated it. She got testy and after two hours of talking and I
still can't believe we talked that long, had that much to say,
and Susan found us and joined in. Darby's four dogs that were
with her dug holes in the shade and lay into them and slept.

Before we pulled up to the beach gate house to pay to get in
we noticed one of the rangers inside hitting "green heads" with a
fly swatter and knew it would be bad. We paid and he warned the flies
were vicious. But we didn't care having already driven three hours
to get there we weren't about to turn back because of a few measly
bugs. Of course a few would be at least pinned to each leg once you
got out onto the beach, swatting at them mostly below the knee and
Susan and Carson took the ocean water, playing the tide and waves
and for a moment looking back at them frisky and aqua and because of
the green heads the beach was splendidly abandoned it seemed free
and Bermudian, especially for someone like me who has never been to
Bermuda. I get there by thinking a top corner spit of Massachusetts
shoreline is Bermuda. My the sunshine is hot, the water terrific,
two sailboats spot along a far horizon. I've decided to walk the shore
from the bird sanctuary over to the town beach where it seems
strangely vacant. Again, the flies. I pass two sun bathers sitting
up with hats and sunglasses and towels wrapped around
their legs. We smile a greeting that is all possible because we are
today suffering all together. I notice the flies stay off as long as
I move and move quickly. My jeans are rolled up to the knees where
it is as deep as I can walk in the water along the shore. I turn to
see where Susan and Carson are, how far have I gone? And to my
surprise not too far; all this time they have been quietly swimming
parallel to my walk. We rejoice. Stopping the flies start biting.

own

Worked early this morning cleaning out our septic tank with a
septic pump owner and his truck. Unwrapped all the hoses. The slimiest gloves in
all the world on my friend, and a glint
of a post-earring in his woodchuck head. What in the world is
this community coming to? He wouldn't be caught dead five years
ago wearing such an ordeal. A country boy. Chipped front teeth,
mommy written all over his body and chunk.
We sucked up the tank. I dug out the trap door and
covered it later while it was still raining.
Good for years more since we use only one john, two sinks and
one tub in the whole house. No hot water unless
heated on the cookstove. Simply crafted by candlelight baths.
You know one of the worse jobs I ever had was digging
out a septic tank — homemade job, steel drum —
across river for a summer house A-frame. Once hunting camp which
I'm sure put the tank in. Never pumped, couldn't with the river.
Pipes backed up, real chaos. I was hired to dig out the tank,
all the pipes, replace. I was 32 and happily getting paid.
Hip deep in shit and not my own.

I'm supposed to give someone named Dot Robins a call. She has
a key to a spring house that my plumber friend Denny would like
me to take a look at. Denny has been a plumber thirty years. He
has a squeaky friendly voice over the phone when he calls to talk
and the voice doesn't change that much when you're with him all
day working. In fact it gets better because he likes to joke and
we have in cellars, crawl spaces, ditches, yanking up submergible
pumps. I haven't seen this spring house yet but Denny says it is good
size, maybe 16 x 20 and he isn't prone to exaggeration. The spring
is on a dentist's land who lives here part-time and Denny
does all of his plumbing and heating. He trusts Denny, goes by his
word. Denny asked the dentist to call me about repairing the spring house
foundation where rock had fallen away but the dentist could
never reach me. I later spoke with Denny who elaborated on the job.
Not only stonework was needed but the inside collar ties were rotting
and the roof was in poor shape. Probably needed a new roof, or layer
over it with steel sheets to slide the snow load off. Denny was
humorously perplexed just how I would get in to work those collar
ties since the work area was over no floor, or no nothing, just deep
water. I haven't seen this yet. Dot Robins has the key and I have to
call her to arrange for picking up the key and getting directions
to find the place. I need to find the place. You see talking
over the phone with Denny and joking like we do we both have
this vision of me in the spring house in waders doing the job,
or swimming or drowning. My curiosity is up. I've made plans to
call Dot Robins this evening and drive out to her place tomorrow.

Dot Robins turned out to be OK. Gave us expert instructions how
to drive through her town of jumbled back roads over hill and dale
to find her place and pick up the key to the spring house. But Dot is
90 and maybe didn't understand so when we got there it turned out she
didn't have any key to the spring house, but to the main house and it
was no good because the owners were away and she wasn't quite sure
where in the house the key to the spring house might be. No problem.
We had a flashlight, we would poke around. We stood half in the front
foyer and kitchen to Dot's little home as we decided about all this.
She expected us but we imagine the house is always this tidy. A peach
on the cast-iron white sink drainboard with a sharp knife beside it.
Not a hair out of place. Old phone still on the wall. Old license plate
with 3-digits on the car. The lawn mowed. She said the spring house
was up the road and we'd see a falling tree butt sticking out of the
woods. We did. Dot and her family once drank from this spring.
Now new houses share the water as part time residents; airy houses
built to bring the outdoors indoors because the people don't go really
outdoors too much. The spring house has a few holes in the roof from
fallen tree limbs and continued neglect has begun serious rot on half
the rafters. There is a gaping hole at the foundation that needs
attention before a skunk drowns in the drinking water, and since we
don't have a key and are using only a flashlight to peer through
heavy hardware cloth, we're guessing at the total labor. But to fix
the hole we figure 100 yards from the road, over a slippery stone wall
bring six bags of cement and mortar on our shoulders and all the
stone in Vermont is there and we can fix it.

Continues hot. We worked all morning on apple tree jobs —
broken by harsh winds in August and have to clean the mess
up and trim the trees back to looking in good shape. Susan
with me handling the logs and brush. Carson was up at the
farm house putting potato crop away into boxes; he now has
a good sense at that. Plays with the kittens around the
barn. Then reads in the truck. We wave to him from down
below. Climb the pasture back to the door yard with heavy
chain saw and wet sweat clothes. Bandanas tied around our
heads. Can't wait to drive the six miles back home to swim
in the river. Being cooler nights the river now holds a
colder water. We found out. At the river, just before
sliding off bank ledge into the water, Susan says she can
still smell or taste the apple wood on her face.

June – August 1995

Bob Arnold

A LINE OF TALK

I walked up to a brakeman
to give him a line of talk,
he says if you've got the money
I'll see that you don't walk.

Jimmy Rogers

PREFACE

Jim Koller has had most of these questions from this interview knocking around in his head longer than I have—his questions got me on the stick to write these short essays, and they have been a line of talk in our friendship over the last decade. When Jim and Leslie and the kids visit us, or vice-versa, Leslie, Susan and the kids turn in early at night knowing Jim and I will stay up late talking. Some of my talk I've remembered in these essays. Both Jim and I make a living working with our hands—building and landscape work—and we also write poems and have edited literary magazines. It's no big deal. Others have done it. Speaking for myself, writing poems and hand labor are both one, they work off one another, and combining the editing of a poetry journal are the things I love to do. The hand labor earns a pay check, but moreso it earns the poems I write, and the editing derives from a literary enjoyment of gathering poets into the same pages, no matter their poetic landscape; the poems simply have to be good. Not just good to me, but good for poetry. Like when you hear a Woody Guthrie song, *that's* good. Bad is easy to smell. It's the same idea Whitman lit into our heads when he wrote: "who touches this book touches a man"—we've heard it a hundred times, but how many have you read? How many even get published? I try to find these poems built into such a book, and when I find them I want to put them into other hands.

Robert Frost wrote good poems in his early years, they were poems that felt lived-in, and curiously read as if they were written before Frost knew what he was doing—which doesn't mean he was ignorant—rather what Olson said: "we do what we know before we know what we do." Later, when the world ate him up and gave him four Pulitzer prizes the poems have already suffered from too much pollination; they had become only poems, down right expected of him. That treatment would kill anything that bleeds. My point is that his early poems talked a real talk, made a poem sing/made the reader sing, brightened the eyes to a connection of life and words. And to find these words you have to hunt, become a reader—a doer—and one good book will always steer you to at least one more good book, and finally to the man Whitman knows you can touch. In these essays when I write of the outsider I'm thinking of the writer with no easy definition or identity, call him what you want. It is Montaigne who is always reminding me "The reader who is not willing to give an hour is not willing to give anything." What isn't explained in these essays is yours to find—it's out the door, the tip of an ear to a sound, and how much you really do want to find. Don't kid yourself.

When Jim and I get together to talk it is usually after a separation of many months, and in my case, months of being with Susan and Carson, working outdoors, talking to myself, piling up books to read at night. To some it might sound too simple, romantic—where are the bad days? they ask. Fortunately I can't accommodate them. Why people want you to be as miserable as they are, is anyone's guess. My bad days are mine, I don't waste them into a poem unless it naturally flows in that direction. I'd rather work it out where bad days begin, in my gut. Sametime, the best love poems are never written. I've been lucky and Susan has helped, and so have other friends—just a crow flapping up river sets a pleasure. You notice these things and follow them through. When Jim and I talk he might be sipping whiskey, Leslie gives Susan jam they've brought from travels through the southwest, and little Bert and Ida Rose really smile at littler Carson which makes him smile. I want to take it all in, Susan and I talk about the visit later and months fill in between the next visit. Other friends visit and we all talk about what we're doing—share books, music, go places with the talk and the silences between visits. Jim talks less than I do but when they return from a cross country car trip he likes to get out the map and show us where they've been, even though he has crossed this country more times than I can remember. It excites him, he may not always show it, but it goes into the poems. Poets put into poems what they do. My feeling is that the less they do, the more literary tricks show up—gumballs, forced language, because they're-poets-and-they-must-write-a-poem! Spare us.

I have a photograph near my desk of Van Wyck Brooks and Jaime de

Angulo; it's a favorite of mine. Brooks is wearing a sweater, tie, and suitcoat standing proud into the eyes of the camera; de Angulo is on horseback in a ragged shirt looking sideways from the camera. What a meeting of the minds! Eastern establishment shaking hands with western soil, reminds me of Emerson seeking out John Muir in the Sierra. Like Emerson, Van Wyck Brooks had a generous mind; it was a mind that stayed open, hung on the lip of vulnerability, took chances, and because of that nerve both achieved more than most American literary historians in finding the gist and flesh of our literature. Brooks went looking for Jaime de Angulo because he knew de Angulo, like any good writer, must first live away from the pages of his writing. I first read Jim Koller as a teenager, looked him up and published him in my twenties...we've been visiting, working, talking, sharing things ever since. "A Line of Talk" is some of the hours.

INTERVIEW QUESTIONS TO FOLLOW WITH THE TEXT

1. We have spoken often of the writer as outsider, coyote & buffalo, part of no organized or even informal group. Could you elaborate on this concept, detailing why these particular writers are relevant to other writers & the general public?

2. Some have said that they thought the outsider we speak of might truly carry the traditions of an American Literature that those in either the university or the closely-knit groups of writers often found in cities have lost sight of. If you think this is likely, have you anything thought relevant?

3. What part does work with one's hands have to do with writing?

4. What is your political/social stance? How does this affect (or effect) your work? Should writers concern themselves with political/social situations?

5. You have published Longhouse for years. Would you explain your approach to publishing? If you were to start it all over again at this time, how would you do it differently?

6. Is poetry as it exists in our society of any value to the general reader or public? What do you see as the state of poetry, i.e.; healthy, out of touch? How can things improve?

Jim Koller

I. OUTSIDER COYOTE BUFFALO

The question of how relevant the outsider is reminds me of how you can ask someone to draw out the interior plans to a city or country land-scapes—how that city or woodland is comprised—and the map drawn will detail a territory that only reflects the interest of the mapmaker: the middle-class show no slums. The weekend countryside dweller's map is the exact mileage to the nearest town. The city and countryside lose their identity among their residents, and most times that unmapped place is where the outsider is. The relevance of the outsider is as relevant as those lost horizons, even though they're right under our noses, we pass them by.

The outsider is that saint or visionary who has one, or many, experi-ences in life where he looks into the heart of nature and God and never turns back. Van Gogh had many. Coyote sees what the outsider sees but many gods talk to coyote. Turf is important, especially west of the Mississippi, but a few have been spotted east. His messages are found from signs integral to the eyes, hands, groin, heart. Coyote moves among us like dirt, water, blood. Buffalo has a passion for self-creation. Has no set locality, but wherever he is, lives in harmony with his life and craft which becomes his instincts. Fame means nothing, he works best in isolation or directly facing the amplifier. Outdoors, to coyote and buffalo, is more important than indoors.

To simplify, I'll integrate for most of the discussion the terms—outsider coyote buffalo—into the name outsider. These three should be relevant to other writers but usually that isn't the case. Like the mapmakers, writers stay in their groove—and if they read—they read what is comfortable to them, or expected of them: writers that eat-what-they-eat, talk-like-they-talk. That explains the echo you hear when reading about these writers. The outsider is just that, *outside*—out of town, blowing his horn on the corner, etc. He's Thoreau at Walden, Muir in the Sierra, Lew Welch driving cab in Chicago. Their families can't figure them out, friends (the few) shake their heads, the manuscript pages are folded and hairy, and repeatedly rejected by a clone of publishers who live for today. The outsider lives in yesterday today tomorrow and most likely is read in the tomorrow but is too busy living to care. Some editors want the outsider to be read now and publish their work, taking chances as editors should...nothing may come of it. The outsider makes the real *realer*. Students love it; read it on the sly, children invented it, and the outsider takes note.

With literary gimmick, distant theory, or reference pages that accumulate half a book, life is the outsider's book—and if he is a poet—all music is his rhythm. It would seem natural for the general reader to enjoy it. No schools are needed to curl up with the outsider's book; simply an awareness, and a desire to bring as much of yourself to the book as the outsider reveals to you. Thoreau reads best out of the lunchpail, not in school. Writers that write in school read best in school.

For some reason we expect writers to be famous before we read them. Look at Isak Dineson and the recent unburial of *Out of Africa*—the book is now called a "movie tie-in," and what do we watch on the screen but a Danish woman finding her independence take soil on African ground. A nut case in her lifetime to many, but romantic and durable on the screen. The book has been around for years...(Hemingway spoke well of it at his Nobel Prize ceremony)...along with Jack London's *Martin Eden* there is no better example of a writer who followed her heart, withstood the struggle, broke rank, and busted her hump physically with the land, its wildlife and people—which many years later produced a book on that life which has no modern equal. On the movie screen it's fantasy and safe, off the screen it scares us.

Barbara Moraff has nitched out a life these past twenty years in Vermont which I think scares some people. It's off the screen, she lives down the road. A mother, potter and poet, who I believe has written some of the most songful poems Vermont will hear. Edgy, lamp-warm poems with rats in the firewood, and you can pour it all over snow and eat it. Of course where the tar road begins not many have heard of her and bookstores don't stock her books and she isn't that easy to edit anyway, since it's life we're talking about here—*made into poem*. That's architecture built with two hands that fits exactly back into two hands. There is no house, love, or poetry that is built better than that.

II. CARRYING TRADITIONS

I don't want to whitewash any group, but if we consider the outsider—writers like Whitman, Dickinson, Melville—and they all certainly fit the bill: runaways from their homeland in love with their homeland, who worked best as loners and died as mysteries to the public, then we know the outsider has carried the tradition, since no writer worth his weight hasn't been influenced today by one of these writers.

Otherwise, I guess it depends on whose American Literature? There seem to be a few, depending on where you look. Let's take Whitman and Dickinson as examples and attempt to tie them to the flesh of poets working today. Whether the university poets or professors like that or not, we're going to find the poets that most of them have never heard of, or won't read. Whitman asked us to "look for me under you bootsoles" and today's bootsole poets, who have carried the tradition, would be poets like Ed Dorn, James Koller, Bob Kaufman, Janine Vega, Thomas McGrath...workers, singers and visitors, who have all made books from a life lived in many combinations and have shown us they are here to stay. Each one is an outsider, or coyote, or buffalo, but they don't call themselves that, someone else does. Emily Dickinson lived so quietly as a poet in Amherst that few knew a poet was there, just like Lorine Niedecker in Wisconsin. But Louis Zukofsky and Cid Corman clearly knew Niedecker was there, and made connections. Even though you had to special order Niedecker's books of poetry just one year ago in most bookstores, poets who have come from her work were already writing and talking, and it skips a stone back to Lorine, Emily....

I imagine a closely-knit group, be it in the city or country, has good merit. Though reading the headdress of poets and writers that flock to writing seminars at Bread Loaf every summer has no merit. I don't blame all poets—a job is a job—and occasionally a good poet, a shaker, is found visiting Ripton, Vermont, but it's not the norm. The norm is the same type of poet. And the only tradition I think Bread Loaf is sustaining is keeping those New England clapboards white. Of late I'm more skeptical about the poets that move from the city to the country to bake the country poem. Not much of a tradition there, more a personal search for the good life without any roots ever watered into the grounds. Poems galore are written while the firewood is buried under the first snow. Getting your shit together is the oldest tradition.

III. HANDS

Working with my hands has everything to do with my writing, but my hands usually want to say less about it and do more off the page—look for the rhythm in my poems—that's the hands.

There are piles of books of good examples that show the sense and rhythm of working with one's hands and Eric Hoffer's *Working and Thinking on the Waterfront* is one of the best. The work is not explained as much as it is just there—it's a job, his life, it's daily. The thinking was something he did as a workingman, not the other way around: one hour of wood splitting for eight hours of deskwork, that wasn't for him. He unloaded freight on the docks of San Francisco as a longshoreman, made his pay, and at night and days off wrote his books of philosophy and politics, and he made pretty good money from those books. But he was always his own man—definitely a buffalo writer. The writing and handwork tied together into a human pulse that moves the pages of *Working and Thinking*, and you get a clear idea how one couldn't live without the other for very long.

But it's not for everyone. Wallace Stevens probably raked leaves, at most, in Hartford and he wrote great poetry. The poem, or "building god through the labor of seeing" as Rilke said it, that revelation, comes as it has to independently for the poet. A good ear can hear what is true and what is false, that ear has to be trained and then trusted. So you don't hear the hands in Stevens, but you do feel the interior of the body, something tropical, and glimpses of lightning.

Working with my hands is what I do—I learned at an early age—and have tried to surround it with books ever since. Working in the family lumber business, learning the building trade, unloading boxcars of western spruce (smelling the west), listening to workers joke and gripe...later on teaching myself stone work, feeling the hands hurt, talk back, begin to sense what it really is to *touch*. If one is going to write a poem about felling a tree, or planting a tree, it can have all the correct words, technique, order—but if it doesn't give the reader the tree: roots, sky, ground, work of hands, then the poem isn't anything but words without the lights on. Don't give it to another poet to read for authenticity, let a woodcutter read it. Watch what he says.

IV. BODY SOUL NAME

I consider anything political which knows its rights. We've got a malamute and its minus 5 degrees this morning and the only place where there is sun is near a backyard apple tree, and he is sitting right in that place of sun. Won't move. And Jack knows he doesn't have to move, the day is his, and he is causing no one harm—he is living according to his nature, as Thoreau said everyone should do.

To be political, to be anything, is to give yourself completely to whatever you are doing. Some writers work all day at their trade and at the end of the day walk to the mailbox with their writing and wait for a check...the next writer might suggest for this writer to walk past the mailbox and around the corner and see that he has a burning nuclear plant slushing on the shores of his favorite river...and a third writer will drop his bags beside these two writers and begin to talk about the open road. Politics is the footing in the process of being alive, and for the writer it should sound familiar: "In the beginning, was the word"—it's where all good writing starts, with a footing.

The Eskimo say a man is made up of three parts: body soul name. That's as political as I am and I believe it's about as political as one can get. You can vote for this and vote for that but if you don't put your money where your mouth is, it only proves the shame of the vote. It's twenty-four hours. It's body soul name. If lived true to form it draws man through politics and back to man—most stop in the politics stumped. The best of our writers moved from man and into politics and back to man, everyday, because they take gambles and make it their business, it's part of their survival and what finally puts an edge to their writing. And there is a crushing machine out there waiting to spit them out into sameness—so they can be safe, like everyone, employable. They tried it with Vallejo, Mayakovsky, Brecht, and lost teeth for it.

Walter Lowenfels wrote "the revolution is to be human" and that's akin to the Eskimo body soul name. The writer must be human. Not a great man in his books and a piece of cold iron in person, it's easy to be a nice guy on paper. It's to be an activist full-time, which in society quickly shapes up into being an outlaw. An outlaw has to be careful who he talks to, how he avoids the law, lives quietly and has no need of a big stick. If he chooses the big stick, or the big stick is put in his hands and it feels good for a few days, like Hemingway, then he's going to have to slug with it the rest of his life.

The activist, the writer, the one-with-words, watches Washington, Moscow, Belfast, Beirut; if he doesn't, no one else will. TV follows these places like a puppy. The writer has the ability to frighten governments, make it run around asking questions like "*Exactly who are you?*" Tom Paine had that power. Victor Jara was murdered because he had that power. The writer composes poems to the bear, the sound of high-heels, Larry Bird at the foul line, and the next day works on poems of our murderers: Pinochet, Marcos, Kissinger. A writer/activist is someone who climbs 80 feet into a redwood tree to save it from the assault of the lumber companies and is buried an hour later by the logger who cut it down, because he is also an activist, who has to put food on his big table. Better to go after the corporate leaders in the shiny city who think of redwoods as patio decks. Too many activist/ writers get their photographs into *Time* or on the back of a book jacket...the best activist is hardly seen, the results are seen. Look how frustrating it is because Salinger or Pynchon won't show their faces to the public. They both know that without a face they move better around us.

V. LONGHOUSE

In the early 1970s I found a plot of land to work off of, built a cabin on it to house myself, the books and tools, and shortly thereafter began Longhouse in 1973. My approach to publishing is to gather all walks of poets into the same bundle of pages and make it somehow jell. To inform my readers with poetry and an understanding that the reader has to be included in the lifestyle of the publication—since I believe in financial independence of grants/funds, no ties are encouraged with anything but flesh. As an editor I'm after the serious working poet; any style/region. The idea is to move the poetry around...to excite people, make readers, bring readers and poets together.

When I started out I was involved with very few poets. The tough part was locating the poets I wanted to publish, and they lived everywhere: California, Wisconsin, New England, Kyoto. So I hit on a few poets I had been reading and admired, but didn't expect much since they didn't know me from fox. Hayden Carruth, John Clellon Holmes, Ted Enslin—each one responded with enthusiasm at what I was doing and put their shoulders to the wheel by sending poems, donations, other poets to contact. The important thing back then was they *answered*, many don't. Word got around. Before long I was trading publications with other publishers like Jim Well, John Judson, and Rosemarie Waldrop (all poets, too) who were each generous with their trade and knew that publishing a book didn't stop with the book: there was a sharing and a life devoted to it. At the start the magazine was called *Our Poets Workshop*, which was soon chopped down to *Workshop*, and by the time I met Susan and the cabin got a second story and the garden was widened, it all became a home in the name *Longhouse*.

I think we've done pretty well. Nobody owns us, and we have about 100 readers, and those 100 readers are the type to pass the magazine around to another 200 readers. It's not how many readers you have, it's what type of reader, and ours seem to be after that range of poetry light. I've lost count of how many issues, broadsides, booklets we've published, in fact the early issues were given away so free I don't even have copies. But someone's got them...most likely Tarachow, Giannini, Lewandowski, Levy—those are the poets of my age, each a personal friend, who have been the meat and potatoes: the give and take: for an editor.

I doubt I would do much differently if I was starting all over—in fact I try to change gears every few years within the Longhouse—smaller off-shoot publications like *Poets Who Sleep* and *Scout*. The tone of the entire publication reflects a habitat with fresh water flowing by, exactly what Susan, Carson and I have here on the Green River. It's homespun, printed by us and collated on the kitchen table. At the start we published more frequently and were publishing poets from the U.S. and abroad—today I'm more interested in the outsider, the buffalo, as I like to call him. It's a writer near extinct who for years has roamed the literary world from the fringes, but like the buffalo he is a pathmaker, a road builder. This type of writer believers in no separation from his life and craft, the language grazes through it. I'd like to collect a small library of these buffalo writers into simple made books and place them in the right hands. Now, the "right hands" isn't always the person who already knows the song—if that were the case we'd read only one another in our little cliché and be the same idiots we point our fingers at. Emerson said "give me initiative, spermatic, prophesying, man-making words"—that's the secret. Some poets gave me eyes and now I want to share those eyes.

VI. STATE OF POETRY

In one of Lorine Niedecker's poems she offers—

> There are two kinds of artists,
> Those who write for people and those who write
> For art's sake.

It's that simple, and I like a combination of both. Poetry should be of value to the general reader, I've seen it so. If I visit a school to work poetry and on the first day I see faces blinking eager but unsure, I know there are reasons. Most of the general public is that way with poetry because it takes time to warm up to a poem. It's a job of the poet to shed some warmth. It's been drummed into the public, usually by schools, that poetry is a "mystery" we have to solve. Symbolism is attached. Very serious discussions take place...the poem is then frisked for meaning, once found it is disemboweled and pinned to the barbed wire fence...same thing we do with anything wild, which is where poetry originates. After the mystery has been solved and those funny lines stretched out into a "meaning," the public can then enjoy it. Maybe. I see a lot of people in the backrow asleep.

I one time read a poem of mine about stone work to a group of teachers that asked to hear the poem, and I received gestures of appreciation after reading it, but no spark. Later on, walking out to my car, I met up with a crew of maintenance workers spreading sand off a pickup truck onto ice and one of them, a friend, for a lark, hollered over for "a poem." I had the stone poem fresh in my head and recited it, a short poem, and at the last line all three nodded their heads and raised their shovels in salute. *That's* spark. They could have thrown the shovels at me hating the poem, that would be spark. Poetry needs spark. Poetry is written from a spark.

To reach people the poet has to write like the whole person that he is, who just happens to write. The reader has to do the same—give that whole-ness—wake up past that state of semi-anesthesia. It isn't the language that scares the reader, rather the gooey pretense, that air some poets strut because they have nothing else. Poets are tuned into the sharpened verbal tide hashed together with being alive. They work on the page or as story- tellers, and it takes work to read that page or to listen well. Some carpenters will build an entire house without ever touching a handsaw. Reading books and listening are handsaws—they bring you closer to others and make you meet yourself.

For the reader to sit down with a book of poems he has to be in-spired to sit, he won't sit for nothing. So if a poet has written a poem about a hawk he has to bring that poem alive on the page for the reader and the hawk. He can only do that by being-hawk. Fancy words won't help, only the ability of the poet's experience with language and a hawk will have the reader feel-hawk. It has to have feathers, claws. It has to be the flight of the lan-guage matching the flight of the hawk—and the reader isn't stupid; he'll love it, and read on.

The state of poetry had become a State. Since government funding has perfumed the scene it has both assisted poets and smaller presses and made most junkies for the money—a fine example of colonialism. Some haven't lost their integrity, a little money one year didn't hurt after years of the writing struggle...but whenever anything is government funded it is be-ing watched, pegged, reeled in with red tape, and so is the recipient. That's the bureaucrat's job, he has nothing better to do. Editors and poets have plenty to do: they need to publish magazines and books that gather the best minds of their generation, and it doesn't matter if it's twenty-five copies or 1,000: you're publishing, you're moving, you're making true connections.

Poets need to get into the schools to excite the kids, the kids are just waiting for it. He has to show students and teachers that Cummings was delicately smart as well as a wild-and-crazy-guy, not a duffer like their poet friend who has tenure. Poets need to work with the school basketball and football teams and share the poetry of pro-athletes Alex English and Todd Christenson; it won't be Shakespeare, but it will say more to them NOW because it's poetry written where they're coming from. Once inspired, one thing leads to another. Poets of the 80s were listening to Bob Dylan in the 60s and some are still listening while reading Pound and Petrarch; things connect. Poets have to get into the schools and tap these roots into the soil. On the job, more gingerly, the poet shares—not expecting immediate results—but like a gardener waters, weeds, hoes, gets dirty, relaxes, and the rows somehow flower straight. If they don't, plant another row.

Over in Europe poetry can still be found nailed to a post or tree (just like Villon's time) and a friend, while over there, read one he liked and mailed it back to me and I nailed it up on my wall in Vermont. That's connection. A poem having a friend think of a friend and then sending it over to make the tie. That's the strength of the poem and friendship, and it was up to me to nail that poem back up, or pass it along...to the next nailer.

A fine poet in San Francisco, George Evans, recently passed on a poem my way and it was one he knew I liked. George Oppen's "Forms of Love," printed handsomely on a straightforward placard that he said was running on 17,000 buses around the country. That's a lot of nailing up, and one sure way of improving things: get poetry visible to the people by choosing a poet of strong human examples, then select one of his poems that will ring in the ears forever, or at least for that day. That's enough, that's everything. It educates, it has people stop to read (they do) and gives the gift of a good poem to the people. Maybe it will agitate a few to question the poems that run in *The New Yorker* each week (many don't seem to ring like Oppen's).

To have healthy poetry we have to have healthy poets. Poets that walk the countryside like Wordsworth and Basho...who jump to that clickety-clack of the city, like Paul Blackburn...who feel the land and look into the eyes of the people they write about. We have to have poetry editors who don't complain, especially within the small presses—so what if no one is reading the books you publish—the idea is to publish good poetry that will eventually find good readers. Whitman took his poetry door to door. Find your readers, cut back your distribution before losing your independence; unlike the large publishers the small press publisher shouldn't be in it to get fat, it's for the poem. If you make a buck and don't lose face, terrific. Poets have to read everything, or at least if you read Wilbur then read Whalen. And vice-versa. The healthiest poets I know help each other, and make their living faraway from poetry and with poetry; they don't have their eye on any marketplace, but on the muse. And the muse was the guy talking to himself last night in the laundromat...the muse were the geese you heard flying over so high they were out of sight.

Green River, Vermont
Winter 1986

Ryan Walsh

ANOTHER LINE OF TALK

It's been more than fifteen years since Bob Arnold and Jim Koller first collaborated on "A Line of Talk" and much has changed in the world of publishing and editing. RIVENDELL *often relies on exchanges via email. When I contacted Arnold electronically, he graciously provided the following.*

RW: You've written of the Outsider Coyote Buffalo writerrs. Who do you see as some of today's young buffalo writers?

BA: To tell you the truth, I'm not too sure how happy I am any longer with this term "buffalo writers." It immediately throws up many images in my head—as if forcing these young writers to wear weird buffalo horn hat of some sort, to Bob Marley's "Buffalo Soldier" in head-nodding Reggae beat, to our literal buffalo now being chased around Yellowstone Park by pesky recreation snowmobile clubs. In these parts we now have bison petting farms stuck on a commercial byway between a Wal-mart and a Super Stop & Shop. It hurts to think about it. The reference has become immensely clunky to me. But fifteen years ago when I was mapping out answers for Jim Koller maybe the "'buffalo" was one way to survey a safe-harbor for these poets I admired and often learned from. Buffalo meant "becoming extinct," like the nickel, like the long drawn terrain the animal once roamed. These days I'm more concerned that human beings are going to be allowed to live and be humane. Is there a poetry in our living as there should be? I receive no poetry from computers because it all seems so stupid to have to turn a machine on to get turned-on. I love books. I love small press journals and the more homemade and fascinating by that certain touch, the better. Certainly if a friend happens to send a short poem by email I'll be more than happy to read it...but I do better walking around the house putting down pages of text and picking it up later. I've thirty years of correspondence and neatly stuffed trunks of many spinoff books by poets I can't yet part with. They come in all the time. Poets I love are on the shelves in books and loose pages sent and manuscripts and self-published masterpieces all together like a cook's corner. Poetry recipes dirtied up with smudges of sweet spices. How in the world can a computer do better than that? And this is how I've come to find poets—some find me, some I come upon in journals once traded like wildfire with mutual minded editors that got stocked on shelves in the hundreds. All through the mail system. Read every page, every poem, seeked the poets out.

There is far less of that now. It's tough to afford the costs on all ends. I can't afford the price of new poetry books so stake-out a few favorite bookshops and read for a few hours at each visit, but I hardly ever walk out without having bought something. Better a used copy. Old habits are truly meant to die hard. The young poets, or forever-young poets, I really like and have had the good opportunity to publish the last many years would be folks like Greg Joly, neighbor as the crow flies and crackerjack letterpress printer (Bull Thistle Press). He built his own house to house his press in. He is also a dedicated scholar to the life and works of Helen & Scott Nearing. Alec Finlay in Scotland came here to ice-skate once on our small pond and nestled a few days with our family. He's a one-man band of making poetry move internationally: CDs, visual presentations, publications, unique anthologies, and all his way is like a poem itself. I like Joe Massey out in Eureka who works paper projects and shoots on the Internet easy as pie. He has poet friends in Philadelphia who also excite the wavelengths: Fran Ryan, CA Conrad, and of course Gil Ott has done great work in that city for years. Alan Chong Lau is sumi artist, poet, musicologist, and grocer. I last saw him in Seattle's Chinatown packing out celery sticks and later we published a little book of Alan's with the celery in there. Maybe the Pacific Rim has that benevolence for poets because there is a whole crew of them I like on the Olympic Peninsula who live by their wits and write mighty stuff. Often translating Chinese poets like they're blood brothers.

Say, "Finn Wilcox, Mike O'Connor, Tim McNulty" out loud. Just down the road in northern California is here-to-stay Jim Dodge. Great stories & poems. Or his good friend Jerry Redden who letterpress prints like an angel in Berkeley. Tsering Wagmo is Tibetan but lived in San Francisco when we published her blossoming orchard-like poems. I just remember I left the upper Pacific too quickly and missed Sally and Sam Green: remote island press magicians (Brooding Heron Press), homesteaders, poets. The real deal. Same with Stefan Hyner in Germany, tireless translator of worldwide backcountry poets, carpenter, editor of the occasional *Gate*. Peter

133

Money sinking new family roots in Vermont. Michael Hettich's often dreamscape poems triggered from his little garden of eden in Miami. Both Bill Scheffel and Andrew Schelling breathing out poems from mountain altitude Colorado, or else Andrew on some scented trail leading Mexico to India. Charlie Mehrhoff/Scarecrow/friend of the plateau/ he's out there somewhere. Cornwall bred but Slovenia wed John Phillips now back in St. Ives and writing some of my most favorite short poems. Same with Gary Hotham in Maryland, and John Martone in Illinois who publishes his tel-let press like nobody's business. A mound of books now. All top-notch. I know and adore many other women poets but they are all older than me, so I guess they don't qualify! I was a visiting poet twenty years at a local girls' boarding school and worked with hundreds of singers and writers—some with that certain verve—but have only heard of one, Clare Muldaur, who went down that garden path.

RW: I see that Longhouse has a website (www.longhousepoetry.com), and so I wonder: how does the outsider coyote buffalo writer navigate in today's internet-powered global village? How has Longhouse reconciled working in such a world?

BA: Well, living *is* relating, no matter how you do it. And I'm old enough now to have experienced in the building trade fork-lifts taking over from the manual yardworker—all day unloading a boxcar of western spruce and neatly piling each board into a shed behind him. Or seeing handsaws get to be more Skilsaws get to be the ever present chop-saw, or nail gun or next new toy. Whether the bowsaw or the chain saw? I say both, because I've needed both. I wasn't getting too many jobs walking in with a bowsaw, but it's my decision at keeping the bowsaw handy and part of me. So the internet and such technologies are simply one more tool—kept practical and they'll work for you. And this is how practical I am: I know next to zilch about comput-ers.

Susan read your question over my shoulder and whispered to me (we were in a library): "but *you* don't do the website, I do." And it was Jim Koller who five years ago preached the sensible merits of the computer to us who were struggling to sell books out in the woods from our tiny bookshop, twelve miles from any town, dirt roads as far as you could think. No one was coming. The paper catalog was reaching the devoted but no one else, and it was killing us in printing cost and mailing. So Susan taught herself how to organize a bookshop out of a computer while I built the bookshop, read the books, and became the packing clerk. I still tear my return addresses right off the envelopes and tack them to my plank wall. When I get too many, Susan logs them on the computer. Longhouse publishing skips along just as easily as the mimeograph days—I still manually layout everything cut and paste style—and then Susan does everything in-house web design with Adobe PageMaker layout. On a Mac. If I sound clumsy it's because I have little idea what I am talking about. Not exactly ignorant, just that Susan is so good at it. When all is ready we take it down to a photocopy shop in one of the college towns that are really sick of seeing us all these years with fussy projects, but it gets done. We hand make all the books back home by the woodfire listening to music or watching the entire history of world cinema. We end up giving away half, selling a quarter and saving the other quarter until hell freezes over (only to give those away, too!) It remains practical as long as it remains your lifestyle, and we now have a little family all involved.

Our 17-year -old son Carson writes and publishes over the internet his weekly music journal *Track*. All responses return to him, from all ages, by email. You just don't buck what works. He also takes the time to print out each issue and tacks it up in bus-stop shelters, libraries and music stores. The vast majority of our bookselling orders arrive by the internet. It works like a charm if you daily pay attention. On the other hand we buy the majority of our books in bookshops and from people, hardly ever on the internet. It's a personal decision. Way too much is made of this goliath global village. Who in the world told you to buy a cell phone, advocate corny transmitting towers on hilltops, install a fax line, buy all the latest software and stare at a lit screen for hours and hours and hours each day? Nobody. Poetry will outlast us all.

Charter Weeks
PORTFOLIO OF PHOTOGRAPHS

Everyone knows that the camera captures the moment. Indeed, our lives are nothing but an endless stream of moments strung together. Even in the act of recognizing it, it is gone and another is upon us. Perhaps that is why photographs are so evocative; they remind us of how exciting the present is despite the fact that all photographs, of necessity, depict the past. We cannot look at the images of Walker Evans or Dorothea Lange or Wegee or Garry Winogrand or W. Eugene Smith without making a vow to pay attention to what is directly in front of us.

Images in general and photographs in particular are also evocative because we can discern our own experience even though we have not experienced this precise thing. Almost every day when I look at the newspaper, I see some picture I wish I'd taken. Even people's snapshots excite me. In a funny way, all photographs are snapshots, it's just that some people have learned to be more disciplined about what they shoot...and also what they throw away.

The ubiquitousness of the camera has made the photographer transparent. Except for the occasional Hell's Angel who's threatened to make me eat my camera, I have found people either oblivious or accepting of someone walking around shooting pictures. Photography, along with collage, is a kind of democratization of art. I pick up my camera and stalk the world of reality I am immersed in and bring it back alive for everyone to see. You can't beat that for excitement.

Charter Weeks
Barrington, NH

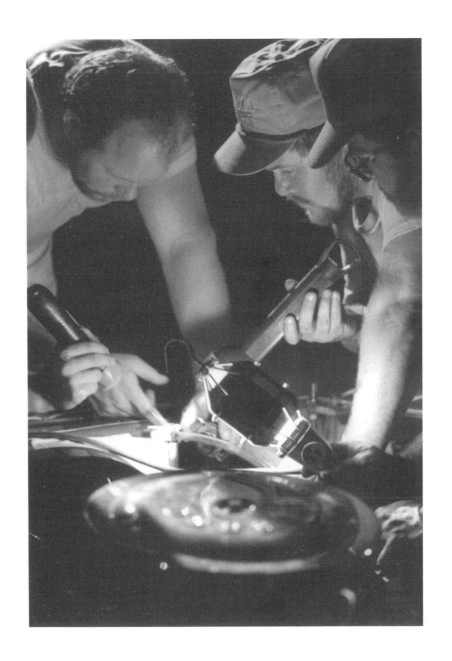

David Budbill

Broken Wing is the story of a Rusty Blackbird with a broken wing who can't fly and therefore is trapped in the north country for the winter, a winter for which he is totally unprepared. It is also the story of The Man Who Lives Alone in the Mountains and how The Man gets involved in the bird's struggle to survive.

Broken Wing is also a meditation on birds, death, personal identity, the nature of being crippled and music. In the early chapters of the book, as The Man's involvement with Broken Wing's daily struggle deepens, The Man Who Lives Alone in the Mountains thinks more and more about birds and their place in his life.

CHAPTER 5: THIS TIME TO WATCH AND WONDER

The Man's attentive and concerned involvement with Broken Wing continued throughout December and into the darkest and coldest time of the winter while at the same time he learned to step back, distance himself, from the little bird's struggle to survive.

While it was indeed the darkest and the coldest time, the center of winter, it was also to The Man Who Lives Alone in the Mountains, the brightest and best time of the year. The snow banks along the sides of the road grew higher and higher and the mercury in the thermometer dropped lower and lower—some nights down to 25 or 35 or even 40 degrees below zero, and on those nights the blue-black dome of heaven revealed a myriad of constellations across which flowed that dense river of stars people call The Milky Way. And if the sky was that clear at night, then usually the days, even though they were short, were brilliant also. Light flooded through the windows of his little house and filled The Man's days with an intense clarity. Oh, how The Man loved these days of deep snow, sharp, stinging cold, brilliant blue skies and blinding white light.

The intense cold and deep snow isolated The Man and his bird friends from the outside world, yet this made The Man happy, not fearful or sad. The woodshed had ample wood for the wood stove; he could stay warm through the coldest time, and there was plenty of food for both himself and his feathered friends. The Man felt as though he and his bird friends were cut off from the rest of the world, hidden in a secret place far toward the interior of a strange land of cold and snow, and these notions made The Man happy. The insularity and solitude that these winter days brought him filled The Man with an odd and quiet joy, and because of the isolation and remove of these deep winter days, The Man knew a kind of relaxation   during this time that he knew no other time of the year. He enjoyed himself and the short days, long nights and the world around him with a renewed, intensified and quiet pleasure.

The sameness of these days, the cycling of light and dark, blended as the days passed one into the other so that the days followed each other seamlessly except for an occasional storm that came to add another foot of snow to the already snowy landscape. In the sameness of these days The Man found not only pleasure, but greater focus and an intense passion as well for now he could attend to his inner thoughts and to the endless turning of day and night—in other words, both his inner and the outer weather—and to, of course, the birds he loved so much who kept him company just outside his windows.

In this time of pensive reflection, this time to watch and wonder, full of stillness and light, The Man Who Lives Alone in the Mountains one day sat down to write another letter.

Dear Howard,

That time of darkness and light, cold and emptiness is here. I want to tell you about what happened yesterday. Another bird story.

I got up before sunrise—which isn't very hard this time of year since the sun doesn't come up around here until well after 7:30—and went about my morning chores. I started a fire in the stove, put the water on to boil, went to the bathroom and peed, brushed my hair, washed my face, and brushed my teeth. Details! Details are important! When the water boiled I made a pot of tea.

Sometimes, of an especially cold winter morning, I like to get back into bed with my tea and not stand at the window.

While the fire warms the house, I drink my hot tea under the warm covers, and I watch out the back window to a different bird feeder and wait for the dawn.

When dawn came yesterday, or just before the dawn, when the morning light began to overcome the darkness, a single Chickadee appeared at the feeder and began her breakfast. In less than ten seconds a dozen of her brothers and sisters and cousins were at the feeder also.

This morning as I watched the little birds, I wondered at the way they always seem to arrive together in a group or very nearly. I know Chickadees don't sleep together, but rather roost each to him or herself. How then did they all get to the feeders at just about the same time? Is someone the leader? Does she wake up the others? Does she sing a few notes? Do they "sense" the dawn while their heads are still tucked in the warmth and absolute dark of the down beneath a wing? Do they all get hungry at exactly the same time? How do they all know to get up and come to breakfast together? Are they simply social creatures who enjoy each other's company and would never think of eating breakfast alone? And where does that social, collective impulse, this ability to act and be together, come from? These questions got me to wondering about other kinds of birds.

Lately in the afternoons there has been a large flock of Redpolls—in other winters it might be a flock of Pine Siskins—sometimes as many as fifty, pecking and scratching across the surface of the snow beneath the feeders finding whatever it is they find in the husks and hulls and refuse from the feeders above. They look for all the world like a flock of tiny chickens as they hunt and peck and bob, but then, and so unchicken-like, suddenly—away they all go all together in perfect unison, up into a nearby tree.

Sometimes this upward flight has an obvious cause like a threat from an approaching Shrike or the yap of a dog, but often there is no apparent cause for this flawless, unified and simultaneous rising up together. How does that happen? How do they do that?

I've often seen the same thing driving down a wintertime dirt road as Snow Buntings who have been pecking along the surface of the road gathering sand and gravel for their gizzards get up and blow away in a swirl as if they were a little bunch of dry leaves caught in a dust devil.

Much larger birds do this also, like the wintertime flocks of Evening Grosbeaks who also visit the dooryard feeders and who can, it seems at will, also display this perfect-unison-take-off from the branches of an Apple tree. And in the spring, large flocks of black birds, Starlings and Grackles and Red-Winged Blackbirds, literally fill up the naked tracery of the branches of a poplar tree—hundreds of birds together in one flock—and then suddenly and simultaneously all lift off and exit at exactly the same time as if all these birds were really one bird with many wings.

And, in a way, more amazing is the same phenomenon among fish. Many times I've seen huge schools of fish, sometimes thousands of individuals in one school, moving together this way and that, up and down and away, waving back and forth like a fan, like a relaxed hand, in the water, again, as if these thousands of fish were a single individual.

In all these examples the group moves together, simultaneously, without a leader, or so it seems.

How do they do that? Is it that they have some kind of collective mind or soul that lives outside each individual? And if this mind-soul does live outside, away from, each individual, if it lives in the space *between* the individuals of the group as a whole—whether it is a flock of birds or a school of fish—and if this is the consciousness of no particular individual but rather the consciousness of all, of the group—if all that, then: are these individuals not really individuals but only parts of a larger individual? Are they only the arms and legs and fingers, fins and wings, of a bigger individual called the flock or the school?

Can it be that the mind-soul of this larger individual really does exist in the empty space among and between the members of the flock, yet controls the entire flock from that empty space?

And how can these birds be individuals one minute, sitting on a shelf feeder pecking open a single sunflower seed and arguing, fighting with each other, and in the next moment lose, or give up, their individuality to the group, to that larger mind-soul, that bigger individual, called the flock? How can they do that?

Could I, could you, give up my, your, own individual self to a larger flock of humans and if I or you did that what would that be like? I'm not sure about you, but I am, I fear, too much the solitary individual to ever be able to do such a thing.

What I'm talking about is why I'm so attached to Broken Wing, my Rusty Blackbird friend. As my bird book says: *a secretive and solitary bird—They seldom occur in very large flocks, and do not as a rule associate with Red-Winged Blackbirds or Grackles.* We are two of a kind, he and I. Both of us cast adrift on this white and foreign sea. And, well, as you know, birds of a feather flock together, even if only to remain apart. Another loner, like me. Which is the problem. He and I are loners and yet we're also more than that.

Each bird is an individual first and a member of a flock second, just as you and I are. Yet some individuals are more inclined to be members of flocks, like Grackles, or like you, Howard, living there surrounded by others of your, and our, kind, while some individuals, like Broken Wing and I, for whatever reasons cause us to be that way, are more solitary and less inclined toward being members of a group or flock.

Yet now that I say that, I know although it's true, it's also not true. You and I both know full well that each and every single bird or fish does not give up its individuality to the group, at least not all the time. Rather I think what they do and how they move so perfectly in unison together is not by abandoning their individuality but rather by some kind of higher form of communication within this group of individuals. And this higher form of communication is something most, almost all, human beings never experience.

But you and I have experienced it. I know you already know what I'm talking about. I'm talking about when we used to play music together, you and I and our friends.

I think birds in flocks are like we used to be, when we played together, how we could jump into a tune and play it—without any discussion before we began of what we were going to do—because we all could communicate so well with each other on our instruments, we all understood each other so well musically, that there was no need to talk.

And once we really took off and entered that other world, call it The Tone World—which is what William calls it—once we were in The Tone World, there really was some kind of collective personality that took over, that made us one being, a flock of four or five, like the birds and the fish, and we, I'm sure, appeared to those listening to us to be, a single, new and different person, a single instrument playing, which, of course, is exactly what we were.

And yet none of us ever gave up playing our own individual instruments or playing out of our own personal and individual lives, and because of that each of us played our own individual instruments out of some deep place in our own personal and individual selves. We were each like snow-flakes, each one of us absolutely different from the other, yet all of us, while we were playing together, made together a single song. We made a new and different person while we played together. We were, at those moments, just like the birds and the fishes, don't you think?

It's not that flocks of birds or schools of fish or groups of musicians are, when they are together, a single living thing with a collective personality, or that they are always only separate individuals who are just great at communicating with each other as they play together, it's that they are both those things and both at once, at least we were at those times when we really did leave this everyday world and pass over into The Tone World.

The thought of being my individual self within the group, yet also joining the group, becoming part of that larger mind-soul, that bigger individual, called the group, the flock, and thereby knowing a kind of higher communication between individual souls, the thought of all of that, the thought of being there with you and the others, of sharing life and music with all of you, all of that sounds so good to me!

Oh, Howard, I'm so homesick! Thinking about all this makes me so lonesome for you and for the others, for the street, our neighborhood, for the music and the noise of the city, for those times we played together. I want to do something, make something, create something with a group, with our group, and not always, as I do here, alone. Alone. Alone.

On the other hand, I read a poem the other day by a Chinese poet named Hê Chih-chang called "Coming Home," which, by the way, was written more than a thousand years ago:

> I left home young. I return old,
> Speaking as then, but with hair grown thin;

My people meet me, but they don't know me.
They smile and say:
"Stranger, where did you come from?"

You see? What if I did come home? Who would know me? What good would it do? No. This exile is my home now.

I know you and alot of others back there think I was out of my mind to come here all those years ago, and staying here all these years has just proved to all of you that you were right! But I couldn't help it. I had to come here. I had to leave there, I had to leave home. I couldn't stand it there anymore. When I came here all those years ago I was just trying to be who I am and not who somebody else says I am, and that's what I'm still trying to be.

Do you know that great quote from Thelonious Monk? "A man is a genius just for looking like himself." Well, it takes a lot of courage and work to look like yourself, "simple" as that may be. And, Howard, sometimes the sacrifices I have to make to look like myself are almost more than I can stand.

I know another poet, I can't remember his name right now, who got it right when he wrote:

> When I was young I dreamed of home and in my dream
> I saw a place remote and in the mountains.
>
> Now I'm in that place and I call it home,
> but home is still nowhere I can find.
>
> It must be nowhere is the right place,
> and when I get there I'll be home.

And until I get to nowhere, I'll be here.

And yet, so much of the time I am sad and blue. So much

of the time I am so lonely, sad and blue. And sometimes, I just don't know what I'm going to do.

Your Friend,

The Man finished the letter, put it in its envelope, sealed it, addressed it, put on his outdoor clothes, and as he walked down the lane to the road and the mailbox, his eyes welled up with tears.

He opened the mailbox door, put the letter in, closed the door, put up the flag, turned and headed back up the lane toward the silent house.

***

Broken Wing's wing continues to mend. He can even fly a little. Then he is attacked by a local house cat and almost bleeds to death in the snow before The Man can rescue him. A blizzard comes, and The Man has to go to bed without knowing whether Broken Wing will be able to survive the storm. He wakes to discover Broken Wing has survived, spring comes, Broken Wing finds a mate, and all seems right with the world. The Man wakes from his dream to discover that it is neither spring, nor has Broken Wing survived. Rather it is only the morning after the storm. As the days and weeks pass and The Man doesn't see Broken Wing, he understands that Broken Wing has not survived. In the spring as the snow melts, one day The Man finds Broken Wing's body. He buries the bird and writes his friend Howard a letter meditating on death and the death of birds.

CHAPTER 10: THE SUMMER OF MOURNING

No matter how glum and brooding The Man Who Lives Alone in the Mountains was that spring, spring did what it always does, it burst in upon the stiff, winter world of ice and death and turned everything flexible and green and did it with an extravagance and burgeoning excess only spring knows how to muster.

The Man tried to join this springtime parade of life, but it was difficult. Everywhere he went he thought he saw Broken Wing flitting into the dark trees. Every thought he had seemed always to be interrupted by a thought of Broken Wing.

His vegetable garden to which he devoted more love and attention than he did his Apple trees and almost as much love and attention as he lavished on the birds, seemed this summer to offer little help or distraction from his grief. In the past his summer garden had always been such a pleasure for him. All those summertime vegetables and the process of   raising them that The Man had hoped would be not only a pleasure but a solace also this year turned out to be neither.

Rather this summer every time he saw a bug on a broccoli or a tomato plant or on his fence of peas, he saw Broken Wing chasing after it. And then he didn't see him.

Every morning with his cup of tea in his hand, when The Man went to the garden to look around, Broken Wing wasn't there; nor did he land on the hoe handle as The Man rested from his weeding and cultivating, nor on the railing of the porch as the man ate his lunch. And when The Man walked up the hill above the house and along the logging road that runs beside the bog, Broken Wing wasn't there either.

That June in the garden, as he thought about Broken Wing and his mid-winter night's dream, as time passed, his grief for the bird did not lessen but instead grew stronger.

The more The Man actually lived through the events which had also been a part of his mid-winter night's dream, the harder it became to endure them without the presence of Broken Wing. It was as if Broken Wing were a ghost at all the events he should have been present for in his living self. It was as if Broken Wing were a ghost in this entire summer of no Broken Wing, as if he should be living out the life he had had in the dream.

Then late in June two gifts of a sort, visitations you might call them, from the avian world began to help The Man adjust to the absence of his dead friend. And these gifts, these visitations, helped the man feel encouraged, alive, even if only slightly, for the first time in a long time. He sat down one afternoon in his rocker on the porch and put his writing board across the arms of the rocking chair and began a letter.

Dear Howard,

I've been meaning to write to you but, as you know, I've been in a funk since spring. But a couple of things have happened lately that have helped me rise up, even if just a little bit, out of my indigo mood.

I've been meaning to write to you for weeks to tell you about my White Throated Sparrow friend with whom I've been playing duets every morning.

It all started early in June. There's a large Balsam Fir about half way down the lane to the road. A few weeks ago early one morning as I was headed to the road I heard that distinctive and clarion call of the male White Throated Sparrow. So I called back, I mean I whistled back, I mean I tried to. His call is so clear and pure and *high* that I had great trouble getting into his range and key. But I'm getting ahead of myself.

So let me get behind myself.

Before I go on, I want to tell you about a little poem I read not long ago, a haiku, by Richard Wright, yes, that's right, Richard Wright, the author of *Native Son, Black Boy, The Outsider, Black Power* and a collection of speeches almost no one's heard of called, *White Man, Listen!* Here it is:

> Leaving its nest
> The sparrow sinks a second,
> Then opens its wings.

That is exactly right! That's what happens. Details. Details are important! What would we do without poets, Howard, without their eyes and ears and feelings! How would we see and know and feel the world?

Back to where I was.

That first day, the first day when I heard him calling his call from high up in that Balsam Fir and I called back to him, much to my surprise and delight he came barreling out of the branches of the tree and across the lane and into the old Lilac bush on the other side of the lane where he landed and called again. I called again too and he flew back to the Balsam and called again. So I called again also and he again as well. This time he headed for the Lilac again but stopped short of it, wheeled around and came straight at me. I was standing in the middle of the lane. He flew around me several times trying to figure out what kind of an odd looking and monstrous White Throated Sparrow I was and then back he went to his singing perch in the Balsam Fir.

Clearly he was plenty irritated with me for my intrusion into what he considered *his* territory and he'd come out to challenge me. Understanding this, I hollered, "Hey! I been here 30 years! You just moved in last week!" Such logic meant little to him, and he came at me again going back and forth from tree to Lilac to tree as I began again walking down the lane to the road. I think he took my movement away from him as a sign of my retreat and his victory in this territorial battle and I was not about to disabuse him of that notion. That was the extent of our encounter on that first day.

The next day and the next, and any day it wasn't raining, I'd go down on the lane and call to him and he'd not only answer but come out to challenge me. Slowly, I do believe, he got used to me and I to him and he quit acting so territorial. He grew tolerant and patient with me and with my inability to pitch my song into his range. Sometimes I could almost get into his octave but never quite. The best I think I ever did was almost getting there, perhaps a third, sometimes a fifth, below him, yet even though I was singing harmony he'd respond, and on those days when I had to call in unison but a whole octave below he'd still sing with me. I was grateful for his graciousness and magnanimity, his patience, with my inabilities. Therefore I was always careful, or as careful as I could be, to whistle his song with the proper intervals even if I wasn't in the proper key. It seemed to me that he didn't mind so much if I sang in F# while he sang in B just so long as I got the intervals right. After all, change the interval of a White Throat's song just slightly and suddenly you're a Chickadee!

We came, I believe, to enjoy our morning duets. And I noticed over the days that we played together that he often changed pitch and key. He had more than one way to sing his song. I wouldn't say we were exactly improvising together, but we also didn't do the same tune every time either. It was music, Howard, the two of us made there each morning together, and it pleased me and, as I said, my guess is he didn't mind it too much either.

And also this. The two of us there together every morning were The Absolute and Original, Never More Basic Call and Response. You know, it's odd. People think our music is urban, something generated in big cities, but everything about it began in the country, whether it was Africa or here in our own South, and Call and Response is probably the most obvious example of it all and obviously our musical ancestors learned this way of playing from listening to the birds.

In a way, Howard, even though it seems I am about as far away from our music as I could possibly get, what I've really done, I believe, is go back to the source, to the beginning of our music. Maybe that's another thing that keeps me here.

White Throat is gone now and I wonder why. I wonder—no doubt because of the gloomy pallor hanging over me this spring—if he died or was killed by the damn red squirrels that attack everything around here or maybe it was just that his mate and he, as soon as the chicks fledged, got out of here to be away from that lousy, amateur musician in the neighborhood who was always trying to sit in and then when he did get a chance to blow played clams all the time. I'll never know why he left. All I know is he's not there anymore and the silence isn't as pleasing as his song.

157

I also know I miss him. Every morning as we sang he'd display himself to me. His clear, brilliant white throat, and the bright yellow spot beside his eye, shown in the morning sunlight. He was a handsome little fellow. His kind has always meant spring to me. Winter is interminably long here. It seems to go on forever. Yet when spring does come and the Robins and Crows and the great migration of Warblers and all manner of other birds return, it doesn't really seem like spring to me until I hear the White Throated Sparrows sing. When I hear that little song then I know for sure spring has really come. I always think what they are saying with their song is:

> The sun! The sun! I bring the sun
> in the bright spot beside my eye.
> Come out! Come out of your house!
> The sun has come!

Well, what that little White Throated Sparrow didn't know was, his willingness to sing duets with me was the beginning of my return to the land of the living I do believe.

Howard, truly:
There is a balm in Gilead to heal the wounded soul
There is a balm in Gilead to make the wounded whole.

And that balm—need I tell you?—is music.

I hope White Throat will return next year and if not he, then perhaps his son or daughter so that next June also I will have someone with whom to sing.

That's the first thing.

The second thing is: for the past ten days or so there has been a crow hanging around here in the dooryard, actually in the yard, and out around the garden too. He's got a club foot. His left foot is deformed, the claws, toes, talons, turn in, curl under, just as you'd expect, as you'd imagine. And he limps as you'd also imagine he would. He has to walk on those knuckles. He seems to be able to fly all right, up to a tree and perch okay, although he seems, obviously, to have more difficulty than a normal crow would being as he can grip a branch with only one foot and has to more or less balance or lean the other, the club foot, on the branch next to his good foot. Whenever he lands anywhere, on a branch in a tree or on the ground, he has to get himself adjusted before he can do anything or proceed anywhere. Everything is more difficult for him, everything. He reminds me of Jimmy Washington, the legless guy on the rolling cart who used to hang around at the corner of Kinsman and 59th. Remember him? And, of course, he reminds me of Broken Wing, and yet I welcome his presence. I'm glad he is here.

I've been putting sunflower seeds and cracked corn out for him especially. It's almost as if the ghost of Broken Wing has returned in the form of this crippled, deformed, club-footed crow. I'm fond of him. I hope he stays around. I haven't seen him for a day or two though. I hope he's not gone off somewhere or been killed. I call him: Lord Byron. What better name for a crow with a club foot!

Again, with Lord Byron, as with Broken Wing, I've got a brother here with me, a deformed, tenacious, gritty, stubborn, obstinate, resolute, black brother. May Lord Byron fight, may he resist, may he rebel, may he revolt until the last bitter, or not so bitter, as the case may be, moment of his life!

I wonder for Lord Byron, as I wondered for Broken Wing, whether he ever gets discouraged, ever wants to give up, give in, just die, because it's so much easier than to continue struggling. Think how much harder it is for Lord Byron with that club foot just to walk across the yard, just to get through each day.

Or maybe on the other hand when the struggle is the hardest, maybe that's when our instincts, or our will to live or whatever you want to call it, drives us onward ever more strongly.

Whatever it is, what is certain is that this life is a struggle. Need I tell you? And those who don't know it, don't know even half of what it is to be alive.

Which reminds me of something else. I met a woman I know at the store the other day, and we were visiting, and somehow I got talking about the blues and she said, "Well, what if you never get the blues?"

Can you imagine? I was speechless.

And she was serious too. I must have had the look of incredulity on my face, because she looked at me and said, "No, really, what if you never do."

I just shook my head. I wanted to say something, of course, I wanted to say to her, "If you don't get the blues, Honey, you be dead! You may be walkin' 'round, doin' your job, Sweetheart, but you be dead."

But I didn't say it. I just smiled and changed the subject on account of I figured I was talking to a corpse.

Sing 'em awhile, Brother, make you feel a whole lot better.

Which is what White Throat and Lord Byron reminded me of and it's what I've been doing lately, and I'm feeling a little better too.

And speaking of indigo moods, I've had an Indigo Bunting coming to eat the seed heads off the tall grass that grows just beyond the lawn right here near the porch every afternoon for about a week. It's rare in these parts to see these birds so I feel especially fortunate. Always late in the afternoon. What a sight they are.

Your Friend,

He finished the letter, put it in its envelope and sealed it, then set aside the letter and the writing board. Yes, he *was* feeling better, a little better at least.

The Man Who Lives Alone in the Mountains rocked and looked out at the summer afternoon, out past his garden and beyond to the mountains to the east where the Ravens lived and croaked and chortled their way through their lives. And he thought about all the other lives both human and non-human that come and go, come and go, come and go, here in this tiny little place, this slab of mountainside where he lived, and he smiled to himself and knew he was a lucky so-and-so to be here and feeling so sad and blue because he knew it was a sign that he was alive and still in love with this life and his life and this world and all the creatures therein.

Rebecca Rule

How the Neighbor Earned His Nickname

When strangers bought the Colonial on Hosshead Hill, those who live down below—which is pretty much the whole town since Hosshead represents the height of land—especially those who live at the foot of the hill in the area called the Hoof, referred to him as the Neighbor and to her as Mrs. Neighbor, even though they had different names on the mailbox, so maybe they weren't married at all. Live and let live, that's the attitude in Woodford, pretty much, particularly in the Hoof. Why that is, I couldn't tell you—except maybe living in the lowlands humbles a person. Or maybe it's how the Hoof always seems to get the worst of whatever comes along. Like mud season. Mud season lasts longer and the mud's deeper in the Hoof. Gracious Alstead, retired English teacher, says it's more "viscous." I don't know about that, but step wrong and you'll sink. How far depends on your weight and how long you stand dumbfounded; it's not quicksand but it's damned inconvenient.

About the time the mud dries up, the black flies come out. Black flies aren't any bigger or thirstier in the Hoof, but there's more of them. I know. I've counted. Between Mother's and Father's Day, nobody goes outside without a net, unless they're making a dash for it. And the old ones, the slow ones, the spleeny ones with no blood to spare, they wear nets even then.

As soon as the black flies die down, the mosquitoes get going. Hosstail Marsh breeds particularly large, mean ones. Voracious. (That's a Gracious word for "hungry.") It is a scientific fact. A professor spent two summers collecting in specimens in baggies to come to that startling conclusion.

On the other hand, though our climate favors bugs, it is not particularly kind to the rest of us. Something to do with the shape of the valley and the iron content of the soil draws weather—twisters, microbursts, thunderstorms. The Old Westgate house burned three times from lightning strikes. You'd think they'd take the hint and relocate, but they just keep rebuilding on the char.

Course we dread winter. If the weather man says "Cold snap, ten below," it'll be twenty below here at noon after the sun has kicked in. If downtown Woodford gets two feet of snow, we'll get thirty-four inches.

Between slogging through the mud; fighting off the bugs; waiting out lightning storms in the car; plucking tree limbs out of the roof; pumping deluge out of the cellar; and tunneling out the kitchen door to the snow bank to try and locate the mailbox with an ice-pick, the inhabitants of the Hoof are too busy surviving to worry about other people's business—like how the Neighbor and Mrs. Neighbor pay their bills since neither of them goes out to work. A lot of people live together without benefit of marriage, and nobody gets too worked up about it except the Reverend Mr. Claus Titbaum, and it don't take much to get him worked up, believe me.

On the other hand, over to Vermont *everybody's* getting married. And there's quite a few Vermont Titbaums none-too-happy about that.

On the other hand, some of us were none-too-happy when the Neighbors posted their land about ten minutes after they moved in: NO TRESPASSING. NO HUNTING. NO FISHING. NO TRAPPING. DON'T EVEN THINK ABOUT PICKING A BERRY. On the other hand, the Neighbor was none-too-happy about what happened to his chickens. It wasn't malicious or intentional; it was, however, inevitable.

I don't know what he thought he was doing when he erected that flimsy wire pen—three feet high, no top, and not even dug down in the ground. An owl could have swooped in and picked off those little peckers one at a time for a midnight snack. A fisher cat could have climbed in easy. A fox would jump in, jump out with a mouthful of poultry before that poultry could even blink. Same with a coyote, only a bigger mouthful. A skunk, on the other hand, would be inclined to tunnel under and start in on the eggs; whereas as a weasel would go straight for the heads. And it wouldn't take a coon more than a minute to finger open that paperclip latch and saunter in through the gate.

But in the end, it didn't turn out to be any of the above that did in the Neighbor's doomed chickens. Unfortunately for Randy Hickey, it was his dog, Mutt.

At first Randy denied Mutt's involvement vigorously. Mutt was home all night of the night in question, sleeping under the porch. An old dog, arthritic, a great waddling scruff of a barrel-chested St. Bernard Newfoundland cross with a smidge of Bassett in the legs, Mutt hardly ever left the yard.

"Look at him," Randy Hickey said to Chief Harold and Officer Fred when they showed up at his double-wide investigating. "Does that look like a dog who'd ford the brook in high water, run a mile uphill through the woods, and massacre a dozen chickens in the dead of night?"

Mutt lay splayed like a rug on the kitchenette floor. He was under house arrest, pending. "What have you got to say for yourself, Mutt?" Officer Fred asked. Mutt raised his head, regarded the investigating officers with hopeful, cataract-blue eyes, and thumped his big old tail.

"Mutt was seen," the Chief said somberly. "He was seen at the scene of the crime."

"Mutt was said to have been seen," Randy Hickey said. "But that don't mean he was seen. How could the Neighbor see a black dog in the dark on a moonless night?"

"Flashlight?" the Chief suggested.

Officer Fred bent low and raised Mutt's chin so they could look each other in the eye. "Did you go on a rampage?"

Mutt rolled over for a belly rub.

He and Randy maintained innocence right up until Chief Harold shined a light under the porch and Officer Fred raked out a pile of feathers, feet, bits and pieces of carcass which, reassembled, did look something like a dead chicken or two.

"It'll cost you five hundred dollars, Randy," Chief Harold said. "You pay for the Neighbor's chickens, and Mutt can walk away from this incident with impunity."

"Impunity my ass. Where am I going to get five hundred dollars? What the hell kind of chickens were they?"

"Exotic," Chief Harold said.

"Silkies," Officer Fred said. "And Frizzles."

To prepare for his meeting with the Neighbor to discuss the situation, Randy practiced looking sad and sorry in the shaving mirror as he scraped away stubble. He wasn't sad and sorry. He was POed. It wasn't Mutt's fault the Neighbor didn't know enough to build a decent pen. It's in a dog's nature to eat a chicken if the opportunity flaunts itself, just as it's in a man's nature to resent having to pay five hundred dollars for another man's Silkies and Frizzles. *Silkies and Frizzles my ass*, Randy thought, *probably garden variety pullets.*

It was foggy in the Hoof that day as Randy started up the hill. He was walking cross country for his health, but mostly because he couldn't get his truck sprung from garage until he paid the balance on the valve job. In the lowlands the morning mist still hadn't burned off—and probably wouldn't for a week or two. But high on Hosshead Hill the sun shone bright. It radiated through the plate-glass window in the Neighbor's sitting room which afforded a view of the whole of Woodford—the Village, the Narrows, the Ridge, the Parade, North, South, and East Woodford, as well as the fogged-in Hoof.

Randy sank into the plush of a sofa so soft and low once he finished sinking, he was staring at his own camouflage knees. He set his NRA cap like sculpture on the polished slab coffee table. Mrs. Neighbor, skinny and shrill, offered herb tea. Something in the pitch of her voice made Randy's left eye twitch She held out a platter of cookies the size of Table Talk pies. "Homemade," she said. "Oatmeal, wheat germ, soy milk, and carob chips. Bound with raisin puree."

"Yuh," Randy said. "Uh-huh." But he was thinking *skeet*.

Mercifully, she soon disappeared into the heart of the house. The Neighbor pulled a fifth of Wild Turkey from a secret compartment in an armrest. He poured a healthy shot in each of their cups, and topped it off with hot water from the pot and a dip of honey.

"Toddy," he explained.

It wasn't half bad. The second round wasn't bad at all. The third was downright tasty. Randy began to warm to the notion that maybe the Neighbor wasn't such a bad egg after all.

"Too bad about your chickens," Randy said.

"I liked those chickens," the Neighbor confessed.

"Ain't it funny," Randy said, "how attached we get." He meant Mutt and the Neighbor knew it.

"Just doing what dogs do, I guess," the Neighbor said, which struck Randy as remarkably reasonable under the circumstances. Thus inspired, he let it be known that he accepted the fact that on account of the evidence found under his porch by Chief Harold and Officer Fred, all indications were that his dog, Mutt, had mutilated several Silkies and Frizzles, therefore some amount of reparation was due. Though five hundred dollars seemed a dite steep. Besides which Randy didn't have five hundred dollars or any hope of getting five hundred dollars any time soon. "I'm strapped," he said. "I've had to buy my own doublewide back three times from my ex-wives."

Through the window they could see that the fog from the Hoof had crept up Hosshead Hill and transformed itself into a drizzle. It was drizzling all over the Neighbor's golf-course green expanse of lawn. Randy and the Neighbor sipped their toddies and stared into the drizzle for a while. They seemed to be at an impasse.

Eventually, the Neighbor pointed to a tree that had fallen just at the point where lush lawn touched unruly woods. The trunk, Randy guessed, must be three and a half feet through. It was the biggest of its kind he'd ever seen. Must be the fertile soil and abundant sunshine on Hosshead Hill promoted unusual growth. The weathering where the bark had stripped away indicated the tree had been dead long before it fell, shattering limbs, scattering branches. It was kind of a mess, that corner of the Neighbor's near-perfect lawn.

"Maybe you could clean it up for me," the Neighbor said. "Cut it up for firewood. We've got two woodstoves and three fireplaces."

"You want me to work up that tree for firewood?" Randy said.

"Cut it to length, split it, stack it if you will, and we'll call it even."

"You sure?" Randy said.

They shook on it.

"Mutt," Randy said, once he'd staggered home. "We're talking impunity." Mutt was glad to hear it and even gladder to get his supper, which was late.

The woodpile Randy Hickey created from the fallen tree became, for a time, a source of considerable interest in town. I believe I was the first to accept Randy's invitation to take a ride up the hill for a good close look.

"I've seen woodpiles before," I said. "What's so great about this one?"

We pulled off the road at the edge of the Neighbor's property. Didn't dare get out of the truck on account of the No Trespassing signs. Randy handed me a pair of binoculars. "Look close now." I rolled down the window, zoomed in on the pile.

"You're looking at $500 worth of poultry right there," Randy said, proud.

"And is the man satisfied?"

"He will be," Randy said, "until he tries to burn it."

All that fall, locals made pilgrimages up Hosshead Hill just to get a look at Randy Hickey's five hundred dollar woodpile. One guy, they say, drove all the way from Winnisquam and took a picture.

Here's the best part. The strangers who bought the Colonial on Hosshead Hill are no longer called the Neighbor and Mrs. Neighbor—which is a little sarcastic, a little cold, don't you think, in light of all those No Trespassing signs.

A little cold is what they'll be if they try to heat that big house with the cordwood from Randy Hickey's woodpile. Some call that particular breed of poor-burning wood Quaking Aspen. It's famous for having about as much heat in a log as in a stick of chewing gum. Some call it Poplar. Around here we call it Popple.

And that's the story of how the Neighbor earned a new nickname, which means we're warming up to him already. Another four or five years, the natives will start saying "Hey" to him at the dump. After a decade, heck, he could run for selectman and he might even get a couple of votes. On the ballot, if he's smart, along with his given name he'll list his nickname— Popple. We call him Popple and her Mrs. Popple, though neither wears a ring and they've got different names on the mailbox, so who knows. Neither of them seems to have a job, but they have plenty of money. Kind of suspicious, but none of our business. Those of us who live in the Hoof don't have time to worry about such things. We're right out straight getting our own Red Oak and Rock Maple cut, split, stacked, and snugged under a tarp, preparing for the long, cold, inevitable winter.

John Elder

Rita gave me Annie Dillard's *Pilgrim at Tinker Creek* for Christmas in 1977, and it immediately rearranged my sense of literature, lending a new direction to my reading, teaching, and writing. My parents had presented me with a copy of *Walden* on my fifteenth birthday. All those years I had treasured Thoreau's prose, transcribing favorite selections of "Spring" and "Higher Laws" into my journal and reading them aloud to friends. But no comparable masterpiece of creative nonfiction had ever come into my ken: I had assumed *Walden* was unique—the only book on that particular shelf. *Pilgrim at Tinker Creek* finally felt like another one to lean beside it, though, both in the nature of its voice and themes and in the excellence of its prose.

In the second chapter of her book, which is entitled "Seeing," Dillard writes of a girl blind from birth who is given sight by a new form of surgery. This celebrated passage introduces a *leitmotif* for the whole book—the quest to see the world as vividly as a person who is newly sighted.

> When her doctor took her bandages off and led her into the garden, the girl who was no longer blind saw "the tree with the lights in it." It was for this tree I searched through the peach orchards of summer; in the forests of fall and down winter and spring for years. Then one day I was walking along Tinker Creek thinking of nothing at all and I saw the tree with the lights in it. I saw the backyard cedar where the mourning doves roost charged and transfigured, each cell buzzing with flame. I stood on the grass with the lights in it, grass that was wholly fire, utterly focused and utterly dreamed. It was less like seeing than like being for the first time seen, knocked breathless by a powerful glance. The flood of fire abated, but I'm still spending the power. Gradually the lights went out in the cedar, the colors died died, the cells unflamed and disappeared. I was still ringing. I had been my whole life a bell, and never knew it until at that moment I was lifted and struck. I have since only very rarely seen the tree with the lights in it. The vision comes and goes, mostly goes, but I live for it, for the moment when the mountains open and a new light roars in spate through the crack, and the mountains slam.

From the moment I first read this passage and entered into the tangled, funny, alarming skein of Dillard's reflections and narratives, I too was hungry for such intensity. Inspired by Dillard, I renewed my practices of journal-keeping, drawing, and botanizing. They were ways to pursue the goal of seeing the world vividly, of glimpsing life more abundant. I also eagerly explored contemporary American nature writing and began to integrate more and more of it into my teaching. I discovered how central to this body of literature was the hunger for visionary experience that Scott Slovic has defined as "seeking awareness." From Edward Abbey to Barry Lopez and Terry Tempest Williams, the shadows of deprivation and estrangement, historical folly and personal grief, function to make the moments of connection more dazzling, to convey the possibility for transfiguration. This Wordsworthian element also flows into American nature writing through Emerson, who writes in *Nature*, "If the stars should appear one night in a thousand years, how would men believe and adore; and preserve for many generations the remembrance of the city of God which had been shown!" A certain "impoverishment," as Emerson might say, may stimulate the capacity for wonder. One basic difference between Emerson and our latter-day American visionaries, though, is that for many of them the darkness around their moments of revelation also includes a world of ecological catastrophe. This chastened awareness is part of the special value of such writers for readers of today. They acknowledge the perils and the horrors of natural degradation while also celebrating the rewards that can come to one who, in Scott Russell Sander's memorable phrase, is "hunting for hope."

"The tree with the lights in it" is a phrase that sums up much of what has stirred me in American nature writing. "The narrow road" is another key phrase for me, expressing the enormous value I have found in contemporary poets like Gary Snyder, A.R. Ammons, and Mary Oliver—as well as in the haiku tradition of Bashô with which they have such a deep, if mysterious, connection. The latter phrase comes in fact from the title of Bashô's masterpiece intertwining haiku with travel narrative, *Oku no Hosomichi* (*The Narrow Road to the Interior*). I was first led to Bashô, as to the study of Japanese and to the sabbatical my family and I spent in Japan, through admiration for our American contemporary, Gary Snyder. The poetry of Snyder, one of the first Westerners to pursue Zen in a Japanese monastery, offered a stringent counter-point to the Miltonic tradition. His voice both baffled and impressed me. I wanted to learn where he came from by exploring the Zen-based literature and culture of Japan.

I quickly encountered Bashô's *The Narrow Road*, a poetic account of traveling as determined and courageous as it was pervaded by melancholy. The narrative, as translated by Noboyuki Yuasa, begins memorably.

> Days and months are travelers of eternity. So are the years that pass by. Those who steer a boat across the sea, or drive a horse over the earth till they succumb to the weight of years, spend every minute of their lives traveling. There are a great number of ancients, too, who died on the road. I myself have been tempted for a long time by the cloud-moving wind—filled with a strong desire to wander.

The world, and time itself, are travelers. To travel with them is to embrace, and perhaps also to hasten, one's own mortality. Surrendering to the passage of time may be attractive in part because of the ways loss and death themselves seem to offer openings into nature. The gentle sadness, or *sabi*, so characteristic of Japanese poetry registers a doubleness that is oddly akin to the dual impact of the sublime in Western thought. An awareness of one's own fading life, like the passing of springtime, is the soil in which a deeper sympathy may germinate. One of the most famous haiku in this volume of Bashô's describes the poet's response to the scene of a famous sequence of battles five centuries earlier.

> Indeed, many a feat of chivalrous valour was repeated here during the short span of the three generations, but both the actors and the deeds have long been dead and passed into oblivion. When a country is defeated, there remain only mountains and rivers, and on a ruined castle in spring only grasses thrive. I sat down on my hat and wept bitterly till I almost forgot time.

> Summer grass—
> all that remains
> of warriors' dreams.

Though the poet weeps at this scene of failed hopes, he also continually searches out such affecting locales in *The Narrow Road*. They seem, in fact, to provide one of the aged poet's main reasons for traveling so far on foot. Perhaps he finds reassurance as well as sorrow in the supplanting of human hopes by grasses bending under the wind. The prose passage leading up to the haiku echoes the famous line of Tu Fu, "Though the capital may fall, the mountains and rivers remain." Having been led to Bashô by a poet of our own day, I have also been given a heightened awareness of how contemporary writers, too, pace the earth in quest of visions. And of how, like him, they sometimes find in the frailty of human achievements the confirmation of a deeper, sustaining faith.

Many poems by Gary Snyder speak to this point, offering readers a broader historical perspective so that we can better orient ourselves amid the imbalances of the present. A poem of his that has been central for me is "For the Children," from *Turtle Island*.

> The rising hills, the slopes,
> of statistics
> lie before us.
> the steep climb
> of everything, going up,
> up, as we all
> go down.
>
> In the next century
> or the one beyond that,
> they say,
> are valleys, pastures,
> we can meet there in peace
> if we make it.
>
> To climb these coming crests
> one word to you, to
> you and your children:
>
> *stay together*
> *learn the flowers*
> *go light*

Bashô's haiku about the grass of warrior's dreams recalls ancient battles in a landscape that has, apparently, forgotten them. But "For the Children" stands at the edge of an *approaching* catastrophe—in a world of "everything going up, / up, as we all / go down." This poem limns the graph of our time, as use of fossil fuels, eradication of wild habitat, damage to atmospheric and oceanic systems, and human populations all curve steeply up. In all such exponential graphs, along with the visible x- and y-axes, an invisible line defines the right margin. This is the "asymptote" towards which the curve grows closer without ever touching it. Such an upward thrust represents a fantasy of endless growth, blasting through gravitation and other limits of our earth. But another invisible line implicitly cuts across the top of the graph and establishes the limited carrying capacity of our earth. Some economists refer to those who assert such limits as "catastrophians," in contrast their own "cornucopian" faith, which asserts that market demands and technological ingenuity will always generate replacements for dwindling resources. But we are looking toward a world of 11 billion people within my children's generation. Most of the growth is projected for the poorest countries, while the wealthiest pursue a binge of consumerism that skews the distribution of the world's goods ever more grotesquely. A recent *World Watch* report entitled *Beyond Malthus* states that, even at present population levels, it would take eight more earths to make a middle-class American lifestyle conceivable for all of humanity. One wonders where the self-styled cornucopians might expect to find these new planets.

It is plain to the speaker in Snyder's poem, at any rate, that the curve must turn back down. Either we will bend it down by forethought, discipline, and restructuring of our economic and social systems, or those systems will crash and we will come back down to earth in some faster way. This latter prospect casts "the shadow of death" across Snyder's poem. But the speaker here, as in Psalm 23, can also look beyond the perilous present—to "the next century / or the one beyond that," when the planet and its human inhabitants will one way or another come back into balance. The poem crosses over the high passes of our current peril and descends into the habitable valleys of the future. This is the point where a reader can see the opening graph of heedlessness transformed into the beautiful balance of an ancient Chinese or Japanese silk painting. Snyder substitutes the simplicity of a walk and a poem for the self-destructive indulgence of our day. This is another way in which he resembles Bashô, who took to the road in order to renew his own culture's sensitivity to nature, at a time when Zen-based arts were largely presided over by esthetes within the enclosed compounds of privilege.

Poetry is primarily an experience rather than a statement of fact. But one element I love in a poem like "For the Children" is the simplicity and directness of its ending: *"stay together / learn the flowers / go light."* As the

Wordsworthian tradition has entered a world of ecological disasters, a prophetic voice regularly punctuates its cadences—like the pause to look and think that interrupts and shapes a hike. The ending of "For the Children," like many passages in contemporary American poetry, resonates with "The Land Ethic," from Aldo Leopold's A Sand County Almanac. In that essay, Leopold sees culture on the verge of recognizing "rights" beyond the human circle. Such an expansion of our ethical perspective, he says, has become "an evolutionary possibility and an ecological necessity."

Snyder's poem, with its similar awareness of the ecological movement, expresses the eagerness to wake up that has long throbbed in America's nature writing as well as in our poetry of the earth. Thoreau writes in "Where I Lived and What I Lived For" that "We must learn to reawaken and keep ourselves awake, not by mechanical aids, but by an infinite expectation of the dawn." He adds, " Only that day dawns to which we are awake." Mary Oliver, in her poem "Turtle," evokes a pond in which a snapping turtle rises slowly toward the soft beauty of teal chicks. She breaks into her own rising sense of horror, though, to ask and answer a question that reorients her both as a poet and a citizen of nature.

> But, listen,
> what's important?
> Nothing's important
> except that the great and cruel mystery of the world,
> of which this is a part,
> not to be denied....

Such admonishing, inspiring voices have made all the difference in my life. Confused as I have generally been about matters of theology, as well as where my path is and which way I am supposed to walking on it anyway, a brisk reminder to wake up to the present can feel life saving. Here, too, the testimony of contemporary American literature is amplified for me by the Zen tradition that informs Bashô's poetry. One of the chants used during times of sesshin, or intensive retreat, at many American Zen centers is the Zazen Wasan, or "Master Hakuin's Chant in Praise of Zazen." One stanza of it goes:

> How near the truth
> Yet how far we seek,
> Like one in water crying "I thirst!"

Like a child of rich birth
Wand'ring poor on this earth,
We endlessly circle the six worlds.

      Just as Snyder's poetry and Bashô's have felt mutually illuminating, so too have I found that Japan's haiku tradition has brought me back to our Vermont poet Robert Frost with renewed appreciation. It is characteristic of haiku to imply a specific seasonal reference. One of my favorite haiku by Bashô goes "*Kare eda ni / karasu no tomarikeri / aki no fure*" (On a withered branch / alights a crow, / the end of autumn). Within each season there are seasons. Peter Milward in fact translates the haiku's last line "the fall of autumn" in order to emphasize this point. The spring of autumn, one might say, comes when colors bloom in the hardwoods; its summer, in the golden needles of the tamarack. But when most deciduous trees have become bare and the only tonality in the sky is the crow that alights to make the bough bounce once under its weight (Bashô's onomatopoetic *tomarikeri*), one experiences the season's completion and culmination. Haiku rarely depict peacocks or other conventionally gorgeous natural objects. Rather, they mark a particular moment in the turning year and bring into sharp resolution a single object in the world. As they hone in on the awkward, incongruous, or homely instances that are the haiku poets' stock-in-trade, these brief strings of syllables suggest that anything in the world we can truly see will contain everything we need. Like Thoreau's world in which dawn and spring are both perpetually available for one who is awake, haiku offer a meaningful, and entirely adequate, world waiting for our notice. Bashô was a poet, not a priest, and was careful to specify that, though trained in a monastery, he had never attained enlightenment. But the stanza quoted above from Zen Master Hakuin echoes his vision of a world thronging with haiku that need only to be perceived.

      Dillard specifies that she finally sees the tree with the lights in it when she is wandering beside Tinker Creek "thinking of nothing at all." One of the most valuable contrasts between Bashô and Milton or Wordsworth is his avoidance of arguments, logical propositions, and elaborations of all kinds. Another haiku by him goes "*Meigetsu ya– / ike wo megurite, / mo yoh sugara–*" (Full moon of autumn– / all night long / I walk around the pond). *Meigetsu*, the "famous moon," appears at the end of each September. Japanese devotees of the haiku tradition love to recite poems that are closely associated with such highly specific seasons through which they are passing. Sometimes they write them out on long thin placards of wood and hang them from trees to participate in a tradition of responsiveness to nature.

Bashô and his lineage have helped me recognize how many of Robert Frost's poems encounter our own Vermont landscape with an equivalent vividness and specificity. Snowshoeing around Bristol and Starksboro in those January and February weeks when the evergreens are packed with snow, I love to pause by a hemlock, push on a branch with my ski pole until it releases the small drift that freighted it, and say Frost's little poem "Dust of Snow."

> The way a crow
> Shook down on me
> The dust of snow
> From a hemlock tree
>
> Has given my heart
> A change of mood
> And saved some part
> Of a day I had rued.

This poem entered into my heart several years ago, on a day when the tracker Sue Morse was taking a group of my students and me around her land at Wolf Run. She recited it as we all paused beside a snowy hemlock, in what was for everyone a striking moment. When I do the same with other groups of students now, I feel that I am entering into a lineage of celebration—of the place, the poem, and all the people who have loved both of them before me.

Another poem of Frost's that serves as an important marker of the Vermont year is "Nothing Gold Can Stay." Growing up in the San Francisco Bay Area, I did not encounter such strongly marked seasons as we know in Vermont. But an arresting seasonality has become central to my sense of place here. When Rita and I were in graduate school in New Haven, our last year before moving to Vermont, we lived in a third-floor apartment on an old-fashioned street called Sheldon Terrace. As spring arrived and we were already beginning to box up our books and otherwise anticipate graduation and a move, we looked out our front window, right into the top of one of the mature maples that lined the sidewalk. It seemed to be full of crisp yellow flowers—beautiful, intricate, and unfamiliar. We gazed at them, even opening the windows to lean out and get closer, before figuring out that we were really witnessing the moment when the buds opened and the new leaves emerged. The tiny new leaves, not yet greened up in the sun, pushed out of the sheath with all their tips and angles clustered together in a lacy bloom for the first day or so. Frost's poem helped us to place this phenomenon, and to remember it again, here in Vermont, each spring.

> Nature's first green is gold,
> Her hardest hue to hold.
> Her early leaf's a flower,
> But only so an hour.
> Then leaf subsides to leaf,
> So Eden sank to grief.
> So dawn goes down to day.
> Nothing gold can stay.

Even in such a short poem, a Western poet like Frost will usually reflect about his observations in ways that Japanese poets avoid—preferring to leave such reflections up to the reader. In this sense, perhaps only the third line of Frost's poem is really a haiku. But I love the rest of it too, especially the line "Then leaf subsides to leaf." Each season is both an arrival and a departure, and what we see is always a process. There is a sadness in the ceaseless turning of our living world, as well as in the literature of nature, that reverberates with Virgil's lines in the *Aeneid* about "the tears of things, mortal affairs that touch the mind." For Virgil, these tears arise from the inevitable sunderings of human history and from the evanescence of all life. The beautiful forms of nature are the traces of life's passing. But the arising and subsiding of life is also its fulfillment. Without it there would be no leaf, no gold, no mystery in the spring treetops. From a poem like "Nothing Gold Can Stay" to those like "In Hardwood Groves" and "The Leaf Treader," Frost focuses on each phase of the foliage's annual cycle of unfolding, greening, reddening, and fall. As he says in "In Hardwood Groves," "the same leaves over and over again." The landscape's arc—up, across, and down—from spring to fall gives us human inhabitants a yearly opportunity to identify our own mortality with the integrity and beauty of the landscape, to ground ourselves and let ourselves go.

I once had an experience in the late September woods near Bread Loaf that related both to Bashô and to Frost. The Dalai Lama was visiting Middlebury College for several days as a participant in a Buddhist-Christian dialogue. I was asked, as a wildflower fancier, to take him and his entourage on a walk through the woods to see some fall blooms. I was of course excited to do so. The wrinkle was that someone in the college's public affairs office had told the press about the event, and when we arrived at the trailhead, a cluster of photographers was waiting. They backed ahead of us as we strolled, shutters crackling like brushfire. Then, as we paused to inspect a stand of steeplebush beside our path, a particularly brash photographer stooped over to pick up a crimson maple leaf, thrust it into the Dalai Lama's hands, saying, "Here, your Holiness," then stood back expectantly with his camera. The Dalai Lama inspected the leaf carefully, then held it forward for the photographer to see, while saying the single word, "Transience." It was the teaching of the Dharma, and a quiet celebration of the wholeness of nature. It was an echo of Bashô, there on a path where Robert Frost had also walked with an eye out for leaves.

The other influence on my growing love for Frost's poetry has been the decision Rita and I reached about a decade ago to make this region of the Green Mountains our home for the rest of our lives. We had always appreciated the beauty of this landscape and loved our teaching here, mine at Middlebury College and hers at the Lincoln Community School. But, as Californians, without thinking much about it, we had always seen this location as temporary. Our extended families were still in the West, and the world was full of places we might want to go, jobs we might want to hold. Having enjoyed ourselves in this mode for over fifteen years, though, we gradually realized Vermont was where we were in fact *living*. Our children had grown up entirely here, and these seasons had shaped our adult lives since the completion of our formal education. Recognizing and celebrating this fact, and deciding that, quite independent of our specific teaching jobs, we would never leave our home here, has felt so liberating. Like a commitment to marriage, our decision removed a range of potential distractions, allowing us to deepen a chosen and committed relationship with place.

One immediate upshot of our decision was, for me, a desire to study the natural history and human history of Vermont more systematically. While hiking around the nearby mountains and reading the chronicles of early settlers here, I kept a journal in which the poetry of Frost came to play an unexpected and notable role. Not only was he a fine naturalist and an observer of the shifting seasons, he was also alert to the twists and reversals of settlement here. He saw northern New England as a postagricultural region, one where many of the hill farmers had already left and where the forests were crowding back in. Such a landscape, for Frost, offered an opportunity to meditate about the relationship between wilderness and culture, and about loss as the vehicle for a deeper sense of history and community. The hardwood groves where hill farms were once maintained stirred him as the summer grass of warriors' dreams did Bashô.

Of all Frost's poems, the one that most informed my sense of our family's home was "Directive," from the 1946 volume *Steeple Bush*. Its opening, especially, captured this paradoxical landscape of loss and recovery.

> Back out of all this now too much for us,
> Back in a time made simple by the loss
> Of detail, burned, dissolved, and broken off
> Like graveyard marble sculpture in the weather,
> There is a house that is no more a house
> Upon a farm that is no more a farm
> And in a town that is no more a town.

Vermont is a state where wilderness is recovering—as registered by both the burgeoning of wildlife and the designation of portions of our Green Mountain National Forest as federal wilderness areas. Such lands, preserved further from development, motorized transport, and permanent human habitation, may feel like refuges from history. Like islands of serenity and solitude where we can escape from the modern world's "all this now too much for us." But we sometimes take a foreshortened view and separate wilderness from history in a way that runs the risk of sentimentality. Ours can be a vison "made simple by the loss / Of detail." Paying attention to the relics of former inhabitants in these mountains, to the stone walls, cellar holes, and abandoned graveyards, we may achieve a more integrated awareness of what it means to dwell here. Frost has helped me to begin paying attention to our family's home ground.

David Carroll

Fishing until Dark: 29 August

In the evening, water sings softly over the lip of the beaver bowl below a knoll of aspen and sweetfern. A three-day deluge, heavy rain circling in on the violent winds from a hurricane's having passed off the distant coast, has recharged every waterway on short and sudden notice. The trout will not have to await the more gradual refilling of autumn rains this year; a flood almost equal to that of the thaw has changed their world nearly overnight. Day's last light has recently slipped away from the highest crowns of the trees far across the wet meadow. Its final traces fade on the few clouds lingering just above the eastern horizon, with peach blushes surrendering to violet. The moon, within a day of its full face and as startled-looking as ever, now advances up and out from behind a dark, solitary pine.

I descend to alder thickets at land's end, to watch and wait. The dark shadow I have been anticipating darts in the water, and against a moon-pale section of the pool's bottom I see the nearly square tail and the white-edged fins. A small trout moves at twilight. In the oncoming darkness, black animal shapes appear; furtive, small, sudden mammals emerge from grass and ferns and race about the opposite banks. Mice, moles, or voles...I cannot tell what they are as they run with quick splashings in and out from cover. One, perhaps a water shrew, literally runs across the water, leaving a rippling, silver trail in lieu of footprints. The moon brightens and becomes burnished gold as the sky goes rose-violet all around it. Thin clouds, on their long, slow journey somewhere, go purple-gray, taking a touch of silver from the moon. My only fish connection so far has been with medium-sized pickerel taken on a green-gold strike close by the weedy bank. He shook off the hook and was quickly away, happily for both of us.

I cast just short of the upreaching fingertips of silky willow across the pool. The rising water and the weight of its ripening berries have brought the brook and silky dogwood together, and its fruits lie in the current's caress. I work alder borders and dogwood sweeps, the nightlike darks beneath the ferns and sedges. As I retrieve, there is a sudden taking, at my feet, just as I was about to lift my line out of the water. One is so easily lulled along a stream, and the alertness that should accompany even the last inches of a line's play in the water is hard to maintain. I set the hook too sharply, and am in the alder branches at my shoulder. Even in this dusky water I saw enough to identify a brook trout. They are settling themselves back out throughout the brook; the wild trout have returned with the rains to reclaim their springtime haunts.

I leave the moonrise and the burbling water at the dam and make my way into inky thickets where nightfall has already taken over, along the quickening run below the dam. Trout can see better than I. Their gold-ringed eyes are adapted to seek food on either edge of daylight, so that they are able to detect the tiny motes they pursue in the earliest radiating of pre-dawn light or on the star-brightening verge of night, when it seems that water holds the last of the day's light longer than the air does. It is at these times that many stream and river insects make their moves, and trout are attuned to them, capable of tracing their shadowy darts toward the surface, or their flickering movements upon it. Only night itself can close the lidless eyes of trout, who hover in the darkest undercuts, or the blackness of sunken logs and trailing fountain moss. The darkest night has its even darker shadows, and here trout sleep, open-eyed, suspended in drifts of water, shifting at times to hunt by starlight.

I come up out of the brook and begin my ascent of the knoll. Earth seems less tangible than water now. The landscape itself blurs and dissolves with the nightfall's advance, yet its features are sharply defined in reflections on the water. A single whippoorwill call, a solstice echo somewhat out of place so late in the season, sounds above the faint murmur of the brook. Not long after, the first star appears in the eastern sky. I make a wish, bid the trout good-night, and leave the darkening brook to continue flooding the shadow-landscape through which it flows.

drawing by David Carroll

Terry Osborne

Roots of Air

1

North of our house on Cobble Hill the Connecticut River valley stretches away toward Canada, lined by two states—Vermont to the west, New Hampshire the east—and by two ridges, one on either side of the river. On any map the ridges appear to lie parallel, unconnected, three miles apart. But from our back deck, you'd swear either the map was wrong or your eyes were playing tricks, because the undulating hills aren't straight at all; they seem to sink and taper and curve and finally join each other about eight miles away, resolving this section of valley into an oval bowl—the Vermont piedmont to the left, forming the west rim; the New Hampshire piedmont to the right, forming the east; the blunt, granitic outcrop of the Fairlee Palisades enclosing the far end; and Cobble Hill itself defining the near. Down the middle of the bowl, at its bottom, invisible from our perspective, runs the river itself, the terrain's chisel, once forceful and unpredictable, now dammed to a gentle roll.

The land's contour is what stands out most. It owes its rolling shape to the glacial scrubbing it's had, most recently by a mile-thick ice sheet that pushed south through this bowl about 80,000 years ago and stayed for the next 65,000, before withdrawing back towards the Arctic. During that time the ice depressed the earth's surface hundreds of feet and filed down the tops of the mountains and littered the ground with rocks, gravel, and sand it had carried south with it from what is now Canada. There isn't the same jaggedness to the ridges here that you find in the Rockies or even in the higher peaks of the White Mountains in New Hampshire. These are just foothills, after all, smaller formations left humped and rounded by the overgoing ice, and so, though they raise the horizon and obscure the land beyond, they do it softly, with a feathered seamlessness between themselves and sky.

The hills are completely forested; the only breaks in the woodlands are the weathered patches on the Palisades' southern face, cliffs too steep and dry to accommodate much but clinging junipers, bristly sedges, and in the warmer months a pair of nesting peregrines. As forest types go, this one could be classified a "transition forest," where the coniferous, boreal forest of more northern latitudes meets the deciduous forest common to areas south of here. In his book *Reading the Forested Landscape* ecologist Tom Wessels describes this region as "a mixing ground where more than one hundred species of woody plants find the limits of either their northern or southern ranges. This mingling of species creates a region with a far greater diversity of plants, and plant communities, than any other area in the northeastern United States."

The forest must have been particularly impressive before Europeans arrived, during the thousands of years the native Abenaki lived in it. We know that its enormous white pines drew the attention of the first French and English wanderers here; so valued were those trees that King George III of England eventually laid claim to them by including in many towns' charters a clause ordering that "all white and other Pine Trees fit for masting Our Royal Navy be carefully preserved for that Use, and none be cut or felled without Our Special License." That Royal order was more or less ignored, and over the next hundred and fifty years the forest, white pines and all, was leveled by European settlers who began moving up to this area from southern New England in the mid-1700s and began transforming the colonial woods into American farmland. During the last hundred years, however, an equally dramatic change has taken place: the farming industry has moved to the wider spaces out West, and so hillside woods around here have regrown where fields and pastures were not long ago. Though today's forest isn't nearly as mature, nor quite as diverse, as the one that stood here three hundred years ago, I imagine it colors and textures the slopes in a similar way.

As wooded as the hillsides are, it would be easy to forget that any open land exists out there. It does, though. Just not very much of it anymore—a fraction of what you'd have seen two generations ago. These days it's confined to the flatter, more fertile ground on the valley bottom, where it's almost entirely invisible to us from our deck—except for a corner of a field we can see, probably three or four miles away, through a gap in the trees—and almost entirely dedicated to cows: fields for hay and corn, pastures for grazing. A handful of families in this section of valley still make at least some of their living from dairy farming, but as I've said, the agricultural way of life that was brought over from Europe and then governed this landscape for two centuries has largely moved West.

Still, for all the predominance of hills in our view, and the absence of open fields, and for all of the shape that river and ice have provided, it isn't finally the land or water that holds sway here, but the sky. The many-faced sky. It can seem to press over the valley like an airborne ice sheet or fill in like soft meltwater where the ridges crease and sink away, or retreat altogether, leaving the air open and pebbled with the patterns of high clouds or stars. Ours is not a culture that charts its destiny seriously by the sun or moon; few of us understand the sky with anywhere near the intimacy that, say, almost every Abenaki did three hundred years ago. So it isn't surprising that I don't know which hill the sun sets behind on any particular day in November, or recognize well ahead of time the telltale cloud progression of an oncoming storm, or notice when a dead star disappears from the night's constellations, or when a new one appears.

But I do respect the sky's presence and influence, the fabric of shadow and light that determines the valley's mood, that often determines mine. I've come to believe during the last ten years that this arrangement of sky over land and water is more than just a stage on which my wife Robin and I play out the scenes of our domestic life; at times it actually seems to direct us. There are days when dark weather fronts pull across to our north, with rainbursts filling the valley like smoke but leaving us untouched, basking in afternoon sun, marveling both at the lucky slant of air that's keeping us bright and dry now and at the twists of life that brought us together as college freshmen. And there are days the sky reverses the divide, when the Palisades' sun-bright slopes against a distant blue seem a cruel tease to us as we labor under a gray overcast, the two of us keeping our distance from each other, feeling as if we've been together too long—I sulking inside a seething depression, Rob tiptoeing around the outburst she knows will come. And there are times when the sky is a single salving cast, as on those nights the emerald swelter of the Northern Lights pulses up from behind the Vermont ridge. Pulling Rob from sleep, I walk her through the house to the back deck, where we stand arm in arm, and beneath the solar breeze and the enormous green ribbons of light fluttering over us like palm leaves, we're inspired to contemplate the mystery of our enduring love.

This valley, then, seems to have built its own character, and influenced ours, through commingled contraries: ground carved by a now unseen river into two straight ridges; two straight ridges bent toward each other to form an enclosure; the enclosure coaxed open by a restless sky; and

183

that sky somehow calmed by the straight curvature of rock. It's a view of freedom gently restrained, gravity on fledgling wings.

Every morning this is the first view I see and every morning it stirs me much the way it did when I first saw it. This valley bowl is one of the few things in life, perhaps the only one, I haven't ever taken for granted, and I can't help thinking that I haven't dulled to it because it won't let me, because it isn't done showing me things I need to know.

Strangely, it wasn't the view that drew me here the first time; it was the house. Ten years ago, in the summer of 1987, I walked casually out of a realtor's office with a secret mission: I was going to sneak a peek at a place I'd just learned was on the market. It took me a while to find it, maybe a couple of days. I suppose I could blame my wandering on the lack of street signs in town then, at least the standard green metal ones with white lettering we have on every corner now; then, there were only wooden ones here and there that people had painted by hand. But the real problem was that I didn't want to ask directions. Part of that was a prideful guy thing: I didn't like asking for help; I wanted to find it myself. Another part was an embarrassment at myself for not knowing where the road was; we'd been living in town for a year, after all, renting a place on Thetford Hill, and I thought I should know. The biggest part, though, arose from a much deeper embarrassment and insecurity: I was afraid that whoever I asked might get suspicious of my nosing around, or worse, might see through me, see me for the self-conscious flatlander I was but was trying desperately not to be.

Eventually, after a day and a half of trial and error—and even subtle direction-asking—I found the road and made my way up it. Rolling slowly into the driveway, a little fearful of running into someone, I rounded the corner and saw the broadsloped Vermont ridge for the first time, risen beyond the house's roofline like a swelling wave. I was awed.

Surprise and luck magnified the awe, I'm sure, because I shouldn't have been rounding this corner at all. Robin and I had already fallen in love with an old farmhouse a mile north of here, a house the owners didn't really want to sell though circumstances had forced them to put it on the market, a place we couldn't afford but that we loved so much we lost sleep fretting over it, imagining whom we could borrow money from and how much of our lives we'd be committing to debt.

Then, by chance, I noticed a listing for this other house in the realtor's office.

"Hey, what's this?" I asked. I was flipping through the listing book absentmindedly, only half paying attention, since I was sure I knew the Thetford listings by heart. But suddenly, unfathomably, a picture of the house appeared. It was as if a leaf, pressed in a favorite childhood book long ago, had fallen from the pages.

The realtor looked up from her work. "Oh, yeah," she said. "That one. I'd forgotten about it."

"Oh, yeah?" a voice inside me was saying. "We've been drivin' all over this goddamn area for the last month, lookin' at houses, and you *forget* about this one right in town? And then all you have to say is, *Oh, yeah?*"

She added, "And the owners are anxious to get rid of it, too."
As she told it, the owners weren't interested in the house at all. They had bought the place for its adjacent land—twenty acres set off to the east that they were going to subdivide into building lots. In the process they had created a separate three-acre lot for the house, hoping they could sell it right away. It was empty and ready to be occupied.

That clinched it. I wanted to see it. I asked for a copy of the listing sheet and said I'd talk to Robin about it when I got the chance. Then, acting only mildly interested though churning excitedly inside, I crept off in search of the house to take an unsupervised look.

* * *

Cobble Hill is a mile-long rise that juts out from the Vermont ridge like a thumb, poking east across the Connecticut valley almost to the river. Its top is a single soft ripple—two crowns separated by a central swale, a graceful undulation between raised ends. Seen from the northeast, the hill seems to stretch out from right to left like a woman lying on her side, the line of her leg leading up to the dome of her hip, then dipping to her waist and rising again along her torso to the higher crown of her shoulders before making a more abrupt scalloped descent toward the river, as if her lower arm were laid out to support her resting head. The house sat just below the crest of her hip.

I followed the driveway thirty yards before coming to a sharp left turn. Blasted through a spine of ledge, the corner was lined on both sides by rock walls—the left overgrown by hemlock, the right by goldenrod. Making that turn, I was blind to everything but the walls.

Around the corner the driveway dropped steeply to the house, so it was just as I came out of the turn that I had the highest vantage, could see everything before starting down. And it was at that moment my heart abandoned that big, beautiful, troubling and unaffordable farmhouse and fell in love with a view of land.

I got out and poked around. The place was very different from the farmhouse we'd been imagining ourselves in. It was a modified saltbox, so its lines were not classically symmetrical, as they were in the other house. It was painted black instead of white. It was twenty years old instead of a hundred and twenty. And when I peeked in through the windows to get a sense of the interior, I could see there wasn't anything near the spaciousness we adored in the farmhouse. I found a narrow galley kitchen, and beyond it a small south-facing sunroom with a wood stove and, connected to them both, a long living room with orange shag carpeting, a built-in bookcase, a picture window and sliding glass door. This place would require a complete reordering of our expectations. Yet I didn't feel disappointed at all; I was already convinced. I was more worried about what Robin would think.

After making a full round of the house, I returned to the back side and stood on the deck, still stunned by the wide spectacle of north-reaching valley. Gazing at it fanned out beyond the neighbors' house and the three black-and-white cows grazing in their pasture, I sensed a deepening of the instant connection I'd felt to this view at the top of the driveway. It was as if I'd come home.

That evening I brought Robin to the house. As we were rounding the corner of the driveway, she gasped suddenly.

"Oh my god!" she said.

"What?" I said, jamming on the brakes, afraid she'd hurt herself or been scared by something. "You okay?"

She was leaning forward, looking out the windshield. "We've got to buy it."

How surprised was I? I thought Rob felt more attached to the farmhouse than I did. I thought I was the only one really dreading the financial burden that place was going to heap on us. All day I'd been readying my sales pitch, thinking of ways to change her mind, to sell her on the advantages of this place and talk up the "positive aspects" of changed expectations. No need for that.

So, how annoyed was I? There she was, the woman who had seemed unchangeably committed to our dream house, looking out the windshield, ready to give it up with her first glance at some other place. "So, tell me," my inner voice was saying to her, "what exactly have we been obsessin' about these last weeks, huh? How important could that house have been to you if you could just toss it away like that? I mean, you are *so* fickle! What's to keep you from changin' your mind about this place? What's to keep you from tossin' *me* away?"

I never said that out loud. Nor should I have, because all that was happening to Rob, of course, was the same thing that had happened to me. But I'd been so afraid she wouldn't like the place or feel drawn to it the way I was, so afraid that I'd have to forget what I'd felt earlier that day, that I couldn't change emotional gears fast enough. The best I could do, sitting in our stopped car at the peak of the driveway, was to feel surprised and righteously annoyed. But the most important thing was that she did like it, she was drawn to it and, like me, was relieved to have found another house to love, one with its own very different, but equal, beauty. One we could afford and actually enjoy.

This is where we live now. This is our home.

What perplexed me then, and does even now, was my instant comfort with the place. It's one thing to find a new view beautiful, and even be stunned by it; it's another to feel strongly aligned with it, to recognize right away a sense of home. Having grown up in Lake Forest, Illinois, a suburb north of Chicago, I knew clearly that this valley was *not* my home. Lake Forest is a residential community built on the wooded plateau above the western shore of Lake Michigan. The terrain of my childhood was lush and gentle, the only abrupt topographical change being a network of deep, narrow ravines that spread from the lakeshore like veins, each ravine tightening and shallowing the further inland it went, and all of them serving as conduits for the land's runoff, draining it all back into the lake.

Around home nature grew at close quarters. Tall, thick-barked oaks and elms shaded our lawn and lined the neighborhood's curving streets. Pines and spruces made fence-like borders between properties. So the only times I saw any distance were when I was riding in a car past the endless cornfields in West Lake Forest or Libertyville, or on my bike three blocks from home, where on the bluff above the lake I might glance east as I was pedaling by, or even stop at one of the cleared lookouts, to catch a glimpse of the horizon, the blended blue of sky and water.

So the view from Cobble Hill did not resemble my childhood home at all. Much more height here, much more distance. And not a single memory. This last quality was something I hadn't considered until I read Scott Russell Sanders's book *Staying Put*. He writes:

One's native ground is the place where, since before you had words for such knowledge, you have known the smells, the seasons, the birds and beasts, the human voices, the houses, the ways of working, the lay of the land, and the quality of light. It is the landscape you learn before you retreat inside the illusion of your skin.

In my attachment to this valley there was nothing so thorough, no preverbal understanding, none of the once-in-a-lifetime intimacy Sanders mentions. Nor was there anything more mysterious—no haunting aura of a past life waiting to be remembered. No déjà vu. Everything about this place—the breeze, the birdcalls, the light and dark, the rocks, the rivers, the history, the people—was foreign.

Well, not everything. Along with my initial awe at the view there was something recognizable—a broad feeling of familiarity, a calm first-time comfort, as when you meet someone new and know immediately that the two of you will be friends. This is a hard feeling to explain, because it's more intuitive than anything else. It might be the shape of that person's face or the sound of the voice that tells you, or the attitudes or compassion or humor or wisdom. It might be that you're reminded of someone you already know and like, or of someone you wish you were. Or it might be that in this one person are collected pieces of all those cues together.

That's as precise as I can be about this valley. Though I had always felt comfortable in northern New England, the feeling that filled me on the deck that first day had little to do with memory and almost everything to do with anticipation, if that's possible. It was a feeling of longing, I now think: a longing to start again and become someone new, someone more consistent and less moody, someone I could actually like all the time; a longing to feel close to a place by choice instead of assuming it by birth, to understand this beautiful, contradictory landscape—which had stepped unexpectedly out from behind a corner—in a way I hadn't understood anything before.

I didn't know how it was going to happen—at the time, I'm sure I didn't even know that it was going to happen—but one way or another it was going to take some learning.

A farmer on the New Hampshire side of the valley told me one day about the trouble he'd had over the years with black bears, how they would come off the piedmont ridge and raid his cornfields. From the pattern of flattened stalks they left behind, he said he knew pretty well what their eating technique was: they'd walk into a field, sit down, reach their arms out and hug the corn into them. Everything within the circumference of their hug was a helping.

This was clearly an annoyance to the farmer, and so I shook my head along with him. But inside I had to smile: there was something so playful and life-affirming in the image of that bear, finding itself in an embarrassment of riches with nothing but time on its hands and a big space in its stomach to fill.

Whenever I think about that bear surrounded by unimaginable bounty, I'm reminded of myself during that first year or so on Cobble Hill, how I reveled in the landscape, learned easily and unworriedly, and pulled life in like a glutton.

Some of the first information came casually, from day-to-day exposure around the house. I began to notice the ordinary left-to-right movement of the weather, and the way the New Hampshire piedmont purpled on fall evenings. I watched the grass in our back field grow four feet tall by midsummer, felt how hard it was to rake up just after it had been mowed. I learned that the black-and-white cows on the other side of the barbed wire fence were called "Holsteins." I saw that the apple trees in different parts of the property bore different kind of apples. I found something that looked to be asparagus flowering like a peacock's crown on the edge of the lawn, far away from where the former vegetable garden was. From the butternut tree out back I felt the sticky softness of the nuts' coat, and tasted the tinny bitterness of the meat.

On my walks, I stayed close to home, traipsing with our dog Griffy through the woods on Cobble Hill, marveling at the various trees, of which I could only identify oaks and maples from the shapes of their leaves. I couldn't tell one evergreen from another. I tested the wetness of the lowlands, stirring up the sulfurous smell of the swamp whenever I sank one of my mud boots in and then pulled it out. Further back in the woods, on a neighbor's land, I bent under lines of blue plastic piping strung from tree to tree, and further still, over another hill, I found a small cabin set against a steep rock outcrop on a south-facing slope. Its door was miraculously open. I crept in and gazed around at the rusted bed frames and tattered chairs, the disconnected wood stove in the corner, the graffitied names of people on the walls and ceiling. I felt as if I'd just stumbled upon a prehistoric cave site.

For the first year or two, I can remember feeling like an awestruck child on those walks. Before I could tell one kind of pine from another, before I learned that the blue tubing was used to funnel sap from sugar maples down to a holding tank or that the cabin was something the neighbors had built as a camp for their kids, I recorded things in the rawest of ways, by sensory imprint and imagination. If there's a purity to experience, particularly as an adult—a way of meeting the world directly, free of the need to name or define things, free of the clutter of thinking too much, free from having to make meaning out of experience—I probably came as close to it on those wanderings as I ever will.

At the time I wasn't aware of myself doing anything intentionally, other than exploring the area around home and enjoying getting to know it. But looking back, I can see that this innocent wandering had the effect of establishing a new "native ground" for myself. It would never be exactly the kind Scott Russell Sanders described, since the valley wasn't my birthplace and I wasn't an infant. But it was my version of it, I guess—an adult version, a reenactment of the original, in which that first year or so of experiences on Cobble Hill imprinted my understanding in a childlike sensory way.

Many walks were full of wonder, and sometimes even a strange magic. On the first day of our first spring here, I snowshoed with Griffy up Cobble Hill from the east end, the "shoulders" end near the river. I wanted to see if I could find my way home across the top of the hill. It's steep on that end, and the snow was thin and uneven, heavy too, so the shoeing was awkward. But I wasn't in any hurry and went slowly, particularly on the upper slope, where the ground was peppered with stumps and branches from recent logging.

Catching sight of a pileated woodpecker as it flew among the remaining trees to hunt for food, I had to keep from laughing and scaring it away as I watched it through binoculars. Cloaked in a long black wingcoat, capped by its red crown, the bird looked unflinchingly stern and ceremonial as it clung motionless to a tree or traveled from one to the next with a shallow swoop and a wing flap or two. But when it moved along a trunk, its aura evaporated: hop hophop hop hophophop it went, straight up the tree, then around it in spirals, making little mincing steps. It was like a

Supreme Court justice trying to look venerable while playing hopscotch in his robes.

"Aha," I was thinking. "I see you now. Both sides of you."

At the height of land I headed in the direction of our house, deciding to bushwhack out of the logged area through a border of young trees. The border was narrow, but when I shoed through it, I felt as if I'd walked into the remoteness of a distant ridge. Griffy and I found ourselves in a small square field, lined on all four sides by trees, with a patch of mixed trees and bushes growing like an island in the center. Though tall evergreens threw a dull shadow over the uphill border of the field, the scene was brightened by a smooth floor of snow, its surface an unblemished white. When I looked up I noticed in the distance a familiar view of the valley to the north.

The combined effect was startling. Here was a place on the same slope as our house and no more than half a mile away that faced the same direction upvalley. And yet who could have known it even existed? It was well back from any traveled road and neatly bordered all the way around. I had this childish fantasy of having found a fort where I could secret myself away, so close to home, yet remote and safe. I could eavesdrop on the world, keeping myself unseen.

I felt something else, though, too, something harder to describe. It was an inkling about the place, a suspicion, like a sharp scent. If I'd known how rarely this pinch of recognition comes, I'd have relished it more. What I sensed was an air of reclusiveness, solitude preferred. A place best left alone. This went against what I could tell about the field from looking around: it abutted a newly logged slope, it was neatly tended by someone, and judging from the barking I heard now and then, it wasn't far from a house. It also went against what I wanted to do, which was to stay and claim the spot, at least to myself. Even so, I couldn't help feeling that the right thing to do was to go. So after keeping quiet a while longer, listening to the emptiness there, I shoed uphill and then halfway across the field, staying as close to the edges as possible, so as not to pock the open snow with prints. Then, turning again, and with Griffy following in my tracks, I shoed off into the woods.

Not every experience was as romantic or certain as that one. Not even close. There was plenty of frustration, countless times when I'd see or hear something and not know what to think, not know what it was. And over time, as I began to recognize how much there was to know and how little I did—trees and birds and rocks, ferns, lichens, insects, all with their own encyclopedic subcategories—the childlike pleasure shrank beneath a growing self-consciousness. In *Nature and Madness* Paul Shepard writes, "The children playing delightedly on the green grass or in awe at an owl in the woods will grow up oblivious to the good in nature if they never go beyond that momentary fascination." So perhaps my deepening dissatisfaction with sensory wonder, and my embarrassment at not knowing the names for what I was sensing, the official terminology for it, was right on cue, the next logical phase of maturation in my new native ground. But it didn't feel that way. It seemed irrational and driven, more self-destructive than mature.

Though this transformation from wonder to antsy insecurity happened slowly, across many walks and in many different places near home, it probably happened most abruptly at the small swamp on Cobble Hill. I went there the first time late one April night, after hearing something through my office window—a steady white noise, like the wash of a distant ocean. Griffy and I followed the sound up the driveway, out onto the road, then up the road a hundred feet or so to the mouth of a grassy corridor leading into the swamp.

The entire swamp was whistling. And it was loud. I couldn't believe how loud it was. Having heard people talk about "peeping," and having recently read a column in our local paper by naturalist Ted Levin, I guessed that I was hearing spring peepers, the inch-long tree frogs that had congregated to mate.

I followed the corridor into the swamp, noticing how the calling in a specific place would stop abruptly as I approached and begin again after I had passed by. Eventually I reached a spot where I was completely surrounded by sound. Though I had a flashlight, I kept it off and amid the whistling relished the volume and pitch. With only my ears as guides, I focused on the sound. I listened to the throbbing of the calls together, a single reverberating mass of noise, high and constant, like the whine of truck tires on the interstate. Then I fixed on individual peeps, listening for the particular cadence of one, and then another, trying to keep them distinct before losing them in the tangle of other calls, this convulsion of male frogs singing for love. It was an overwhelming concert in the dark.

The next time I went back, the calling was as loud and rich and varied as before. But I chose not to notice it; I was impatient to take the next step, to actually see the peepers. For this, however, I was hopelessly unprepared. Ted Levin had subtly warned readers about the time involved in this kind of search: "The longer you squat in the muck, the better your chances of finding a peeper," he'd written. He also recommended shining a flashlight on "rush stems, alder and willow branches, mud hammocks" in order to find a frog—helpful advice, I was sure, except that I didn't know what any of those looked like.

But none of that mattered anyway, because I couldn't even get close to the sound. The same silence that had seemed so interesting on the previous visit wasn't nearly as cute or remarkable this time around. I stepped toward one spot: nothing. Then walked softly to another: more silence. A third spot: deathly still, while back at the first two places the peepers were going full blast again.

What the hell was going on? Wherever I was, the sound was somewhere else, and it was making me paranoid. I began to feel like a buzzing neon sign, blinking out "stupid greenhorn flatlander" to all of those rush stems and alder and willow branches and mud hammocks I hadn't a clue how to identify. And the peepers' loud whistles transformed into catcalls.

The swamp had stirred in me a sharp feeling of incompetence I knew all too well. And hated. And had done my best to avoid over the years. Yes, I'd heard the peepers' kind of mockery before. Lived with it almost every day. It was an outdoor echo of the angry voice I heard inside my head, a voice who spoke to me in words, whose personality was like an unforgiving twin of my own, a Hyde to my Jekyll. He was the one who wanted to lash out at the real estate agent for forgetting about this house on Cobble Hill or criticize Robin for being fickle when she loved the house so immediately. But mostly his attention was turned toward me, his discontent relentless, filled with a searing hatred and derision that made a litany of my own faults, a pronouncement of my every misdeed. And no matter how determinedly I'd turn away or try to ignore him, he'd pull closer and surge and finally fill me like wind to become the only noise I could hear.

"You know somethin', frogman?" he said in his loud, soundless way. "You're nothin' but a stupid shit."

"Is that right," I said.

"You're damn right that's right."

"Well, that's original. Two 'rights' in one sentence. Doesn't that make a wrong?"

"*You* make a wrong."

"Mm-hmm. So what is it now?"

"You know what it is. These frogs, you idiot. How can you not see them? They're all around you! Shit, they're almost jumpin' on you. And you, fancyin' yourself a little Nature Boy. What a joke."

As hard as his angry disdain was to take sometimes, it wasn't unexpected. Over the years the anger had actually become a predictable part of his torment, something solid and consistent that I could brace myself for. What was more dangerous was his funny mockery. He'd start joking and act like a buddy and get me laughing, and sometimes I'd get so involved in the banter that I'd forget what he was up to and lower my guard. Then he'd start in on me for real, and I'd wonder how I could have been so easily fooled. Because the voice never had my peace of mind at heart. The ultimate butt of his every derision, no matter how innocently begun, was me, and the ultimate goal of his every word was to get me to believe him.

More often than not I could deflect his anger or match him joke for joke without feeling too beaten down. But not always. When I couldn't, it was because of his perseverance and power to persuade: to preach and preach and preach until he had convinced me that I was as flawed and hateful as he said I was, or else worse, that I was *nothing*—alone, anonymous, of no importance to anyone, with nowhere to go but six feet under. And on and on and on he would carp, relentlessly, until I was blind to everything but this dark little world of his, this tug of war he'd arranged, the insults he'd rain on me, the arguments I'd have with him—at my desk, in the shower, in the car while stopped at intersections, eventually even in the woods—until it would seem that my only recourse, my best defense, was simply to stop fighting and agree.

The voice had been with me for as long as I could remember. As a kid, I often got down on myself, dwelling on my failures while discounting my successes by attributing them to luck or someone else's charity. That kind of thinking, and even the presence of a damning internal voice, we know today, is pretty characteristic of a depressive mood or personality. Discussing a depressed male patient of his, Terrence Real, psychotherapist and author of I Don't Want to Talk About It, writes: "If we were able to take a psychic stethoscope and listen in to the unremitting conversation looping inside [his] mind, we would hear harsh perfectionist judgment matched with bitterness, mistrust and hopelessness."

We may know this today, but thirty years ago the word "depression" hadn't found its way into popular culture, didn't roll off people's tongues as it does now. Like other mental illnesses it was still taboo to talk about, usually confined to whispers beside the words "hospital" or "asylum" and never applied to any but the most troubled children. While that was true in our house as well, my mother could still see that there was something going on with me; she used to tell me that I was my "own worst enemy," not knowing how accurate a description of my inner turmoil that was, and she'd often urge me to make my life easier by not being so hard on myself.

Instinctively, though, I'd already done that. When my own worst enemy became too much to bear, I simply deflected him outward toward other people, a strategy I've since learned is also fairly typical of depressives. As James C. Coyne writes in his introduction to *Essential Papers on Depression*, studies on depressed patients "suggest that their negative feelings, including overt hostility, are also directed at the people around them." On occasion I found not only that the voice could discount classmates to their face as cuttingly as he discounted me, but that when he did I felt better for a while.

I say "on occasion," but the outward-turned voice must have occurred often enough to make it a recognizable part of my personality. I remember the day I discovered that: I was standing next to my parents at home, beside the dining room table where they always spread out the day's mail. They were reading to me from a generally complimentary fourth-grade report card. But under "Weaknesses" it said something like: "Terry could learn to be more tolerant of classmates he feels are not as capable as he." My parents treated the comment supportively, explaining specifically what it meant, what it was to be "tolerant," but that only added to the humiliation I felt at having any identified "Weakness" at all.

That this one-sentence criticism is the only comment I remember from any grade-school report card is indicative of how hard it hit me then and, I suspect, how true I knew it was. It also shows how well the voice has been preserving my failings all these years. But until that day in fourth grade my critical (self-critical) side hadn't seemed so distinctly bad or unusual or weak to me; it was just who I was. From that moment on, though, I knew I had to do something about it. Since it never occurred to me that someone could change himself, even if that self was hurtful to others, I must have figured I was stuck with me. That left only one alternative: to protect myself from the "weak" me. So I did, by convincing myself I had no weaknesses. I created a flawless image of myself, built a thicker shield of affability and self-assurance around it for protection, and then hid deeper inside the battlement, where it was easier to deny the presence of other people's criticisms.

In a very real sense I was two people then. On the outside I wore the disguise of an assertive and gregarious and confident, often *overconfident*, young man; on the inside I was a scared kid chasing success and its half-pleasure as hard as I could, so that I wouldn't have to hear the inner chiding that accompanied any failure.

Success, I learned, could be had most easily on safe ground, by sticking to things I did well. When as a kid it seemed that I had athletic ability, I devoted myself to sports. Football, hockey, baseball, golf: I moved from one to the next with the passage of the seasons, often being elected captain of teams. Of the four it was hockey I had the most promise in, so I concentrated on that. I went to predawn power skating lessons and summer hockey camps and eventually got recruited by and accepted to Princeton, a place I wouldn't have qualified for with grades alone.

And, at the same time, when it seemed to me I had a knack for words and language, I decided to develop that too. At college I majored in English, and then moved back to Chicago to pursue it in graduate school, and to stay close to Robin, who was starting her own graduate work in clinical psychology nearby. A year later I took a job teaching English at the elementary school in Lake Forest I'd gone to myself. Though nothing was ever immune to the voice's criticism, this path was pretty safe: I was back home; I felt at ease in my job and familiar at the school; I understood the students, because I could see myself in them; I knew rules of grammar and syntax; I could talk about stories and arguments, and their beginnings, middles, and ends.

Three years later Robin and I moved east again so that she could finish her clinical graduate work at Dartmouth Medical School. Even though I was moving away from my true home ground, I was excited. We both were. While in college together we'd made road trips throughout northern New England and had always dreamed of living there sometime, if we could find a way to support ourselves.

Once here I made sure to keep things as similar and familiar as possible. I happened into a part-time job teaching English to first-year Dartmouth students and thrived on the challenge of older minds. But a year later we moved out of the house we were renting and bought this place on the rim of a valley bowl, and all my straight-ahead, face-forward, steady-as-she-goes plans got diverted by my attraction to the landscape.

There was a year or so of pure joy, as I've described, of tripping through the woods naïve as a child, when it seemed that I'd found a place where the voice couldn't touch me. But that ended: I must have worn out his grace period for naïveté. He started reminding me that as childlike as I felt, I wasn't one, that I was an adult who knew nothing about the landscape. Nothing.

I suppose I could have turned away from the valley then, retreated back into more familiar territory of teaching and sports, where the footing was surer. But I didn't. I think it was too late by that time: the landscape had already imprinted itself on me. So instead, I tried to quiet the voice by treating the valley like a piece of literature I didn't understand, a skating technique I couldn't do: I decided to learn it, to find names for the things I didn't know.

I started with the most basic information. I learned the place names in the valley, all the towns and villages whose borders fell within the bowl. On the Vermont side, from Cobble Hill north, there was East Thetford, site of the first European settlement in town; North Thetford, which flourished as a rail town after the railroad arrived in 1848; Ely, lying half in Thetford, half in the town of Fairlee, whose train stop, for the last part of the nineteenth century, served the Ely copper mine, nine miles away; and Fairlee, where Samuel Morey, the inventor of the paddlewheel steamboat, spent his final years, never understanding how Robert Fulton had gotten (and taken) credit for Morey's own invention. Heading back south on the New Hampshire side there was Orford, where Morey lived most of his life, and where a line of seven beautiful Federal-style homes, the earliest of which was his, still dominates the Ridge near the river. And south of that, Lyme, one of the most active Underground Railroad stops in the area.

Next I identified the various hills in our view. Following the Vermont piedmont north from Cobble Hill (elevation 873 feet), there was Thetford Hill (939 feet), Houghton Hill (1,472 feet), Potato Hill (or High Peak) (1,703 feet), Ely Mountain (1,468 feet), and an unnamed peak I eventually called Oven Bird Hill (1,569 feet); the Palisades (902 feet) were straight ahead; then there was Cottonstone Mountain (1,760 feet), Blackberry Hill (720 feet), Sunday Mountain (1,800 feet), Kenyon Hill (1,309 feet), Breck Hill (660 feet), and Post Hill (988 feet) coming back on the New Hampshire side.

I bought field guides on birds, trees, and wildflowers. The first wildflower I identified that spring was coltsfoot, a slender, dandelion-like bloom growing beside a path across from our driveway. I learned that one way to tell a Scotch pine from a white pine was by the number of needles in each needle bundle: two for Scotch, five for white. I discovered that the chickadees so numerous at our bird feeder in the winter were black-capped chickadees.

Along with the first bits of bookish knowledge came a renewed sense of accomplishment and conquest. I'd begun learning names for the things I'd been seeing, and given the rules of knowledge I'd grown up under—that nothing was known unless it was named—it confirmed that I finally knew something. In fact, I began deriving more pleasure and reward from identifying what I was seeing than from actually seeing it. And I wanted more of that, and I wanted it faster.

Hurry.

Run from the voice.

Faster.

The quicker I learned something new, I thought, the less likely the voice was to make me feel stupid out there in the valley. And so the speed of the learning became its own measure of success.

Looking back at myself then, I'm reminded of a chipmunk I saw one day in the butternut tree behind the house. Poised on its hind legs, it pulled thick, drooping catkins from the branches, eating them the way we might eat an ear of corn: it held each catkin by the ends and spun it, chewing a single mouth-wide strip around the circumference in quick, choppy bursts, before dropping it and plucking off another. As I watched that assembly-line meal—one catkin, then another, then another—I remember thinking what a waste it seemed, all that hurry, all that catkin left untouched. All of it done with such joylessness.

3

I happened upon the tree near the top of High Peak in the early summer of 1989, on one of my early walks along the Vermont ridge. We'd lived on Cobble Hill almost two years by then, I'd just begun taking my explorations out into the valley, and Robin was within weeks of delivering our first son, Carry.

I'd started my climb on the west side of the hill, the side I couldn't see from home and hadn't explored before, so the ground seemed charged, potent with unknowns. And it didn't disappoint. It surprised me with its topography, the spine-and-gully formation lying across it like ribs that took me up, then down a little, up further, then down a little again, like a tide carrying me out from shore. It surprised me with two peaks at the top instead of one, paired knobs separated by a hollow. And it surprised me with its high openness, made by recent logging, which had cut a swath up the south side of the hill into the hollow.

Later, after coming off the peaks, I wandered along the west edge of the ridgetop for a while. Eventually, I found myself in a gully with a raised wall on my left that sloped uphill away from me. Concentrating on my footing, I had my head down most of the time, but at one point I glanced up to find the most surprising sight of all: a fifty-foot tree in full leaf, its base raised five feet off the ground. And below it, cast in patchy sunlight, where its roots should have been, was the leaf-lined trough of the gully, and nothing else. In the instant it takes to be startled, it occurred to me the tree had no roots, or else roots of air.

After the initial shock, I walked closer and investigated, trying to understand what had happened. It looked as if the tree, a maple, had been blown down years before, almost entirely uprooting itself in the process. Its top had come to rest on the uphill ground to my left; down by me, it had fallen across the gully like a drawbridge across an empty moat. A branch that had been perhaps ten feet off the ground when the tree was standing suddenly found itself upright above the gully when the tree fell over, and it just kept growing. Now, years later, it had become its own tree, taller and thicker than the fallen one out of which it had grown and which supported it now, serving as its base, a cylindrical platform five feet above the gully floor. I raised both my arms onto that fallen trunk, and leaned against it.

"Pretty little theory," the voice said.

"You like it, huh," I said.

"Oh, yeah. A branch growin' into a tree on top of another tree, and all without roots. That's priceless."

"Well, that's what it looks like, doesn't it?"

"Not if you know anythin' about trees."

"So you know about trees?"

"One of us has to. Listen, it's simple: if you've got a live tree, you've got roots."

"I don't even know enough about trees to say whether that's true or not. Aren't there any kinds of trees that stay alive some other way?" I asked him.

"Oh, please," he said.

"Okay, then where are this tree's roots? They aren't underneath it."

"Man oh man. You're not really that thick, are you?" he said, then added slowly, in a singsongy way, as if to a young child, "Why don't we try lookin' where the rest of the roots are?"

The original tree's roots were to my right, but from where I stood the entire root base looked to have been upturned, yanked out of the ground long ago when the tree had fallen. Still, some of those roots could have held, I guessed, at least enough of them to feed the new tree. But when I walked around the base, I found the underside completely exposed—a giant earthen hand, upright, looming taller than me, its torn roots poking like spindly fingers from the edges of its veined palm. The more I surveyed the broad underside of the base, the less I could explain how the tree was still living. There seemed too much rootedness open to the air, too little still planted to support both the new tree and the solid platform of the original one.

"Here we are," I said. "Now, show them to me."

"It's not the kind of thing you can just show. You dig underneath the base, you'll find 'em. Go ahead. I guarantee you they're there."

I said, "Guarantee, hell. You're not really sure, are you? You could be wrong."

"Not likely."

"But possible. For all of the guaranteed roots you've shown me, they might as *well* be growing in the air."

I meant it, too. In the shadow of that base, with no live roots visible and all my other explanations shot to hell, I half-dared to believe that magical airborne roots were possible.

And, in fact, they are. In *Volcano*, Garrett Hongo's memoir of his return to his childhood home on the island of Hawai'i, he describes the trunk of an enormous native tree fern called *hâpu'u*:

> Its stump is its root, a bundle of matlike fibers that take on sustenance from the rains. The standing trunk is actually a bundle of fibrous stalks . . . surrounded by an absorbent, spongy matting that knits everything together. This matting is, in actuality, a system of intertwined aerial roots. . . .The villagers here in Volcano know that you must water *hâpu'u* from the *top* of its trunk, not at its base.

Later, a friend tells Hongo about *hâpu'u*'s life cycle:

> The *hâpu'u* gets to a certain point when it's too old or too heavy to support its crown—about thirty or forty years. Then it collapses, and you'd think it'd die, but it just sends up another shoot and makes a joint back from the fallen trunk up to the canopy again and lives for another thirty or forty years until it collapses another time and sends up a new bundle of roots and fronds. A tree can fall a bunch of times, make a series of joints like you see around here

and send up a new crown every time. . . . It's *immortal!*

I didn't know about *hâpu'u* that afternoon on High Peak. I would have wanted to, I'm sure, but it's good that I didn't. I probably would have used it as I used other book-fed information in those days—to squelch my insecurity and answer the voice. Instead, without a concrete explanation for the floating maple tree, I had to rely on the thing that had first propelled me so happily through Cobble Hill's woods: raw wonder. And, god, how freeing it was then to remember that uncertainty didn't have to turn savagely inward, that it was still possible to revel in something's impression, and *believe* it, even if for an instant, no matter how fantastic the impression might be; I felt like a child again, out ahead on a walk, conjuring the ordinary into the magical before the doubting adult arrived.

So when I learned of it, I greeted the existence of *hâpu'u* with the wonder it deserved, and not greedy affirmation. What a miraculous world it seemed, to have room for a tree like that, growing upside down and rightside up at the same time, both its roots and leaves in the air, rising from its fallen self like a phoenix from its ashes.

I also greeted it with gratitude, for if something like *hâpu'u* could exist, then so could a floating maple, and so too a New England valley bowl where straight ridgelines managed to bend themselves and meet. If *hâpu'u* could flourish, then perhaps there was hope for a man who had pulled himself from his home in the suburbs of Chicago and, chased by the enemy voice inside him, suddenly felt like an insecure boy in that valley. Perhaps he could discover home there and grow securely into it. Perhaps he could learn from its contours the complex ways of the land, and then those ways could teach him how to soften and bend the lines of his own divided nature—lines that made him feel split in two sometimes, bouncing back and forth between boy and man, dumb jock and capable teacher, greenhorn flatlander and valley nature lover, hurried chipmunk and unworried bear. Perhaps he could come to understand through his own experience what he had dared to believe for a moment one afternoon on a hilltop: that a living thing could find fertile ground where you might least expect it, in the invisible firmness of air.

Wesley McNair

FROM THE FOREST AND THE TREES: FOUR SEASONS FROM
A JOURNAL ABOUT PLACE AND POETRY

All spring the tree that inspires me most is the dead elm my dogs and I pass on our daily walk. It is so tall not even the vines that climb its sides each spring can reach its highest branches; yet they go as high as they're able, decorating it with a lovely, green lace. From the castoffs of weed and decay, this surprising elegance.

***

Listen to northern New Englanders explain the location of a house, gravel pit or pond, and you will eventually hear the expression "over in there," or "down in there," as in: "Stay on the main road until you come to a general store on the left, then take your next right. Their summer camp is *down in there*." Thus does the landscape of forest, hills and hollows make its way into native speech.

***

Kinnell, Oliver, and Kumin have all written poems about picking and eating wild blackberries in a New England August, but no one has written of the leisurely talk which goes on in the blackberry patch and is partly why one goes there, taking a family member or friend along for the purpose. "Good pickin'," somebody says far off in the patch, and "They're loaded today." Nearer by, a woman tells of all the quarts she put up last year, and her companion tells about the blackberry cobbler she will make for her grown son. Then they recall picking, good and bad, in other patches and other seasons. Hearing such voices as they drift across the bushes, one could be in heaven—God, listening to each innoncent reflection, and to each affectionate joke: the man's voice asking his wife stuck in the briars, "Who's winnin'—you or the thorns?"; the woman threatening to bake him a "green pie."

***

September. The leaves in the surrounding forest begin to turn, and the ache inside comes back, that yearning for more of it, for fall to tear one open with its fierce oranges and blood reds, to carry one off in October winds, and November rains.

***

On a frozen weekend in February, William Stafford stays with me and my wife Diane between readings, bringing great warmth to our house. After he leaves I find this poem on his pillow, left as a gift—a poem another poet might have saved for publication, though for Stafford, the pleasure the poem would give us was publication enough.

McNair's Place

Because it is Maine, snow still lingers
till its own good time in reticent places
or turns its face in shadow away,
and any farm stays only partly yours,
retaining its Indian posture, no matter what
    century it is.
Even towns have a habit of straggling off
rough at the edges and allowing old barns
to hang around leaning along Maine Street
reminiscing with stands of woodbine and
    popple and wild grape.
What sheriff could arrest a land like this
when the red stars come out to patrol the dark?
Snow backs off, streetlights hold still;
out there in a surge of trees, galloping
hills escape all the time where our country
belongs to the world and knows no law, no
    owner, no state.

***

"Nature's first green is gold," says Robert Frost, referring, perhaps, to that yellow fuzz one sees in trees that are just budding and leafing out in the springtime of northern New England after a long winter. Yet for the maple tree, the first green is brown—a russet which, one discovers on closer view, belongs to tiny leaves in the exact shape they will always have, astonishing as a baby's hand. Without the brown of maples in the forest, we would not see the yellow of birch and poplar half so well. Their brown sets the contrast that makes visible not only nature's gold, but the whole spectrum of early green in the trees coming back to life each May in northern New England.

***

A Mercer neighbor, Denis Culley, tells me about a horse—his old work horse and friend, Dick. For some time now, the old-timers in our town have been advising him to get Dick a mate. "A horse gets lonely without one," they all say. Unable to afford another horse, Denis now goes out to the pasture on spring and summer nights after the work is done to stand quietly beside his horse. Of all the love stories I've ever heard, this is one of the most moving.

***

How beautiful is the texture of talk on summer nights when we sit with friends on porches or, as I did last night, on the back lawn in deck chairs under the trees. Its intimacy and directness reminds me of James Carse's description of talk in *The Silence of God*, "To speak from your heart is to receive the listener into your heart." One often hears that the modern age has abandoned poetry; yet communicating in this way, we are almost speaking poetry. How, then, have we abandoned it?

***

The poet does not believe in miracles, but in mysteries.

***

According to Bei Dao, the Chinese poet and dissident, it is important for any poet to have a small group with whom he can share his secrets. So saying, he suggests a definition of poetry as a code which, shared with others, gives special knowledge and power to the sharers and the poet alike. It is a definition shaped by his life under political oppression, and it reminds us of the capacity poetry has to change us and our world.

***

Trees again. On a November drive shortly after moving from New Hampshire to Maine several autumns ago, my homesick wife Diane began to cry about the "friends" that had been taken from her. When she dried her eyes and I got her to talk about her grief, I discovered it wasn't people she meant, but the great, old maples that had stood at the edges of our property and our lives for fifteen years.

***

On CNN's "Headline News," of all places, a Buddhist turns up to speak about suffering, and then gratitude. Gratitude is rare among Americans, he says, because in a capitalist culture, people are conditioned to want and get, so receiving is what is supposed to happen. In fact, we are never fully satisfied with what we receive and only want more. Unable to know gratitude, the Buddhist explains, we remain spiritually childish.

***

But gratitude exists. This January, from the front window of our house in Maine, Diane and I watch snow coming to rest on the distant trees around our property, which seem suddenly enormous, as if the snowfall had made them grow. One has a low branch with twists in it like a dozen elbows. Another has three small branches that open at the very top, making a tiny tree. Our new friends.

***

Another spring, and I have just read Philip Booth's musings about the cost of "whatever trees were felled" for catalogs that come in the mail from the retailers. I, too, am troubled by this. Yet I am also troubled by the combination of hurt and resignation I see in the face of Clayton Brann when he tells me during his annual spring delivery of firewood to my house that the recession has stopped the production of catalogs and newspaper inserts. Clayton is a simple and unschooled man who would have difficulty replacing his work in the woods. "You wouldn't think a little thing like that could affect a man's living," he says. "But it does."

***

Place is not only a noun but a verb; one cannot come to know it without locating oneself in it, a slow and interior process. Looking out my window in one more October as I write this, I see blowing and falling leaves whose altered color is so familiar I have not looked closely at them until now. They are part of me, together with the damp chill from last night's rain I experience though I am indoors, all carrying a feeling that belongs to this season and no other. What have I learned that I didn't know I knew from autumn—its bright warmth against the cold, its whirling change against the skeletons of trees—what but that the world is two things at once: a surface and an underneath, a source of celebration and of sorrow, a yearning and a giving in, life that goes on and death that takes it away.

***

The place where I live, how wild it is. This weekend I fly over it with a friend in his small airplane and find nothing but forest all the way to the horizon; yet on the ground in my Maine town I hardly notice the surrounding trees, they seem so far from houses and roads. Now when I see deer entering our fields or a moose stumbling across a sidestreet, I will understand they know my region as it really is: a continuous underworld of green, opening into a dream of light.

***

After a fall morning spent among the trees in the forest of poetry, I too stumble into the street, out to take my daily walk. Everywhere, this strangeness of houses and people walking to their mailboxes or tending their gardens. Everywhere this assumption that life is all here, out in the open.

Walter Clark   Sam Manhart

Canoeing Maine: a Journal
September 1998

At some point we will be heading toward something, a flowing river or the trip's conclusion, but today we are still outward bound. It's more than a measure of half-way points and margins in the maps. Every place and point of water felt more and more remote. The wind on the Umbazooksus Lake. A heron watched us as we left the marsh for the open, shallow lake. If not threatened by our passing, he did notice us, these rare visitors to his home.

drawing by Francelia Clark

Day 1, Moose Island Campground – Moosehead Lake

≋ I'm sitting against a pine tree, feet braced on a rock, hat cocked against the western sun. Sam Manhart and I are on a tiny granite island four miles north of Greenville, Maine, where we launched our canoe. I hear the speaking sound small waves make against rocks, and also the muted voices of those with whom we share this camping spot: three couples, a radio and three dogs, one of which swims in front of me with thumping paws.

The desire to go down the Allagash one more time has been on me for several years. A generation ago Francelia and I made the trip with four Michigan undergraduates. I mentioned it to Sam Manhart, a former student and present staff member at the University of Michigan's New England Literature Program, and he picked up on the idea so quickly we seemed already afloat. Last night Sam arrived in Hancock, NH, after a two day drive from Michigan and we set about getting our stuff together. It's seven hours, more or less, from Hancock to Greenville, which is almost exactly at the point where a line drawn north and south through the state of Maine crosses a line drawn east and west through its mid-section. It is 125 crow miles north to St. Francis, the border hamlet on the St. John River, where Folsom's air service will pick us up. It will be about 180 miles by water. Last night we admitted the seriousness of what we were about to undertake; the grand unprotected lakes, white water and six miles of carry. Then we set about packing with the special cheer that such serious considerations entail.

⅗ How strange it was to sit/kneel in the bow of a canoe today. I'm used to a sailboat's cockpit, or the stern of a canoe. I have sometimes weaseled my way into the stern under the dubious auspices of experience and seamanship, but that flag isn't flying here in northern Maine. Walter and I have agreed to swap the helm each day, and I was more than happy to get my sea legs (i.e. swollen knee joints) with him steering. I like the bow and its closeness to the water. I looked down at the ruffled wake we made, lulled visually to the point where it begins. I felt the rush of it past my calves through the thin shell of canoe.

When Walter mentioned this trip last spring, his eyes lit up like a ski bum's on a deep powder day. I knew there was something real out here, and this afternoon began to confirm it. The fuzzy distance of a far shoreline came into focus and the mountains that I know are islands in the lake inched closer. As the afternoon went on we marked our progress by the ski area to the east as it crept from a profile view to that more resembling the view of a trail map. When we landed at Moose Island, my knees reminded me of the many trail maps I've followed on skis. My legs weren't too excited about straightening, and even less enthusiastic at the prospect of standing. I hobbled around thinking about Francelia's comment that after a few days we will have worked out all the aches.

Night has set in. The stars have thickened and the few house lights along the eastern shore of Moosehead are shining out over the water more clearly now, illuminating in tandem Blair Hill and the Scammon Ridge. There is no moon. As I lie on this slab of granite looking up at the night, my muscles and my mind relax, and I realize that I have not had real silence this past urban summer. Its presence now soothes my ears the way a television being turned off soothes my eyes. I am in New England. I can slow down now, the cities are behind me.

Most of the lights on the far shore have gone black now, and I think about the next few days of paddling north, away from house lights and houses, roads, telephones, and telephone poles. Even the loons are quiet.

Day 2, Moose Island Campground – Moosehead Lake

♒ Walter predicted that the threatening rain would hit, and it has. We both scurried to our tents as the drizzle turned toward a heavy, all day rain. I'm very cozy in my sleeping bag. After three days of driving, of going and going and getting to the start of this adventure, it has begun in earnest and I can afford to put some time into sleep, some time to sleep....

...but now it is three o'clock in the afternoon and the day is shot to hell for canoeing. I light a cigarette and watch it more than I smoke it. I need a project more meaningful than eating dried apricots. I'm going to memorize some poetry. I open *The Complete Poetry of Robert Frost* and find "Too Anxious For Rivers." Just above the title, on the same page, are the last few lines of "Directive."

Here are your waters and your watering place.
Drink and be whole again beyond confusion.

My course is set.

~~~ To the roll call of things forgotten add twine and even the simplest map of Moosehead. We have plenty of Allagash maps. Was it a mistake to leave our folding saw behind?

The sight of me trying to set up my tent for the first time on this trip would have amused Thoreau. On every trip I have to re-learn basic camping skills. Things usually come together by the third day, which is about the time trip sleeping patterns get established.

We talked just now and decided to stay here. Sam is philosophical about our decision in the light of high waves on the lake. I am pleased by this. I wouldn't have been as wise at his age.

Day 3, Deer Island Campground – Moosehead Lake

~~~ Awoke two or three times during the night. Up at 6:30. Big white caps. Lovely shafts of sunlight piercing clouds to the east. Mist rising from hills to meet low scud. Coffee and journey-bread for breakfast. We sit and talk in the warm sun to the lee of an enormous granite ledge while only a few steps away the blast rages.

Three couples set forth an hour ago in their rented pontoon boat. The deck was awash, the pontoons out of sight, and they were sowing garbage bags as they went. After a few hundred yards the ship careened laboriously about, returned to port and off-loaded half the crew and a mountain of baggage. "Enough beer for the Wisconsin State Fair," said Sam.

Late in the morning the wind seeming to abate, we set off with some misgiving, making our way back toward Greenville so as to begin with some lee protection and then come up on the inside, or western shore [Thoreau's route], where we could make easier landing in case the wind rose. The run to the bottom of Moose Island was fast. Sam did fine in the stern, though he later confessed that his experience in lake waters was not as extensive as on rivers. The wind we then headed into was brisk, but the waves were manageable and we got along quite well. Between the head of Moose and Black Sand Island we got into uncomfortable cross-chop and shipped some water over the bow. We stopped to rest in the lee of the island, then headed up lake through two miles of unprotected water, the wind moderating as we went, and then along the east shore of Deer Island, past the fishing camp at the head of the island and through the narrows formed by Deer and Sugar Islands to this lovely spot, arriving a bit past four. There was time to rest, do laundry, swim, build a fire, eat a leisurely supper and quaff hot beakers of Gatorade.

I'm sitting in front of a fire, across which I can see Mt. Kineo to the northwest. There isn't a cloud in the sky, just lovely autumnal orange-red glow. The lake in front of the fire is absolutely still, but farther out a line of dark breeze scumbles the silver water. Tomorrow will be a long day if the good weather holds.

   ❧ I was a bit tight in the stern today, as Walter could easily tell. We did have some waves to deal with, but our passage was entirely doable. Walter said, "If we do ship some water, it'll be all right," which I interpreted as, "Relax, don't worry, these waves aren't that big." I tried to keep the canoe headed directly into the wind and waves and tried to relax a bit, and gradually did both. The situation reminded me of something Nate Way, a friend of mine from Utah, said to me in the desert one time. We were mountain biking, and I was braking too much on the steep descents. I was more accustomed to the mellow terrain of West Michigan and was biking timidly. He said, "You need to bike like you ski. Let the flow take you and relax into the right balance. Ski it; your tires are your edges." I tried his balance/flow theory, and it worked. If biking is similar to skiing steeps, canoeing in choppy waves is akin to skiing in a mogul field. I loosened my hips and let the canoe's motion dictate the motion of my lower body, anticipating the bump and flow of the next wave. My thin smile began to broaden. I was still a bit relieved when we landed at the south end of what I think was Deer Island for a short break. I felt for the first time this trip that familiar little pulse from the cherished adrenal glands that only truly registers when you no longer need its sweet assistance.

By late afternoon the wind had given up. We paddled to this campground on glassy water. Tonight after dinner we had a poetry read around. I stumbled through "Directive," butchering it rather effectively. It was a strange transition from the inward memorization of the poem to the actual voicing of it. I knew the string of images but was surprised by the sound of my words. A few times I caught myself listening to the sound of the last line instead of surfacing the next. I'll try that again in a few days. Walter has gone to his tent and I'm sitting here in front of the last glowing fragments of fire as night deepens. We have a long day planned tomorrow and I should get to my sleeping bag soon.

Day 4, Seboomook Point Campground – Moosehead Lake

By seven this morning we were paddling out into the mist. The shoreline behind us disappeared very quickly and we were wrapped in white. Walter took a bearing on Mt. Kineo last night, mystically predicting this early morning fog. We navigated by compass and the only sound was the slight rush of paddle through water. My eyes had given up trying to penetrate the horizonless cloud and my ears had taken over. The sky began to turn blue overhead and the mist burned away, retreating to the northwest. We had our first unobstructed view of Kineo, still five or six miles off.

We paddled into a bay that was full of dead wood and were approaching the shore of Kineo when a big fox came running into, and then out of, view. It was in front of us and gone so quickly that we were left with just the smile of the moment and the sunlit face of the Kineo cliffs. An Indian trail summits Mt. Kineo, ascending above the low crags that face Rockwood Village   before dipping into the thick forest that crowns the island. On top of Mt. Kineo is an observation tower. As I climbed the tower's steps, the size and scope of Moosehead Lake came into view and I began to get my bearings. Walter pointed out the tiny white specks of houses at Northeast Carry on the horizon. After he had started back down the mountain, I stayed behind and gazed out over the water and mountains and forest in every direction. I tried to cement that view, that place, that afternoon in my memory. I then struck a course, due east, for the top of the Kineo cliffs. Bushwhacking in northern Maine, I learned, takes enormous effort. I tried to follow the compass bearing from the trail but the fallen logs and thickets of brush made me meander like a stream. I eventually reached the open cliffs and saw the bare rock sloping away toward vertical beneath me. I leaned out a little, both hands clutching a sturdy pine, and took a photograph of the tiny, sheltered bay at the base of the mountain. A southwest wind was rising across the north end of the lake, and the canoe, far below, was a speck of sunlit red. I headed back to the trail going over, under, and ever around the thick obstacles of the forest. My face and hands gathered spider webs, pine needles, and sap. As I approached the beach where Walter was waiting, I noticed that a hummingbird was hovering just beyond the bill of his cap.

WALTER AND THE HUMMINGBIRD

Walter sat chatting with a hummingbird
as my bootsteps trampled onto the pebbles
that beach the lake. Interrupting
their meeting was my mistake.
They eyed one another graciously,
each as much for his own as the other's sake,
fed by the moment's proximity, that of a
canoe's prow yearning through its point of rippling wake.
I can't say what secrets they shared, whether
of flight or verse or the rhyme of the breeze.
Walter turned me a smile as the
hummingbird turned, adjourning downwind
toward the water-lined horizon of trees.

Since the lake was calm and the breeze was behind us we took the whole northeast end of the lake in one go, reaching Seboomook Point shortly before sundown.

Day 5, Thoreau Island Campground – West Branch, Penobscot River

≋ We made a slow start to make up for our exertions of yesterday, but it was only a little over a mile to the carry. The two or three houses facing the lake seemed deserted and barren, but the enormous lawn in front was freshly cut; there was laundry on the line and big juicy apples hung from the single tree that seemed to say "welcome." We had time for one final look at the grand spread of Moosehead before we set forth over the arrow-straight carry road:

Millionaires
Come and drink of this clear water,
And bears.

Shiki

We set out with little ado, carrying the canoe and one big bag on the first trip and coming back for the rest.

On the second trip we stopped at Raymond's Country store. Mr. Raymond is a Bostonian who came to these parts twenty years ago and claims rhetorically never to have been south of Moosehead Lake since. He said that many who retired to live in the Maine woods could not stick it out. "The first summer, it's April to October and the rest in Florida. The second summer, June to September in Maine, the rest in Florida. The third summer they stay only two months and socialize with people you know they have nothing in common with and go shopping in Bangor once a week. The next year the property's for sale."

Mrs. Raymond, who had been silent through most of the discussion, perked up when I said that stocking such a store must be tricky business. She nodded vigorously and said they carry a completely different line of goods during the winter months. Mr. Raymond remarked that mail is delivered by a contract carrier who is not required to deliver on days when there is an inch or more of snow. "Sometimes we don't get mail for a month," said he, leaving us to decide whether this was good or bad.

I had had so much of Mr. Raymond's home-made pizza (from the case of frozen pizzas in the back) that I could barely stagger over the carry, but any road is attractive after some days in a canoe, and we enjoyed this dirt track with its one or two cabins, store, and flock of canted mailboxes at a by-road. Thoreau's canoe and belongings were pulled over the exact same route on a wooden railroad in 1855 and 1857. Towards the end of the carry he stopped to drink at a spring. It's still there, now encased in a blue barrel. So we stopped, too, in an act of practical piety, to fill our water jugs, then pushed off onto the West Branch of the Penobscot River. A significant phase of our trip ended as we passed from the watershed of the Kennebec to that of the Penobscot: a little less than a fourth of the distance. We were glad to get out into the middle of its placid waters and away from the fierce bugs at the landing. We soon reached Lobster Stream, where the river turns from east to north. I had promised Sam a moose along this section, but none obliged. Just beyond sight of the Golden Road, but well within hearing, is the small island at the head of the Moosehorn deadwater where Thoreau's party camped on 16 September, 1853.

The site is on a grassy bluff looking upriver. I think the Maine Forest Service must give it special treatment. There were even several rounds of wood ready for a fire had we chosen to have one. But it had rained off and on all day and we were eager to eat and get under canvas. Midges were urging us on. Sam has been declared cook by acclamation, and I dishwasher. "Speed," "Simplicity" and "Carbohydrates" are carved over the cookhouse door.

I went early to my tent and considered the bugs, which would be camping with us from now on along the rivers. On warm damp nights such as this they can be truly bothersome. Blackflies are not the issue so late in the year, and mosquitoes can usually be kept out of the tent. It's no-see-ums that occupy mind and flesh, raising welts on ankles and wrists, and invective at the dinner table. They infiltrate the tent when you enter and their bite is like the touch of a lit cigarette. Sam claims to have luck with his lighter. Attracted to its flame the bugs immolate themselves. My tent is too small for such tricks. I had thought to distract them by inviting them to make guest entries in this journal, but the results are predictably crass.

"Yum."
"Great entree."
"Type A, Myrtle."
"I feel a buzz coming on."

Good night.

Day 6, Longley Stream Campground – Chesuncook Lake

♌ This morning was sunny. A cool north wind took care of yesterday's bugs, and we had a leisurely paddle down the West Branch of the Penobscot. A few hundred feet upstream stood a moose, a large cow. I fumbled around for my camera and hurriedly snapped a few photos, expecting her to bolt for the far shore. She eyed our canoe with a calm that approached boredom. As we neared the mouth of Chesuncook Lake, the channel widened and the current slacked to a standstill. We stopped at a campground and hiked a vaguely maintained footpath to Chesuncook Village.

We walked into Chesuncook Village and stopped to pick apples from the tree in front of the church. We then proceeded to the village graveyard. Walter had been there before. I think the graveyard is an important historic landmark for him, a record of families who struggled to live here, a measured and maintained location to be revisited in the vast sameness and oblivion of forest and water. He pointed out a grave that said, "NAME UNKNOWN" and explained that it was probably the body of a logger found long ago in a spring's thaw.

We walked to an inn on Chesuncook Lake and while Walter went inside to check the place out, I sat outside near the largest birch tree I've ever seen. There were a few lawn chairs near the inn's garden. I reclined in one and looked out over the lake toward Mt. Katahdin, its profile close and gleaming in the afternoon sun. It was a beautiful day that suggested August, but the locals had already started to hunker down for the approaching winter. When we got back to the canoe, we decided to take a fifteen minute nap.

Evening has come on. I just heard something strange. There it is again. Those are wolves howling. That last one sounded closer than the others.

PREY

There's a new sound amid the silence,
slowly rising above the loon's call
and over the low slap
of lake on land in the north wind.
Wolves are howling a wanton chant
to the forested night; some miles away,
some many miles.
Moose, near and far, must also hear
the wails of the wolves.
They all must hear the occasional airplane

rush overhead.
I perceive myself as prey tonight,
in league with the waking moose
as the wolves go silent
and set out, circling
the scent of their next meal.
My sudden fear predicts
the blue gleam in their eyes
as inevitable truth, invisible
as a distant flight fading from
sound to silence beyond the clouds
while the moose gaze warily out
at the encroaching darkness.

≈ Up in time to celebrate, by accident, the 145th anniversary of Thoreau's stay here. The day bright and clear. No moose appeared before breakfast, but we did see a square-end canoe with kicker, guide and client. Salmon are returning to spawn on the West Branch; we would see fishermen all the way down to Chesuncook. On the river by eight, the bugs hustled off by dry northwest air. In an hour or so we passed the mouth of the Moosehorn. Here is how Thoreau describes this stretch of river in *The Maine Woods*:

At starlight we dropped down the stream, which was a dead-water for three miles, or as far as the Moosehorn; Joe [Joe Aitteon, his Indian guide] telling us that we must be very silent, and he himself making no noise with his paddle, while he urged the canoe along with effective impulses. It was a still night, and suitable for this purpose, – for if there is wind, the moose will smell you, – and Joe was very confident that he should get some. The harvest moon had just risen, and its level rays began to light up the forest on our right, while we glided downward in the shade on the same side, against the little breeze that was stirring. The lofty, spiring tops of the spruce and fir were very black against the sky, and more distinct than by day, close bordering this broad avenue on each side; and the beauty of the scene, as the moon rose above the forest, it would not be easy to describe. A bat flew over our heads, and we heard a few faint notes of birds from time to time, perhaps the myrtle-bird for one, or the sudden plunge of a musquash, or saw one crossing the stream before us, or heard the sound of a rill emptying in, swollen by the recent rain.

Presently we came to Ragmuff Stream, also mentioned by Thoreau, and after a while to Big Island, where the river picked up speed. Many, many fishermen here. Almost all the campgrounds were occupied, as if for a stay of some time, with wall tents, cook stoves on legs, blue tarps, and clothing hanging out to dry. We went through the riffles with no problem and paused at the granite pool for a bite to eat and to prepare for what we thought would be a hard paddle against northwest winds; but the next five miles to Log Boom Camp where the river opens onto Chesuncook Lake proved surprisingly easy.

Day 7, Donnely Point Campground – Chamberlain Lake

♋ At some point we will be heading toward something, a flowing river or the trip's conclusion, but today we are still outward bound. It's more than a measure of half-way points and margins in the maps. Every place and point of water felt more and more remote. The wind on the Umbazooksus Lake. A heron watched us a we left the marsh for the open, shallow lake. If not threatened by our passing, he did notice us, these rare visitors to his home.

Our crossing was unhurried but direct, like the gait of people leaving a church. Walter remembered the alders that marked the Mud Pond Carry. As we paddled toward them, we spotted a faded ribbon tied to a tree at the trailhead/ streambed. I hoisted the canoe onto my shoulders and waded into the murky trench. It was glorious. The portage was two miles. I tried to convince myself that it was five or ten miles, that I'd be under the canoe's yoke all day, that I'd better get used to it. In this context, two miles was nothing. Near the end of the trail, I'd occasionally tip the bow upward and peer out beyond the gunwales at the trees, searching for the clearing that would mark Mud Pond. The trail rose gradually from water to gloop to mud to a relatively dry path that ended in a small field. I plopped the canoe down, pleased. As I approached Mud Pond for the second time, now only carrying a backpack and my paddle, I heard a churning in the water. A large moose trotted past the put-in. I waded waist deep into Mud Pond and watched her retreat. She ran about fifty feet along the shoreline, turned, saw that I was watching her, and rushed onto land through a thick stand of alders and spruce. As soon as she hit land, she was gone. The thick forest hid her immediately.

The person who named Mud Pond had a flair for description. As we crossed, the blades of our paddles completely disappeared with each stroke and

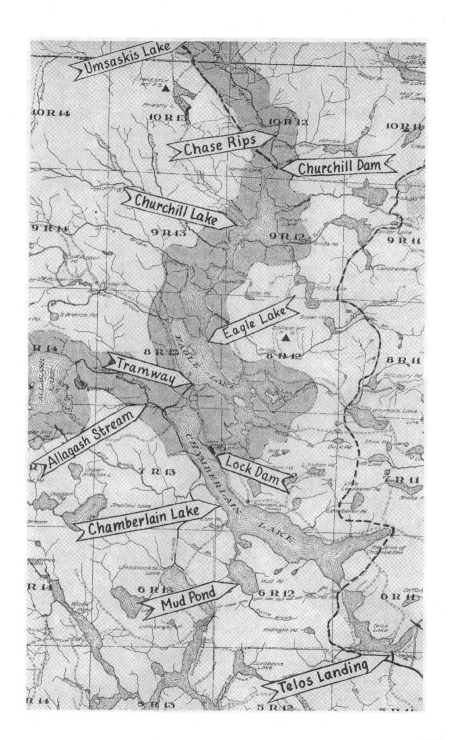

emerged with a fine layer of black silt that washed away and was replaced, leaving murky whirlpools at metered intervals behind us. We found the channel that would lead us to Chamberlain Lake and saw no sign of the dam that might have been built, used, abandoned, and all but forgotten in the years between Thoreau's passage here and ours today. We paddled down part of the rocky and fast-flowing creek, then walked down the rest of the way to a small bay on Chamberlain. Our thoughts turned toward dinner and bed and we weighed our options. Mud Brook Campground didn't sound very appealing to me. The name suggested bugs and muck. Donnely Point sounded regal, like something to aspire to.

〜 The middle of the night, if one has no anxieties, is good for thought. For some reason I seem to find myself thinking of prayer. If a stray prayer comes along in the middle of the night I make it welcome and hope to send it on its way refreshed.

We were comfortably off by eight, making good time to the bridge at Umbazooksus Stream, which we negotiated without a carry. "Umbazooksus" means "meadow" in Abenaki, and the stream did indeed wind lazily through an enormous meadow. The air smelled sweetly of swamp grasses, the volatile odor caught at dusk from autumn car windows. After awhile the stream narrowed and we had to walk the canoe over rocks in fast water. The gate was up at Umbazooksus Dam and we were able to walk right through into a landscape different from any we had seen so far. The horizon was low and very close on all sides. No mountains could be seen. The forest came down gently to the water wherever you looked. The lake was motionless and wild with no human sign except for the dam: not a beer can, not a piece of faded wrap, not a circle of fire charcoal. The dam itself seemed no more than a single word in a conversation with many pauses. There was a ring of raw earth around the lake like rust around the edge of a bathtub in an empty lot.

> Tourists and ranger gone home,
> An old fellow in a red hat
> Fishing from a beat canoe
> Vanishes in falling snow.

〜

As soon as you shoulder your way in through the alders that guard the carry entrance you are in dark, dark woods. Umbazooksus Lake could as well be ten miles behind you. In another couple of hundred yards there is an abandoned clearing beneath huge pines. A blind man had a small store here in the early lumber days. He and several others from the Mud Pond area are buried in the Chesuncook cemetery we visited yesterday. This morning there is only this hushed space haunted by forgotten purposes. Some half-burned logs suggest that snowmobilers lunched here last winter, and at the outer edges tangled in moosewood lie remains of earlier times, a barrel stove with rust like lichen, the head of a peavey without a handle, and most evocative, an upside down coffee pot with its bail sticking absurdly in the air.

> *I am awe-struck*
> *To hear a cricket singing*
> *Underneath the dark cavity*
> *Of an old helmet.*
>   Bashô

This carry and site must have been in use long before westerners appeared. There is convenient water and protection from wind. The carry is the most direct way from Penobscot to Allagash waters. Thoreau had his most trying adventure along this trail. He and Ed Hoar lost the trail when their guide pushed ahead. As so often in *The Maine Woods*, Thoreau managed to make light of a bad situation, describing his route as "a well swamped road..."

We then entered another swamp, at a necessarily slow pace, where the walking was worse than ever, not only on account of the water, but the fallen timber, which often obliterated the indistinct trail entirely. The fallen trees were so numerous, that for long distances the route was through a succession of small yards, where we climbed over fences as high as our heads, down into water often up to our knees, and then over another fence into a second yard, and so on; and going back for his bag my companion once lost his way and came back without it. In many places the canoes would have run if it had not been for the fallen timber. Again it would be more open, but equally wet, too wet for trees to grow and no place to sit down. It was a mossy swamp, which it required the long legs of a moose to traverse, and it is very likely that we scared some of them in our transit, though we saw none.

Today was about as fine a Mud Pond passage as one could ask for, but still tiring. Adventures and difficulties lie ahead, but it is unlikely that we will have such a demanding day again. We have broken the back of this trip.

Day 8, Little Eagle Campground – Eagle Lake

♌ In skiing, there are moments when falling is not an option. If you slip from a traverse over rocks or miss a turn at the top of a steep chute, you could easily find yourself fluffing off to the big sleep. Today Chamberlain Lake struck me as a body of water in which tipping the canoe was not an option. I was not convinced that the canoe would stay afloat if we tipped. It could easily fill with water in the choppy waves and disappear downward with a last maroon glimmer, leaving us floating with paddles in our hands. And there we'd be, but with a swim in front of us; no dry clothes, no food, no cigarettes, no shelter, and no fuel, in that order. Oh, and no hiking boots to walk out in because they're also tied to the canoe, along with the maps which might indicate the general direction of the way out.

We were alone with the lake. Walter has expected to see a ranger each of the last few days, but none have materialized. Looking across the water, I could see no sign of the dam that our map claims is there. After a while of looking, I marked a white something that I thought could be the dam, but, with time, it looked more like a blob of granite in the sun. We decided to bow to the winds and cross Chamberlain well to the north. I was more than happy to hug the shore and head for the protected bay of the Tramway Carry.

The lake was still a bit choppy close to shore, but not choppy enough to keep me from reciting "Directive" to myself. I'd start, "Back out of all this now too much for us..." And continue until I either goofed up the words or one of us said something. Walter talked about the forest around Hancock, New Hampshire, following a trail of syllables home from the wilderness.

♒ The Tramway is a mile-long endless chain used early this century to haul logs from the St. John watershed to that of the Penobscot. My unreliable guess is that each link weighs about thirty-five pounds. At the time of its building—no easy task out here in the middle of nowhere—Canadian and American lumbermen were contending to determine whether logs would go down the Penobscot to American mills in Bangor, or down the Allagash to Canadian mills. Its job was to haul logs from the Eagle Lake watershed, ostensibly Allagash acreage, across the height of land to Penobscot waters. It was later replaced by gigantic steam tractors, and then by a railroad [1927-1937] which ran from Chamberlain to Umbazooksus Lake. As we walked along the carry, its rusty linkage straggled through the brush beside us like a mythological serpent. At the north end, transshipment terminus for logs from thirty miles of lake between here and Churchill Dam, the woods covered a veritable machine shop, an enormous junk pile of indecipherable wheels, cogs, bolts and boiler plate, grown through or shaded by good-sized trees. A clearing in this muddle showed signs of recent activity. Two abandoned railroad locomotives had been levered to a standing position, by means of wedges and blocks of heavy staging. A page stapled to a tree gave their history and the name of the small organization which is currently restoring them. We marveled, looked into everything, climbed aboard and pulled an imaginary whistle, then had lunch and set forth on Eagle Lake.

As we came out into the fullness of Eagle Lake, between Hog and Farm Islands, we were able to look back to Pillsbury Island where Thoreau's party made its most northerly encampment in 1857. This is where we left our phantom companions behind.

Day 9, Pine Campground – Thoroughfare between Umsaskis Lake and Long Lake

✍ We arrived at the dam and concentrated on beaching the canoe smoothly. We'd not had an audience since we put in at Folsom's in Greenville, and a calm landing seemed an important validation of the last week's paddle. We met Mike the Ranger and shuffled bills out of our wallets for our Allagash camping and the portage fee. Walter mentioned that we had not paid for any camping on Moosehead and the Penobscot. I almost stepped on his foot, but Mike didn't care that much about the money; the Penobscot wasn't his drainage. He was a good guy. He gave Walter the official safety spiel for the Chase Rapids while I walked the canoe to the Chase put-in. Mike even gave us a roll of toilet paper.

We decided to run the rapids well ahead of a small group with brand-new canoes. There's just no gauging the skill level of people with shiny new boats.

Walter asked if I was nervous. I told him I was a little nervous and laughed, adding that it usually brings out my best. I had to speak loudly over the growing rumble of the rapids, and then we were in them, slamming up and down through the standing two and a half foot waves. We managed to keep the boat pointed downstream and into the crests of the waves. Walter scooped water from the boat as it filled. Then he flipped backwards in the canoe to redistribute his weight with the agility and grace of a Chinese acrobat. He scooped, and I steered and howled. We covered six river miles in under an hour and had to paddle hard to gain the shore where Mike had left our gear.

The river flowed fast and we spent the afternoon avoiding rocks. Their depths varied, but most of the big ones had the evidence of the river's summer use scraped on them in green or red paint. Walter called them bubblers. I called them mean customers or big berthas or whatever silliness sprang to mind. The Allagash slowed to a deadwater as we passed the marshy poke logans of the river's delta where it meets Umsaskis Lake. We crossed the lake and paddled under the bridge that marks the Thoroughfare to Long Lake, arriving at Pine Campground rather proud of the day's exploits.

I read the poems I've written on this trip to Walter tonight. Saying a poem challenges its shape, puts it in a new and different arena. In Walter's words, it extracts it "from the silences we've enjoyed here." Walter listened very intently. He asked to hear each of the poems a few times. He had some encouragement, and his criticism was right on; I need to cash in my images. They hang there at times like forgotten Christmas tree ornaments. I need to trash the ornamentation, to grow my poems with roots, buds, bulbs, and their consequences. They should respond well to light and to sight and to their own sounds. That sounds like goodnight.

Day 10, Outlet Campground – Round Pond

〰️ Sam cooked a champion supper tonight—a superb dish of crab meat, pesto, pasta with dried black beans sprinkled on it. Definitely the best meal of the trip; we both agreed. And Sam's standards are high.

We took this morning off. I got up at seven, wrote a bit, took a leisurely poke around our corner of the entrance to Long Lake, and walked up the road from the Thoroughfare bridge for a ways. There's nothing like a canoe trip to make a dirt road exotic. Saw flowers and beer cans, but no telephone poles.

When I got back, Sam was up and starting to pack. We set off down Long Lake a little before 12:00. The water simply spilled through, dropping eight feet in twenty-five yards, and the temptation to run it was in the air, but we would have been sorry and Sam had too much common sense to even listen to any thoughts I might have had. There followed another ten miles of river with good current, down which we paddled as hard as we had coming through Long Lake. Reaching Round Pond, we paddled another mile and a half along the shore and pulled in here shortly before four. Tomorrow will be a long day as we hope to pass through the checkout point at Michaud Farm and find a camping spot close to Allagash Village.

Day 11, Big Brook South Campground – Allagash River

⚡ We were no longer headed away as we paddled from camp this morning. We were paddling home. We thought we were out of the woods already, with a casual two day float in front of us, a gentle run-out.

I never saw the rock that flipped us. I saw a few rocks downstream and was leisurely planning to avoid them when Walter said the word "left" four and a half times with exponentially growing volume and urgency. I was in the stern and "left" was my department. Kerploop. Over we went with Walter's last half syllable and just enough time to look at each other that last, dry moment. Walter emerged from the river and bellowed an heroic laugh, a roar. I joined him and we laughed in the sunshine as we wrung out our sopping everything. The grit was back, under our finger nails and in our teeth. The rest of the day we gave the Allagash the respect it deserves, and we stayed afloat.

We stopped at Hosea B Campground to change into dry clothing, and I suspect that our freshly showered appearance lasted all the way to Michaud Farm, where Ranger Scott invited us into the Ranger Station. It was a mild day, but he had a fire going in the wood stove, and the heat was sweetly penetrating.

We decided to view the Allagash Falls from the water, and were soon headed downstream to the accompaniment of distant thunder. We landed at Big Brook South Campground and pitched our tents as the rumbling grew louder. We'd just finished erecting the tarp over the standard-issue Allagash picnic table when the sky opened up. It poured for twenty minutes, thick sheets of rain that obscured the view of the river just thirty feet away. It left standing puddles three inches deep, but the forest here is pine, and the duff quickly filtered the water down to the greedy evergreen roots.

I stay up a while after Walter turns in. I watch the embers slowly hiss to a dark orange and eventually head to the river, a bailing jug in hand. I kneel and fill the jug and turn back toward the tiny glow. The only sounds are an occasional pop from the darkening fire circle and the constant, hushed rolling of the Allagash. I pour the water on the embers and head for my sleeping bag, promising myself and the river that I will come here again. I silently thank Walter for the sparkle in his eye that began this adventure last spring as I tiptoe past his tent.

≋   To go back to the day's beginning, we were up early at Round Pond and on the water by 7:30. Made good time, despite gray weather and intimations of thunderstorms. It seemed the world was our oyster. Perhaps we were guilty of hubris, but in any case the river god caught us napping. It happened so smoothly and suddenly that before we could even name what was happening we were in water up to our chests, puffing and gasping and feeling for the bottom rocks that kept sliding out from under. I edged upstream, and we grabbed for the paddles before they could float away. Everything else of value was tied in, except for some wet clothes wedged up under the bow. We managed after a bit to work our way over to a little islet, not more than a few tufts of grass, and when safely lodged began to laugh in nervous excitement and relief that our predicament was not worse.

We came to Allagash Falls, our last carry. There we met a fellow with a soft voice and an odd smile who, as we later admitted to one another, gave us the creeps. We first saw him preparing to take a swim above the falls, and I had a horrible suspicion that he was committing suicide and we would find his body endlessly circling below. Then he showed up for a visit as we were preparing to launch. We chatted for a while and he mentioned that his partner "was somewhere around." Sam had an immediate premonition that the fellow had murdered his partner. At this point, however, we had passed beyond reach of the social contract, and callously took to our boat. If murder ensued, the news hasn't yet reached the papers in our part of the woods.

Day 12, Hancock, New Hampshire

≈ We were up early today, knowing that we had much ahead of us. We hadn't a dry piece of clothing between us, thanks to yesterday's flip and the storm at supper time, and we were eager for exercise. Everything got packed in as tight as possible, no matter how wet, for we might have to transfer to our plane in mid-stream.

This last section of the Allagash was particularly beautiful with straightaways ahead seeming to dive into steep hills whose sides were mottled with black evergreens and brilliant deciduous trees. The maples were at their height of color, and the lurking cold of mid-October was already present here at the top of Maine. The river gave a very perceptible impression of descent. After a couple of hours we began to see houses, and not long after entered an enormous S-curve which concludes the Allagash like a signature at the end of a manuscript. The Saint John was just around the corner. We landed at a bear-hunting camp which had a small store/eatery in front. Folsom's answered the phone right away, and we agreed to meet them in three hours about fifteen miles downriver at a little island on the Canadian side. It was something to step out of the chill into a stove-warm room. Twenty deer eyed us glassily from the walls. What free space remained was covered with photographs of hunters who had gotten their bear. The preferred position was kneeling with the bear's head resting on the hunter's shoulder—so one could see the two grins at once. Off in the corner of the room there was a barrel stove, a small dance space, some music stands and two stuffed fisher cats. We ordered from the menu, chicken nuggets from the freezer for Sam, Dinty Moore stew for me. Had a nice talk with the owner and guide, Kelly, who asked us about our trip with courtly grace. He must have to listen to a great many such stories. So then we set forth, a bit reluctant to leave the warmth and the calories.

Although the Allagash had been high, the St. John lived up to its reputation of having little water after spring. We had enough for easy running, but not enough to make the rapids feel overmastering. The pace was faster than on the Allagash and we found ourselves approaching our rendezvous at the precise moment appointed. But, when an hour and a half had passed, we paddled to the opposite shore and called Folsom's and asked what the story

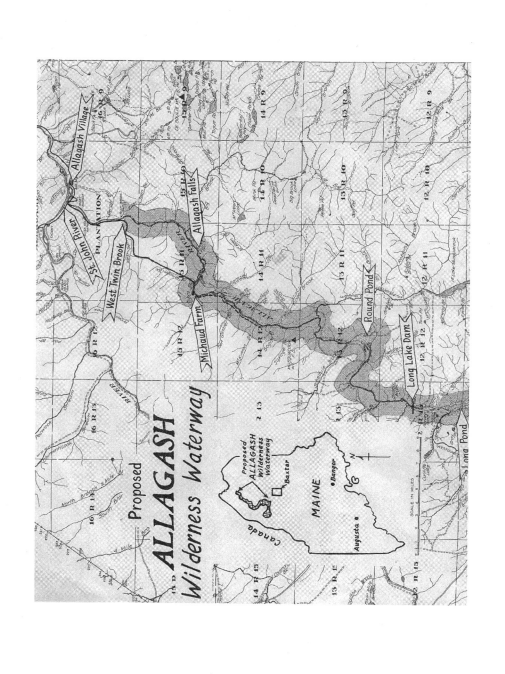

Proposed
ALLAGASH
Wilderness Waterway

was. The plane had had engine problems.

᷂ Our pilot, Rick, agreed to fly over the course of our trip. I pressed my face to the window and looked down at the Allagash and out at the low mountains of northern Maine, spread out like an intricately colored, wrinkled tapestry. Watermarks and landmarks zipped past in reverse order: Allagash Falls, Round Pond, Long Lake, and the Chase Rapids. I saw our camp-ground on Eagle Lake and the large rock where I'd seen seven mergansers take flight. The long profile of Chamberlain Lake appeared, and off in the distance lay Gero Island and the northern part of Chesuncook.

Throughout the ride, we'd been passing huge tracts of clear-cut, and I asked Rick how he felt about the timber companies. He had a lot of friends that cleared the forests, said they made good money at it. I asked if it was back breaking work and he replied that it used to be, but that now they have machines that allow a two man crew to work independently, one working a contraption that stripped a tree of its branches and chopped it clean near the base, and one driving the logging truck. It was all natural, accepted by Rick as an inevitable part of the landscape and the history.

We landed in Greenville with heavy rain. We thanked Rick for a safe flight and headed for the highly recommended Frog Rock Cafe. It was wonderful to have coffee poured into a clean mug in front of me, and I basked respect-fully in the warm condescension of the honeysweet service. "More coffee, hon?" "Yes, maam." I plowed through about a million calories: chili, one bowl full. Reuben, swimming happily in grease. Blueberry cheesecake, yes!

And then we were on the road, talking about the what ifs of our adventure now that they were safely behind us. We drove south and soon we merged with the flow of trucks on the rain soaked interstate. How quickly we met civilization and its big lights.

᷍ The ride home was without event, though we pushed to make up for lost time. Sam told me he had asked Rick whether he picked up many canoeists who had made the entire trip from Greenville to Allagash Village. "You are the first," was his reply. THAT made us feel good.

᷂ We arrived at Hancock, New Hampshire, around midnight, and I took a short walk down the road from Walter's house. The stone walls reminded me of hiking through the woods of Kabeyun, a boy's camp on Lake Winnepesaukee where I first got to know Walter. We have returned to a familiar corner of New England that has the feeling of home. Thoreau must have felt something like this when he arrived home to Concord from Maine, returning to the regularity of the village and the blueberry patches he knew like the back of his hand. He must also have felt the strong tug of the Maine wilderness. He traveled there three times. A part of me wants to go canoeing tomorrow, to drive north and buy food, rent a boat, keep going, but the inner voice whispers "sleep" to me.

Things to Look Into

Parker Huber's *The Wildest Country: A Guide to Thoreau's Maine*, published by the Appalachian Mountain Club in 1981 and now, unfortunately, out of print, is the indispensable guide if one wants to follow Thoreau's *The Maine Woods* routes.

If you want to know more about logging in this area, Fannie Hardy Eckstorm's *Penobscot Man* is authoritative and rests on observation, since her father, a lumber boss, sometimes took her with him on his visits to lumber camps.

Bashô and Shiki translations are from R. H. Blyth's 4 volume *Haiku*.

Charles Pratt

An English Teacher's Advice: When You Don't Know What to Write, Start Where You Are

Mid-February. In the day, weather permitting, I'm pruning apple trees. In the evening, by the fire, I'm falling asleep over *Walden*. To be more precise, I've just finished *Walden*; I've been waiting until I finished to write this, in the hope that Thoreau would show me a direction. (Find your own direction, he told me.)

My other winter activity, whenever possible, is visiting my children's children, and watching them explore directions.

Thoreau says, "I have frequently seen a poet withdraw, having enjoyed the most valuable part of a farm, while the crusty farmer supposed that he had got a few wild apples only. Why, the owner does not know it for many years when a poet has put his farm in rhyme, the most admirable kind of invisible fence, has fairly impounded it, milked it, skimmed it, and got all the cream, and left the farmer only the skimmed milk." Too much cream is bad for the heart; skimmed milk is healthier. I try to put my farm in poetry and to farm it, too. The farm's most valuable part survives both efforts.

"The farmer," Thoreau says, "is endeavoring to solve the problem of a livelihood by a formula more complicated than the problem itself. To get his shoestrings he speculates in herds of cattle." The real goal, he makes clear, is not a livelihood but a life. I have discovered in myself the soul of a small businessman. I love exchanging my product for money, when the product is something as sound and satisfying as an apple—or a poem, for those with a taste for poems. The transaction registers a thrill in a deep level of my being.

Here in February, when I look back at the day's end, the ground is littered with prunings. I'm tired. I know that I have done *something*. I hope that I've done it right, and that the apple trees will forgive me if I haven't, recover from my mistakes, cover for mistakes.

There's a link here with children, and grandchildren.

Where better to be than where I am?

Dudley Laufman

MOUTH MUSIC

1. Mouth Music

Lived on a farm he did, up Cape Breton way, back from the sea a bit, but with tide. Said they dragged the river bottom each spring to bring up the sludge you know for to spread on the fields.

Did you go to the square dance? I says. Oh sure, says he, and many's the time I tuned up the dance, too. Tuned up the dance, says I, what do you mean by that, you went around and tuned up the fiddles? Hell no, he says, I tuned up the dance. We hummed the tunes don't ye know, mouth music we called it, some call it lilting. Here's Miss McLeods Reel for ye. Deedle di de didle di dum deedle dum; See now how it goes. We used to dance out on the weather gray wharf in the salty inlet, spruces by the rocky shore and gulls above wheel-ing mewing. Four old men with white beards sat in the first row, they were the first rate tuners. One of them always held my sister on his knee. We younger chaps stood in the second row, being second raters. I'll tell ye, there's a power of music in the tongue, makes toes itch.

2. Some Dancing Masters

M. Violet

was a little man dressed in green velvet, scratching a *pochette* and yelping out steps to half naked Iroquois men and women (bet he liked that part) as they capered and leaped about the long house. *Un pas en avant, un pas en arriere, encore une fois.* Wooed one of the half naked women. Took his pay in beaver skins and bear hams.

Clement Weeks

wanted to be a fiddling dancing master, one that would be fond of women, rum, sleep under hedges...that kind. Instead he became a master dancer, his favorite being Black Joak, Hunt the Squirrel, Lady's Breast Knot, The Lily, Rural Felicity, Sukey Bids Me, and Barrel of Sugar. He may have courted someone but never drank with rummy women or slept beneath honeysuckle dripping pollen. Fiddles floated before his eyes as he dream danced his life away and was buried on the edge of Great Bay where the ebb tide does contradances and the flowing tide does cotillions.

Amos Merrill

was a bear hunter (one every year). Folks said he could fiddle a bear out of the woods, that the bear would dance right out and lay down paws up. No said Amos, I wouldn't do that. Unfair. And I ain't Indian enough to know the proper blessing. No, I'd go into the woods after them. I would think Thank you best way I knew how.

But I fiddled for dances here at my inn on the mountain. Lena played piano and Fanny first fiddle. I played second and called the reels and Paul Jones right in the dining room for the summer guests while the bears watched from the woods.

Today the mountainside is completely forested over. Not a trace of Merril's Inn. But there are still bears dancing to echoes of Amos's fiddle.

Edson Cole

conducted a dancing school in Freedom, showing students how to enter a hall and how to ask a person to dance and how to accept. Playing the fiddle he would show the waltz steps saying, One, two, three, balance with me, if you can't do that go siddown, saying, See this fiddle is my sweetheart. And around the room he would go.

Meltiah Lawrence

has little known about him except that he was the model for the fiddling dancing master in Laura Richard's novel, *Rosin the Beau*, sitting on a stool calling out the changes for Lady of the Lake (thrice each night), Pop Goes the Weasel, and The Tempest. When asked to do the Chorus Jig he said, There isn't a foot in this room fit to dance the Chorus Jig.

There were tales of a mysterious fiddler who wandered the roads of central Maine on foot or bicycle teaching violin and dancing. Nobody knows who he was. Maybe he was Meltiah Lawrence as he was becoming Rosin the Beau.

Or Me

maybe he was becoming me, or I am becoming him. I'm always saying, There isn't a foot in this hall fit to dance the Chorus Jig. And I have a Mazda bicycle.

I walk old roads in late November, the woods brown and silver like a dancing master's coat, like the burlap sack that holds my fiddle.

3. Dancing in County Clare

It is Sunday night. The pub is shaped like a horseshoe magnet. An orchestra plays in one end, their music rough like the broken end of a whetstone. A dance is in progress where the current moves both ways. The girls are mini-skirted and white as gulls. The men are in church clothes, dark as ravens. They rise, glide and dip, slanting in, slapping their feet on the cement like surf under the Cliffs at Dereen.

Julia Shipley

John Says

I set two alarm clocks for 4 am and wake up every hour anyway. I dress in less than ten minutes and leave town marveling at the lights on: are they really up, too? The woman at the Dunkin Donuts hands me a large black coffee and change and says "have a good night." This is the same hour as last call in the bars in NYC. I turn left onto Trombly Hill Road, which turns suddenly to dirt, and pass dark houses and vast fields until I turn up the barn driveway and see the portholes of the huge barn lit.

*

John says, "go get the calf and throw it in the van."

I imagine a delicate, fawn-like calf nestled in the grass. No. It's up and running, a black bull calf. I try to gather him in my arms and lift but he collapses. So I push him piece by piece: head, neck, leg, other leg, back legs, and one final push inside the van and slam the door. As I steer us through the pasture, headlights on, he bawls to his mother whose enormous face fills the driver-side window, heightening the strangeness of taxiing a calf in a field in a van while all my friends are in REM sleep. Amanda's so close I could kiss her black cheek. She's galloping eight miles an hour. Maybe I should put up the window. Two other cows swerve and lurch in front of the van. John calls it a rodeo.

I leave the calf in the van and use a piece of plastic tubing to switch the bucking Holsteins into the barn, and then chain them in their places. John's halfway through the milking. I dip teats and hoe crap and feed hay until we're through chores. "Did you get that calf?" He asks as he fits the last milk machine in the sink and gets ready to start the wash cycle. We walk out to the van and I open the door and show him the animal whose gender means it will never make milk, the animal who will be loaded onto a truck probably tomorrow or Monday. John says, "We'll, he's a nice sized calf."

*

This morning I try to notice the things I've become accustomed to: the hay's whisper and rasp on the concrete as I break open a bale and distribute the flakes. The *moo* that starts out mellow but crescendos with baritone urgency.

There are dialects of moos: absolute displeasure and petulance such as when the herd is going out to fresh pasture and one in heat gets left behind. Some moos trumpet. The grating bleat of calves who plead for milk.

*

I push the sawdust cart down the center aisle and thrust the shovel in and fling shavings under cows. At the end of the barn there is a calf so still it must be dead. I look for one second, two seconds, three seconds, but nothing of it has twitched. It's dead. I ask John what to do.

He says, "Don't feed it."

*

Between morning and evening chores a tractor trailer from Canada arrives and we begin to unload 2000 bales of hay. The chain on the hay elevator keeps bucking its track. We stop and use wrenches and pry bars to fix it, half hanging out of the hay mow. I crank my side then pass the wrench to John and he cranks his, so it's tightened evenly. We begin again. Sometimes a different hold-up. Electricity stops running to the drive motor. Or too many bales on the elevator. Everybody waits.

I thought John stomped on my coffee cup on purpose. I thought last night he said "I wish you'd quit." Today he said, "After Christmas you're gonna help me with naming the heifers."

I looked up at the hay mow where I grabbed all those bales coming in. I realized that I was getting caught in my equipment. When I understand this, things start running again.

*

How cows lay down: they lower themselves so carefully that they lean forward into their folded knees; and then they sink slowly from the back until that moment they can't support their own weight, and drop in a heap.

*

I don't always love it: a waterbowl overflows and floods the stall and aisle; one cow won't take her place and gets herself wedged in with two others; or the whole herd busts through the fence; or just one clobbers the garden or she has her calf in the ravine and how do you get her out now? Or the rubber collar around the cap of the bulk tank falls in milk. And these are just nuisances. But the hoe gets caught in the gutter cleaner and jams it, that's expensive. Also expensive: the clamp wasn't fastened and milk fills the floor. The agitator paddles on the tank seize and the milk won't cool...

and then I push open the barn door to go get two bales for the horses and the air is soft. Light is just beginning to cut open the box of surrounding darkness. Or the goose feather moon is rising or falling into the black trees at the edge of the pasture and my breath condenses, freezing, matching the vapor of the milky way hovering above the manure piles.

*

We're leaving the barn. I'm so tired I can hardly stand. John says "If you leave one light on they're less likely to step on a teat."

Nearly 75 animals inside. 75 bodies all 101 degrees F. 75 heartbeats. Then I realize: most are pregnant again. Now how many heartbeats? More than I can fathom.

Wyn Cooper

Three Postcards from Vermont

Postcard from Marlboro, Vermont

On this very dry Fourth of July, nothing is knee high
except to the grasshoppers, going out of their little minds,
sending messages of love all around, but no one listens,
no one believes, no one hears them above the explosions.

Postcard from Glastonbury, Vermont

In the first five years after World War Two, eleven hikers disappeared inside
these town lines. Those who live nearby will barely get out of their cars here. Not
that there's much to do, except look at the woods, and there's no one to see—64
square miles, and not a single resident. In Bennington, the Veteran's Home has
an unobstructed view of Glastonbury Mountain, rising like bread in the morning. Though the mountain is oblong and the town a square, it's known as the
Bennington Triangle. When I explore the long-abandoned roads, they follow a
path that has nothing to do with the land they traverse. They seem to be spelling
something I can't read, no matter how many times I retrace my route. I think it
is two long words, but don't know which ones. I am welcomed and spurned at
the same time, as if the mountain can't make up its mind.

Postcard from the Wind in Vermont

In fall the wind blows cold one night,
then stays that way for half the year.
I fly inside from wall to wall.

Each bird to its branch, says the wind,
each bug to its leaf, each trace
of lipstick blown away.

Anina Robb

———————————————

Fleeing the City

On the Massachusetts turnpike, crossing states, I'm no musician, no gypsy,
not even a runaway. I'm leaving a city I'm too happy to leave: trash
collections at dawn, potholes, hours spent boiling water. I drop the hatch-
back. The snap of the lock, like applause, clicks into place. I grin wide,
hoping someone will see me. The first hours are bliss: poppies in the   me-
dian, orange sugar-drops, and each pine tree clearer than the one before. I
can see: no smog, no distraction. I think about the few miles of New Hampshire shoreline. How, tomorrow, the cold sea will swish between my toes. I
think my back hurts and maybe I'm pregnant. The poppies close. At the U-
Save Motel, the lobby's sliding door pulls back a red reflection flashing
CHEAP CHEAP. Inside, I ring the bell. A balding man pushes the back
room curtain aside, his forehead flushed, newborn. His pants aren't
buttoned correctly. My breath stops for a moment. Some things are only
bright in darkness. It is just like the day to die with me right here. The friend
I said good-night to on the phone at the rest stop is gone. I own nothing. It's
darker here than in the city. Lonely stars prick through the sky. I only need
one night of rest, I think. Gloom spirited in the comfort of hills. I think I
hear the man say: I could do something for you. But my eyes are already
closed. I cover my ears with my hands and listen for the briny sea breezes
inside of me.

John Hyland

AT THE CORNER OF STATE AND ESSEX

1. *Judy's*

There's this sign above the beer-worn bar: "If you aren't confused around
here – you're not trying hard enough." It sits above a row of red Budweiser
caps and beside another: "Shirts and shoes required, bras and panties
optional." Voices criss-cross quick and slow, creating a web of noise in this
smoke-dust eatery propped at the corner of this street I've lived on for almost
three years now. Been coming in here for half that time, but the patrons still
throw curious, perhaps scornful glances at me as I pass though the door. The
bartender-waitress knows me, remembers my face; her smile welcomes me.
She smiles as I cruise past the bar. And I feel that smile on my back as I slide
into the corner booth and notice a grey-wrinkled man in the opposite corner. I throw my fleece in the corner of the booth. It's late April, but outside
the air is as cold as early March. It snowed a couple days back up here in this
northern country. Almost everyone in here has short sleeves or leather vests
on. That's how it is all through the winter.

As the bartender-waitress shuffles between the packed tables, I light a
cigarette. This is the only place I know where I can smoke and eat and think.
I can't imagine that the Board of Health is here much, and the business
people from downtown know not to come here with their slick suits and
trimmed hair. The ring of the phone suddenly begins to billow into the
clouds of smoke above the bar, where five fellas sit with their "shorts" of
Bud. There are only two beers on tap her: Bud and Busch. And if you ask for
a Sam Adams, you'll probably get tossed out on the pavement. It's Sunday
morning. The phone is still billowing. A fella at the bar wearing a tattered
jean jacket with a looming American flag displayed across the back saunters
behind and lifts the receiver. I can only see his lips move. He turns, shouts,
"Dotty here?" "Just left" comes a voice from another corner. Watching him
place the receiver back on the rotary phone sitting atop the cigarette rack,
the bartender-waitress hurries up to my booth with a coffee. "What'd you
need, sweetie?" There are no menus here. "Eggs over-easy, hash and toast," I

say, placing another cigarette between my lips–she's gone before I say toast; most likely, she's heard that order fifty times today.

Despite the fact there's a three–day-old scruff peppering my face, I am too clean-shaven for this place. I'm too young. And my hair's too short and I'm not nearly tough enough. I glance across the booths and make eye contact with the Old Timer in the corner. He's the only one quieter than me in here. He's chain smoking Marlboro 100s. His hands shake / tremble as he lifts the cigarette to his thin, blue-tinged lips. Beneath his translucent skin, disclosed by a rolled-up red flannel, there's a corpse fighting to surface. No one speaks to him. No one speaks his language; he's been here too long. Every time I'm here he's here. And as I watch him nurse a shot of something, I recall a line from Olson's *Maximus*:

There are no hierarchies, no infinite, no such many as the mass, there are only
eyes in all heads
to be looked out of

I exhale; wonder what he's seen, what he is seeing now as the smoke obscures his vision...I wonder this and know that I'll never know.

Before walking through the door here, I picked up a pack of smokes at the Big Apple across the street. The girl behind the counter was on the phone. I don't know what she was talking about. But I caught this phrase: "yeah, well, sometimes memories will remember." And isn't that just the way.

2. As the First Snow Started

Late night and I wake unable to return to those blue dreams. The racket of fresh snow falling startles me to pull on wool socks and boots, a scarf and hat and meander dream-like into early morning's quiet. I follow the cracked now snow-dusted sidewalk to the twenty-four hour gas station store: delight of snow-crunch; melting wet flakes dripping down my half-waked face. I cross *State*–no sign of automobile or plow, just the streetlights holding falling snow in upside-down funnels of light. I go in the store. The fellow behind the counter is propped-up / sleeping in the corner. I fill a paper cup with hot black coffee, and leave a dollar on the counter. Slowly creaking through the door, I find early dawn still quiet though a vermilion streak of sun has ripped the sky above of this small city. The sky continues to snow. I stop. Lean against a telephone pole. The coffee too hot, I hold it between my hands. Across the street *Judy's* door flies open with shouts of "get the fuck outta-of-here." He stumbles out in thin Salvation-Armed threads, then yells whiskey-muddled words. I sip the coffee. He sways (grey) down the street through the cold. By the way he sways I know he has no place to go; his only choice is to follow the feet he'll be unable to feel in the now imminent winter. I light a cigarette. He turns the corner. As the smoke drifts up, dissipates into the falling snow, the fact of how we move becomes poignant: in strange yet obvious ways we're disbanded to these cycles, this syntax and these sounds in dawn's snow-quiet.

Jim Schley

FIREWOOD

1.

Poplar splits slippery clean, once the maul head finds a route through the log; this wood is massive and moist, like hard cheese. White ash splits suddenly and vertically down the visible lines of grain, whereas yellow birch has fine grain, its ridges from top to bottom continuous and parallel. And sugar maple recoils from the impact, adhering sideways across the saw cut, its grain a knotted whorl of overlapping folds that spiraled as they grew. Each log has its texture, its particular mannerisms against the blade or beneath the blow. Cherry sheathed in dark leather. Hornbeam in a hair shirt. White birch as flaky as the flesh of certain fish.

Our wood is felled on the hillside above the house, where we're culling the faltering trees and those that aren't maples to leave the sugarbush in dominion. Downed trunks are bucked in place or at several landings where they're hauled with a truck or a horse. Not fond of chain saws, and very fond of splitting, I would always rather pay for unsplit stove lengths, or trade my splitting for the firewood we need. One year I split for two households, so we had our own wood for free. At least that was the feeling.

2.

Split steadily, but consciously try not to struggle. Toss whole logs to the low block in the clearing beside the path, eight or ten at a time, then take them one by one, at a cadence. This is one of those tasks that demands no elaborate thinking; actually the effort is pleasing, rejuvenating, and completely absorbing. The six-pound maul head is heavy enough that centrifugal force to an astonishing degree does the work. Whenever fatigued, and I forget to simply concentrate on angle and timing, with little or no muscle added to the downward arc of the maul, I end up tensed to the strike, which translates through the rigid wooden handle as solid concussion, and which frequently will not cleave the wood at all, but sink the maul a mere inch into the log end. All at once I remember the right way, and instead of attacking just stand for a moment with the maul raised up like a banner pole, effectively resting, then let that wedge of steel drop as though its handle were only a rope following and guiding a projectile straight down and often right through the log to bury its edge in the block beneath. The pull is outward as much as downward. A second before the maul head strikes, I imagine the wood fibers parting and opening, then watch as that truly occurs.

Sometimes, in one of these games splitters of large piles invent to extend fascination and absorb the time, I split a large log in steps, nearly but not quite driving all the way through, and after each strike rotate the wood a quarter turn with the lever of the maul handle so that with the final strike the log parts suddenly in four or five sections like an opening blossom or sliced piece of fruit.

3.

South Main Street, the Dorchester road, Route 10, Norford Lake Road, Route 122, Union Village Road, then Alger Brook Road, our spur now known as Blue Moon Road—I made six moves in twelve years. I've stacked wood in garages, sheds, dooryards, and under eaves; stacked with room-mates, girlfriends, house guests, parents, and now with my wife. Moving no longer. At the house we've built ourselves, we build the woodpile along the path that brings you in from the drive, so rows of stacked log-ends line the walkway to the left, with the ground dropping off to the right toward the garden, berry patch, and chicken-run then rising tiers of pines, beyond which we look east across broad swaths of woodland to the Connecticut River valley and further, to the westernmost peaks of New Hampshire.

Our chickens scuffle and carouse as we work, usually preferring to be where we are, at times underfoot despite the smack and rupture of the maul splintering logs. By early fall we hear geese—far off, then closer, then gone in the direction of Maryland's outstretched estuaries. One afternoon a goshawk sat upon a branch and surveyed the slope like a passing feudal lord; that grand gray bird was as tall upon the bough as the distance between my elbow and raised fingertips.

4.

If some September you decided (for no reason but curiosity) to map all the woodpiles in a northern New England town, you'd have a diagram of the town's homesteads. There are probably more woodpiles than vegetable gardens. Yet on many sites, the woodpile will have vanished by May. A map of the woodpiles in the same town in April or May would show only a fraction of those on the September map. And comparing those whimsical maps over a course of years, you'd see how the woodpiles migrate upon the landscape, as people seek an ideal combination of level and well-drained ground, good sun-exposure for drying, proximity to paths for easy access in deep snow....

Locating a woodpile is a measure of how settled we are, how at home.

Four Photographs by Pat Barnes

Albert Dole

Garvin's A Building History of New England

A Building History of New England by James Garvin.
University Press of New England.

As a carpenter in rural New Hampshire, I am surrounded by many stately old colonial and Greek Revival houses that I admire and would like to use as paradigms in my work. I can spend the better part of an afternoon studying the detailing of the cornice of an old church with binoculars, in order to build a pedimented gable similar to it. However, I've learned from working on them that many of these beautiful old buildings are actually haphazardly or even shoddily built—gracefully finished, but structurally shaky. More than once I've heard at work, "They don't build them like they used to, thank God." Although I've seen them often and even reproduced their details faithfully, I couldn't tell the Georgian style from Federal, or even Greek Revival.

So, when James Garvin's *A Building History of New England* arrived in the mail, I was eager to see if Garvin could clear up my confusion. I wasn't disappointed. I know a lot about old building methods from thirty-five years of first-hand experience, but I learned something new or had a misconception corrected on almost every page.

The first section of the book deals with construction technology. After detailing the history of Northern New England's building methods from settlement until World War II, Garvin discusses the evolution of building style in that time period. He explains arcane material so clearly that it is almost always comprehensible on a first reading. Though technical at times, the book isn't a dry read. The writing is good, elucidated by many fine photos, as well as drawings done by the author or excerpted from old ads and builders' handbooks. In the final section, Garvin shows how a knowledge of the progression of different technologies and fashions in doors, windows, moldings, mantels, and stairs may be used to date a building.

Garvin's primary purpose in writing *A Building History* is to further the cause of preservation by trying to convince the owners of old houses to preserve or restore what they own. This is a cause I've served for years, so in addition to my eagerness to get some historical perspective, I was also enthusiastic about the author's apparent motivations. Even so, I approached the book with a certain skepticism. It seemed unlikely that historical patterns could be imposed on the mish-mash of styles, technologies, and methods that I've seen in my work on old country houses. And even though a house may have been built at a given time, who's to say that the carpenter wasn't an old-timer using outdated methods and details to make something that was old-fashioned even when it was new? An essential of living in Northern New England is the sense of isolation you feel from the centers of culture and fashion. (This does not mean that South Acworth, New Hampshire, doesn't feel to its residents like the hub of the universe. It's just that the currents of fashion swirl in the peripheral regions around the hub, generally "down below," south of wherever a northern New Englander happens to live.) A lot of rural construction is done by the owner himself, or whoever turns in the lowest bid. In either case, I supposed that the builder would not be likely to know the current fashion, much less how to build it.

To make matters even more confusing, houses were altered from early on, if only subtly. Sills were replaced with timbers from other structures, doors were brought in from other buildings, cornices were added to gables. I saw an extreme example of this mix of building elements in a house I used to own in South Acworth. I knew from a previous owner that the kitchen had been remodeled in 1948. In 1979, when I remodeled again, I found that the plaster base used in 1948 had been small scraps of sheetrock taken from another house. They had been turned around with the wallpaper still on them and nailed to the new studs so that the backside of the old sheetrock then served as the plaster base in the new kitchen! I also knew from the oral history in town that the house had been moved around 1840 from the foundation of the house next door and set up on a new foundation at its present site. When putting in a second-floor bathroom, I learned that the eave walls had been raised four feet at a time when timber framing was still practiced. It would have made sense to do it when they were moving the building. These and other details made me think of that as a typical country mutt of a house.

I thought about that house after reading *A Building History*. I had just learned from Garvin that tall eave walls were in vogue in the Greek Revival era, around 1840. Bingo! Other details began to fit. The house had wide frieze boards, simple crown molding, wide baseboards, square blocks in the upper corners of the door and window trim, just as described in the

Greek Revival section. Clearly the house had been remodeled in the style current in the time of its move. Only the doors were from an earlier era. In all likelihood they were in the house when it sat on its original foundation. I was beginning to see that even common country houses were influenced by currents of fashion as Garvin explained them. My initial skepticism was dissolving. I now felt confident that I had a basic understanding of the old building styles used around here.

The closest I came to disappointment with the book was a wish for more discussion of commonplace architecture. In spite of Garvin's assertion in the introduction that "poverty is the friend of preservation," it seemed at times as though I were reading a history of the trophy homes of 18th and 19th century northern New England. However, I can see some reasons Garvin had to use the approach he did.

Once when I was a boy, my father told me about the houses in the northern Massachusetts town where he grew up. He said "Of course, most of them have burned down since then." The homes of the rich folk, the ones often featured in *A Building History*, were the ones in which wood heat was abandoned early on. They were more likely to be built of brick, or to have a roof of slate rather than wood. Furthermore, when people who could afford to bought a grand old house that had been well maintained, they were probably less likely to mess around with their new home than if they had bought an old farmhouse whose roof had been leaking for years, and whose once-handsome trim was rotting and falling off for lack of paint. Finally, it was the wealthy who had either the leisure time necessary to keep up with trends of architectural fashion illustrated in the books published in England and Massachusetts, or the resources needed to hire architects or master carpenters who were so informed. The houses of the rich are excellent examples of what was *a la mode* in building fashion at any given time.

Just as the houses Garvin uses as illustrations are primarily those of the rich, they also tend to be concentrated in an area near the coast. There is an interesting reason that up-country houses are not well represented. The hinterlands, with few exceptions, (for example, North Haverhill, New Hampshire) were settled last. The first pioneers in any area were unlikely to include many master masons or carpenters. The early arrivals were probably akin to the young daredevil framers of modern carpentry. Older men who had had the time to master their craft, establish a business, and set up a shop lost their youthful wanderlust.

This assertion is borne out by a look at the oldest houses in New England. Although they are well-framed, according to Abbott Lowell Cummings, one of Garvin's sources, they lack the kind of ornament that seems to be the province of older, more experienced workers. The master joiners did not start leaving England for New England until pockets of civilization had been established along the coast. When they did start arriving, they tended to settle in those areas where there was enough wealth and demand to support them in business, rather than in the "savage wastes." So Garvin's apparent bias toward buildings near the coast is a more or less necessary outcome of the chronological pattern of settlement. This necessity is especially obvious in the discussion of Georgian building styles, because most of the interior either had not been settled or had just barely begun to be settled while we were still subjects of the kings George.

The Monadnock Region of New Hampshire, where I live, is in the hinterlands. It is known for its unspoiled villages, and for being out-of-the-way. I've always thought of it as an area where fashion is relatively unimportant. The old photographs I've seen of the local farming families posing outside their homes make it look as though life was hard and offered little opportunity for anything but satisfaction of the most immediate needs. Now, having read Garvin's book, I can see that even in this backwater, style mattered. I can think of at least two local houses and two churches with fancy trim on their gables facing the street and very plain trim on the back side. The old builders were putting on the style, but only where it mattered most.

Rebecca Rule

THE OLD AMERICAN GIVES NEW LIFE TO CLASSIC STORY

The Old American by Ernest Hebert. University Press of New England.

The title character in Ernest Hebert's novel *The Old American* is a aging chief of the Algonkian tribe. Hebert combines Algonquian (referring to languages) and Algonquin (referring to peoples) to create the word. He combines historical fact with his own self-proclaimed "loony imagination" in a brilliant weaving that began with a single anecdotal thread. The subject of that weaving, the character Hebert conjures from the single thread, lives on the page with such depth of personality the psychicly inclined may suspect the author of channeling a spirit, maybe the spirit of one of Hebert's native American ancestors.

This is true: A stone monument on the corner of Main and Winchester Streets in Keene, where Hebert grew up, marks the site of a log house built by Nathan Blake in 1736. Briefly, the monument tells Blake's story:

> *He was captured by Indians and taken to Canada 1746*
> *Ransomed by his wife Elizabeth Graves 1749*
> *Six generations of Blakes lived on this spot.*

This provides the loom of Hebert's weaving. Here's the found thread that got him going, the line "spoken by an unnamed captor," that "set the fiction into motion."

When Nathan Blake, having left the safety of the stockade to release animals from his barn, came face to face with an armed Indian, he quipped that it was "mighty early in the morning and he'd had nothing to eat."

The Indian, to Blake's surprise, understood. And replied in perfect English: "It's a poor Englishman that cannot go to Canada without his breakfast."

These are the first words spoken by the Old American, Caucus-Meteor, in the novel, and they set into motion the development of a complicated and utterly believable relationship between captive and captor, Englishman and Algonkian, farmer and nomad, young man and elder.

Both men are strong. Both are clever. Both are gifted. Caucus-Meteor is, among other things, a linguist fluent in English, French, and several Native American

253

languages. Nathan Blake is, among other things, an athlete. Both are believably conflicted and flawed in all kinds of interesting ways, some funny, come tragic.

On the funny side, for example, the old man is so vain he wears, always, "a distinctive red turban with white feathers sticking out the last turn at the peak, a strategy designed to conceal a bald head." Nathan, on the not so funny side, struggles to understand his own heart, his misunderstood longings that distanced him from his family long before Caucus-Meteor forced him to leave New Hampshire for Quebec.

The two share a trait that enhances—even more than the backdrop of the French and Indian War—the relentless drama of this story. Caucus-Meteor and Nathan Blake are each highly skilled in reading and manipulating people, including each other.

Each is, in his own way, remarkable self-possessed, self-aware, wise and growing wiser through their adventures.

When Nathan Black runs the gauntlet, he must use his intuition about human nature to save his own life. If those who form the gauntlet choose, they may stab, slice and beat him to death or near-death.

Or they might decide to spare him any injury at all.

Caucus-Meteor describes and analyzes the scene in a stream of thought.

A stick cracks you between the shoulder blades, like the lash of a whip but cutting deeper. You wince—run, Nathan, run. But no, you walk to the other side, offering yourself for abuse. Stones strike your face and chest. You take another step forward, but keep your head up. The old Mohawk with the burn-scarred face grins at you, a man driven insane by torturers in a time gone by. Another stick slashes you across your back, and you cry out involuntarily, as you did the day I burned myself instead of you. I feel that wound now, a tender place like a sorrow or a remembered hope. ... A woman raises a switch to strike you. You see the blow coming, but you don't try to avoid it. You smile at the woman. Are you insane, Nathan Blake?

In a way, Nathan's walking of the gauntlet mirrors the whole of his captivity. His behavior, his actions and reactions determine his face.

Metaphorically, Nathan walks the gauntlet again and again as he adapts to and establishes his position among the Algonkians. So does Caucus-Meteor who, like all powerful leaders, must outwit many enemies, face many challenges. In a way we all walk or run (hide from, crawl through, fear, embrace, finding meaning in) the gauntlets of our own lives.

ARCHIVES

Maxine Kumin, "In Deep," IN DEEP:
COUNTRY ESSAYS (Beacon Press, 1987).

Russel Banks, "In the Pemigewasset," *Sumac*, 1970.

Ray Kass, "White Mountains Drawings," 1968.

Henry David Thoreau, *from* THE MAINE WOODS
(ed. Joseph J. Moldenhauer, Princeton University Press, 1972).

William Carpenter, "California," THE HOURS OF MORNING
(University Press of Virginia, 1981).

Wesley McNair, "Where I Live," THE FACES
OF AMERICANS 1853 (reissued by Carnegie Mellon
as a Classic Contemporary, 2002).

Maxine Kumin

In Deep

Early winter. Foliage gone, the woods reveal their inner architecture. In a strong wind, oak and maple branches creak and rub against each other, cranky as old door hinges. I can see in deep now, deep into this second-growth forest where pastures once were, and farms prospered. I can spot the occasional apple tree and lilac sprawl, the tumbled stone walls and caved-in foundations at a considerable distance.

The deerflies, those scourges of midsummer shaped like tiny deltoid planes, have vanished. Ground wasps that lurked in rotten logs waiting to pounce on the unwary traveler are now in hibernation. Only the deer hunters are left for us to contend with.

Weekends we ride out in threes and fours, horses and people bedecked in extremely orange pinnies—Ten Mile Cloth, the manufacturer calls it, claiming it can be seen at that remove. Each of us has a cowbell tied to one stirrup. I carry a folding saw across the cantle of my saddle. Aurally and visually we make a fearsome procession. Of course the hunters hate us, but these are *our* woods too, and this is our only season for bushwhacking.

Midweek, theorizing that the Sunday shooters have gone home, I risk my neck alone. Riding along old rangeways between vanished settlements I peer down every track. All those roads not taken! Bending low under overhanging branches, sometimes stopping to saw my way clear, I take them one by one. And one by one they peter out like rambling thoughts, glimmering ideas unrealized.

Somehow I am never cured of my fantasy; surely one will carry me through? One day, riding in deep, the perfect trail will materialize, a leafy carpet underfoot, and overhead just room enough—a tunnel for my chestnut horse and me. We will trot for miles this way, admiring the configurations of hummocks and rivulets underfoot with glistens of ice between, and bits of bright blue sky visible over the next rise. Eventually we will come out on the other side.

What is waiting on the other side? Maybe nothing special, maybe only more of the same, dear enough for this watcher. But the quest is real. To get there you have to go in deep.

Russell Banks

_____

IN THE PEMIGEWASSET

1. *Bondcliffs*

Stalking the railroad bed
sunk into the riverbank
            three miles,
            to where the river forks and the railbed
dribbles onto shiny black mulch
below thin prisms of birch,

holding tautly
to the compass—

            although the land
sloughs rockily off now
            as if following
            arcs and wobbles
            of yearlong sun—

to the Bondcliff trail,
            dry sluice of rocks
            bear-sized
            where the brook
            once ran down
            from the cliffs,

I climb back up
            filled with my own weight
            and moving it loosely from side
            to side, like light in a lantern
            and slabbing towards the top.

2. Mt. Bond

The cliffs are soft hummocks
from the top.
A snooze, some scruffy blueberries,
and out and down
    the ridge to Mt. Bond,
    where the tracks
    of a deer
    dot the trail.
  Too high for deer.
I follow deertracks over
and down from the mountain,
leave them when I leave the trail
for the shelter, where the first things
I see
are a nuthatch and a mouse.
Then the East, shaded,
    falling down and away,
    fifty miles.

3. South Twin

Above tree-line on Guyot

by eight o'clock, threading soundlessly
among planes of light
shattered by huge cobbles,

I cruise

the ridge, jog piecemeal west
into slow manes of wind,

drop into crouched pine
and descend to the gap.

Then—climbing again—
the rasp of my breath
comes back, and resting halfway, I listen

to my body's noises—lungs stiffening with chilled air,
heart warmly churning, blood squishing
past cocked ear.

Just before
I make the top, a bomber
from Pease

and across the sky,
east to west,
a roaring gush of noise loyally following
behind, still roaring

when the plane has disappeared
near the western horizon,

then dwindling to a narrow corridor of sound

as I scramble
to the top of South Twin
and full-faced, dump myself into the wind.

4. *Galehead, and the Falls*

As if the moutain were a metaphor,

from South Twin you can see
Canada and Massachusetts by turning your back
from one to the other.

Clattering down to Galehead,
            a clump
of cleared moraine that falls between

South Twin and the Franconia Range
  like a pause,
I eat lunch on the sunnyside porch
of the boarded-up cabin— crackers
and peanutbutter, sardines, cup of cold water.
No fire. Sun humming through high, dry air.
Mountains hunkered up behind me.
  In front, the Pemigewasset sliding out
  and away from Galehead,
  a thick, rolling lawn
  of conifers.

Then I descend again, walking heavily downhill
into the woods, moving fast and clumsy
like a cricket,
   and do not see the sky
until I reach the Falls
and crawl out onto the backs of a roaring
herd of water-pounded grey rocks

and lie there
in the sun and endless noise,
the tough, moss-backed hides of the rocks
tensing gently motionless
beneath me.

5. *East Branch*

From the Falls, I walk the river down
to East Branch. Five or six miles
through new spruce to birch,
   south by the compass
   on the sinking railbed,
yet keeping to the riverbank just the same.
East Branch is where
yesterday
I left the railbed for Bondcliffs.

I glance around for tracks.
A ranger with a Polaroid camera is waiting
at the shelter.
            "Friday night this one's

jammed.   First one from the road,
you know."   Alternatives are beginning
to pile up.
            I walk a half-mile back
towards the Falls and camp there.
A small fire, beef stew, cup of tea.
Sleep comes quickly, is broken late
when I wake from dreams to voices
that speak my own language and float to me
through spruce trees
on slow winds.
            The people have come in
from the road. I will pass them
tomorrow when I leave.

Ray Kass
White Mountains Drawings

Henry David Thoreau

When we got to the camp, the canoe was taken out and turned over, and a log laid across it to prevent its being blown away. The Indian cut some large logs of damp and rotten hard wood to smoulder and keep fire through the night. The trout was fried for supper. Our tent was of thin cotton cloth and quite small, forming with the ground a triangular prism closed at the rear end, six feet long, seven wide, and four high, so that we could barely sit up in the middle. It required two forked stakes, a smooth ridge-pole, and a dozen or more pins to pitch it. It kept off dew and wind, and an ordinary rain, and answered our purpose well enough. We reclined within it till bedtime, each with his baggage at his head, or else sat about the fire, having hung our wet clothes on a pole before the fire for the night.

As we sat there, just before night, looking out through the dusky wood, the Indian heard a noise which he said was made by a snake. He imitated it at my request, making a low whistling note,—note,—*pheet—pheet*,—two or three times repeated, somewhat like the peep of the hylodes, but not so loud. In answer to my inquiries, he said that he had never seen them while making it, but going to the spot he finds the snake. This, he said on another occasion, was a sign of rain. When I had selected this place for our camp, he had remarked that there were snakes there,—he saw them. But they won't do any hurt, I said. "O no," he answered, "just as you say, it makes no difference to me."

He lay on the right side of the tent, because, as he said, he was partly deaf in one ear, and he wanted to lie with his good ear up. As we lay there, he inquired if I ever heard "Indian sing." I replied that I had not often, and asked him if he would not favor us with a song. He readily assented, and lying on his back, with his blanket wrapped around him, he commenced a slow, somewhat nasal, yet musical chant, in his own language, which probably was taught his tribe long ago by the Catholic missionaries. He translated it to us, sentence by sentence, afterward, wishing to see if we could remember it. It proved to be a very simple religious exercise or hymn, the burden of which was, that there was only one God who ruled all the world. This was hammered (or sung) out very thin, so that some stanzas wellnigh meant nothing at all, merely keeping up the idea. He then said that he would sing us a Latin song; but we did not detect any

Latin, only one or two Greek words in it,—the rest may have been Latin with the Indian pronunciation.

His singing carried me back to the period of the discovery of America, to San Salvador and the Incas, when Europeans first encountered the simple faith of the Indian. There was, indeed, a beautiful simplicity about it; nothing of the dark and savage, only the mild and infantile. The sentiments of humility and reverence chiefly were expressed.

It was a dense and damp spruce and fir wood in which we lay, and, except for our fire, perfectly dark; and when I awoke in the night, I either heard an owl from deeper in the forest behind us, or a loon from a distance over the lake. Getting up some time after midnight to collect the scattered brands together, while my companions were sound asleep, I observed, partly in the fire, which had ceased to blaze, a perfectly regular elliptical ring of light, about five inches in its shortest diameter, six or seven in its longer, and from one eighth to one quarter of an inch wide. It was fully as bright as the fire, but not reddish or scarlet like a coal, but a white and slumbering light, like the glowworm's. I could tell it from the fire only by its whiteness. I saw at once that it must be phosphorescent wood, which I had so often heard of, but never chanced to see. Putting my finger on it, with a little hesitation, I found that it was a piece of dead moosewood (*Acer striatum*) which the Indian had cut off in a slanting direction the evening before. Using my knife, I discovered that the light proceeded from that portion of the sap-wood immediately under the bark, and thus presented a regular ring at the end, which, indeed, appeared raised above the level of the wood, and when I pared off the bark and cut into the sap, it was all aglow along the log. I was surprised to find the wood quite hard and apparently sound, though probably decay had commenced in the sap, and I cut out some little triangular chips, and placing them in the hollow of my hand, carried them into the camp, waked my companion, and showed them to him. They lit up the inside of my hand, revealing the lines and wrinkles, and appearing exactly like coals of fire raised to a white heat, and I saw at once how, probably, the Indian jugglers had imposed on their people and on travellers, pretending to hold coals of fire in their mouths.

I also noticed that part of a decayed stump within four or five feet of the fire, an inch wide and six inches long, soft and shaking wood, shone with equal brightness.

I neglected to ascertain whether our fire had anything to do with this, but the previous day's rain and long-continued wet weather undoubtedly had.

I was exceedingly interested by this phenomenon, and already felt paid for my journey. It could hardly have thrilled me more if it had taken the form of letters, or of the human face. If I had met with this ring of light while groping in this forest alone, away from any fire, I should have been still more surprised. I little thought that there was such a light shining in the darkness of the wilderness for me.

The next day the Indian told me their name for this light,—*Artoosoqu'*,—and on my inquiring concerning the will-o'-the-wisp, and the like phenomena, he said that his "folks" sometimes saw fires passing along at various heights, even as high as the trees, and making a noise. I was prepared after this to hear of the most startling and unimagined phenomena witnessed by "his folks," they are abroad at all hours and seasons in scenes so unfrequented by white men. Nature must have made a thousand revelations to them which are still secrets to us.

I did not regret my not having seen this before, since I now saw it under circumstances so favorable. I was in just the frame of mind to see something wonderful, and this was a phenomenon adequate to my circumstances and expectation, and it put me on the alert to see more like it. I exulted like "a pagan suckled in a creed" that had never been worn at all, but was brandnew, and adequate to the occasion. I let science slide, and rejoiced in that light as if it had been a fellow-creature. I saw that it was excellent, and was very glad to know that it was so cheap. A scientific *explanation*, as it is called, would have been altogether out of place there. That is for pale daylight. Science with its retorts would have put me to sleep; it was the opportunity to be ignorant that I improved. It suggested to me that there was something to be seen if one had eyes. It made a believer of me more than before. I believed that the woods were not tenantless, but choke-full of honest spirits as good as myself any day,—not an empty chamber, in which chemistry was left to work alone, but an inhabited house,—and for a few moments I enjoyed fellowship with them. Your so-called wise man goes trying to persuade himself that there is no entity there but himself and his traps, but it is a great deal easier to believe the truth. It suggested, too, that the same experience always gives birth to the same sort of belief or religion. One revelation has been made to the Indian, another to the white man. I have much to learn of the Indian, nothing of the missionary. I am not sure but all that would tempt me to teach the Indian my religion would be his promise to teach me *his*. Long enough I had heard of irrelevant things; now at length I was glad to make acquaintance with the light that dwells in rotten wood. Where is all your knowledge gone to? It evaporates completely, for it has no depth.

I kept those little chips and wet them again the next night, but they emitted no light.

William Carpenter

CALIFORNIA

I think of the California poets,
how easy it is for them.
They have vast open spaces,
they drive jeeps and live nowhere,
they drift from cabin to cabin
on mountains with beautiful Spanish names
and there are girls in the cabins
who love poetry and sleep with the poets freely,
for in California there is no guilt nor shame
nor hunger, life is as a dream,
lobsters crawl up on the shore to be caught,
they shoot seabirds and fry them in butter on the beach.

There are no seasons in California.
You make your own, you move from
places where the sun shines all the time
to places where it rains or snows forever.
If you want June or October or some cross-country skiing,
you go to that place in your jeep
and the season is there always.

It is a good climate for poetry, since it is full
of images. You pluck them from the trees like breadfruit
with your feet or knock them down like coconuts.
It is good also for religion, as the Three Winds
bring secret doctrines from the East,
sesnsual and voluptuous names for the emotions,
creeds that make holy your underground desires,
your daily habits and the parts of your body.

In New England we scratch in the soil with sticks,
find scarce turnips among the rocks,
have no religion at all, fence out our neighbors,
wear clothes, work hard, abstain from sex
and write poems, when we do, on the way to the madhouse.

I spent some time in Midwest, where they
were neither wholly free nor wholly tragic.
They lived, screwed, married, divorced and died
like regular folk. They grew corn and fed it to
their pigs, then shipped them east and west
for slaughter. It made sense.
When I am finished with this rocky ground,
wet weather and neurotic ocean,
I will become a Baptist in Des Moines,
rise early and drive out to the river
to watch the fall migrations.
I will take photographs and keep
a family album, with no poems, for poems,
Maine or California, drive you crazy.

Wesley McNair

WHERE I LIVE

You will come into an antique town
whose houses move apart
as if you'd interrupted
a private discussion. This is the place
you must pass through to get there.
Imagining lives tucked in
like china plates, continue driving.
Beyond the landscaped streets,
beyond the last Colonial gas station
and unsolved by zoning,
is a road. It will take you
to old famhouses and trees
with car-tire swings.
Signs will announce hairdressing
and nightcrawlers.
The timothy grass will run beside you
all the way to where I live.

Contributors' Notes

Bob Arnold was born in the Berkshire Hills and for many years has made a home with his family in the hills of southern Vermont. A stonemason and builder, he is the author of both poetry and prose books including On Stone, Where Rivers Meet, American Train Letters and Once In Vermont. A new long poem, "Yokel," is in the works.

Russell Banks' most recent works of fiction are Cloudsplitter and The Angel on the Roof: New and Selected Stories (both from HarperCollins). He is the president of the International Parliament of Writers and lives in upstate New York.

Kate Barnes lives on a farm in coastal Maine. Her books of poetry include Crossing the Field and Where the Deer Were. She was Maine's first Poet Laureate.

Pat Barnes, a native of Boston, has lived in Claremont, California, for many years with her late husband, the poet Dick Barnes, their kids, snakes, dogs, cats, birds and desert tortoises. She can be found photographing stone walls in Ireland and New Hampshire, or sacred images in Italy, France and Pakistan. Her photographs have appeared on cards, CD covers and book jackets, most recently on Donald Hall's The Painted Bed.

Michael Blaine's poetry and short stories have recently appeared in Comstock Review, G.W. Review, Midwest Poetry Review, Mid-Atlantic Review, and Mid-American Poetry Review. He is the editor of the Delmarva Review, which features writing from the Delaware Eastern Shore. Blaine was born in Oxford, Mississippi in 1968, but grew up on the Eastern Shore. He returned to Oxford to study English at The University of Mississippi and graduated in 1992. Blaine is finishing a Master's Degree in English at Salisbury University in Maryland.

Joseph Bruchac, Abenaki Indian writer and storyteller, lives in Greenfield Center, New York, with his wife Carol in the house where his grandparents raised him. Winner of the Lifetime Achievement Award from the Native Writers Circle of the Americas, his two newest books of poetry, Ndakinna and Above the Line will be published in 2003 by West End Press.

For the past thirty years, DAVID BUDBILL has lived in a remote corner of the mountains of northern Vermont. His most recent CD, SONGS FOR A SUFFERING WORLD, with bassist and multi-instrumentalist, William Parker, and drummer Hamid Drake, is forthcoming early in 2003 on the Boxholder Records label. Budbill's latest book is MOMENT TO MOMENT: POEMS OF A MOUNTAIN RECLUSE (1999, Copper Canyon Press). Garrison Keillor has read frequently from MOMENT TO MOMENT on his National Public Radio program "The Writer's Almanac," and four of the poems are included in Keillor's recent anthology, GOOD POEMS, (Viking Penguin, 2003). Budbill is also the creator and editor of *The Judevine Mountain Emailite: a Cyberzine: an On-Line and On-Going Journal of Politics and Opinion*, which is available on his website at: www.davidbudbill.com.

WILLIAM CARPENTER grew up in Maine. He moved back there from Chicago, hence the envious potshot at west coast lifestyles. He's been living and teaching on the downeast coast ever since, and finally got around to writing about it in THE WOODEN NICKEL. "California" was a mid-seventies response to Gary Snyder's TURTLE ISLAND.

Naturalist-artist DAVID CARROLL is the author-illustrator of three acclaimed natural histories, YEAR OF THE TURTLE, TROUT REFLECTIONS, and SWAMPWALKER'S JOURNAL, (his "wet-sneaker trilogy"). SWAMPWALKER'S JOURNAL was awarded the distinguished John Burroughs Medal for Literature in Nature Writing in 2001. In the same year he received the Tudor Richards Award of the Audobon Society of New Hampshire. In 1999 he received an Environmental Merit Award from the U.S. Environmental Protection Agency. Carroll is an active lecturer and turtle/wetlands preservation advocate. His paintings and drawings have been exhibited at many museums, galleries, and universities. He and his wife, the painter Laurette Carroll, have lived in Warner, New Hampshire since 1969.

GARY CLARK was born and raised in New Haven County, Connecticut. He received a Bachelor of Arts degree in English and Drama from Dartmouth College in 1986, and a Master of Fine Arts degree in poetry from The University of Oregon in 1992. Since the fall of 1993, he has worked at the Vermont Studio Center in Johnson, Vermont, where he lives with his wife and three children.

WALTER CLARK, who co-founded The University of Michigan's New England Literature Program, lives in Hancock, New Hampshire.

WYN COOPER's books include THE COUNTRY OF HERE BELOW, THE WAY BACK, and the chapbook SECRET ADDRESS. His poems have appeared in dozens of magazines including *Poetry, Orion, Ploughshares,* and *Crazyhorse*, as well as in ten anthologies of contemporary poetry. A poem from his first book was turned into Sheryl Crow's Grammy-winning hit song, "All I Wanna Do," in 1993. Cooper has recently written song lyrics that are included in the text of ANYTHING GOES, a novel by Madison Smartt Bell. Bell set Cooper's lyrics to music, and the two recently signed a three-CD deal with Gaff Music. The first CD will be produced by Don Dixon, REM's original producer. Cooper lives in Halifax, Vermont.

CID CORMAN writes a book of poems every day for years now—no vacations.

ALBERT DOLE graduated from Dartmouth with a degree in classics. Instead of continuing study at Cambridge University, he shocked his family by giving up his place to become a carpenter. Since he had seen carpenters rebuild the front steps of the family's house when he was five years old, this is what he has most wanted to do. He came into the trades in the late sixties, when the cultural divide between the "hippy carpenters" and the more conservative contractors was often hostile. Established builders were reluctant to hire him, so he is largely self-taught. His son began working with him at the age of thirteen and is now a full-time carpenter too. In his spare time, Dole plays with his antique Massey-Harris tractor and meets once a month with two other carpenters and a Latin teacher to read Homer in Greek. He and his wife spend as much of the winters as they can in the house they just built in Puerto Rico.

ROBERT DUNN is recovering from a term as Poet Laureate of Portsmouth, New Hampshire.

JOHN ELDER has taught at Middlebury College since 1973 and now holds a split appointment as Stewart Professor of English and Environmental Studies. He is the author most recently of THE FROG RUN, READING THE MOUNTAINS OF HOME and has edited an encyclopedia, AMERICAN NATURE WRITERS, and (with Robert Finch) THE NORTON ANTHOLOGY OF NATURE

WRITING. He lives with his family in Bristol, Vermont.

THEODORE ENSLIN lives in Milbridge, Maine, and is writing sporadically. He has finished most of the work that has seemed important to him for over fifty years. His new book, IN TANDEM, is out from Stop Press (London), and one called NINE is about to appear from NPF. Bob Arnold, at Longhouse Publishing, is planning a little one, A FOLDER FOR L.N., this winter.

DAVID GIANNINI has published twenty-three collections of his poetry, including ANTONIA & CLARA (Adastra Press), KEYS (leave books), OTHERS' LINES (Cityful Press), STEM (White Pine Press) and ARIZONA NOTES (tel-let press). His work appears in national and international anthologies and magazines. He has worked as a gravedigger, bee-keeper, and professor at Williams College, The University of Massachusetts, and Berkshire Community College. He presently works as a psychiatric social worker—case manager at The Northwest Center in Lakeville, Connecticut. He lives in Otis, Massachusetts, with his wife, Pamela.

DONALD HALL has published fifteen books of poems, most recently THE PAINTED BED, which Houghton Mifflin published in April of 2002. His other books of poems include WITHOUT, THE OLD LIFE, THE MUSEUM OF CLEAR IDEAS, OLD AND NEW POEMS, and THE ONE DAY.

MARIE HARRIS is New Hampshire's Poet Laureate. Her most recent book is YOUR SUN MANNY: A PROSE POEM MEMOIR (New Rivers Press). Her children's book—G IS FOR GRANITE: A NEW HAMPSHIRE ALPHABET—is out from Sleeping Bear Press. The poems in this issue are from a sequence titled "Safe Harbor."

GEOF HEWITT's latest book of poems, ONLY WHAT'S IMAGINED, is available at better bookstores, from Amazon.com, or straight from Hewitt himself at P.O. Box 51, Calais, VT, 05648.

BILL HOLSHOUSER is a native of North Carolina and a resident of Cambridge, Massachusetts. His poetry collection, NAKED BREAD, was published in 2001 by Every Other Thursday Press in Cambridge.

DAVID HUDDLE's novel LA TOUR DREAMS OF THE WOLF GIRL appeared in 2002 from Houghton Mifflin. His new collection of poems, GRAYSCALE, is forthcoming from LSU Press in 2004. He teaches at The University of Vermont and the Bread Loaf School of English.

CYNTHIA HUNTINGTON's third book of poems, THE RADIANT, won the Levis Prize and will be published by Four Way Books in April 2003. She directs the Program in Creative Writing at Dartmouth College.

JOHN HYLAND recently completed his Masters in English at The University of Maine. He's edited the *Stolen Island Review* and organized the Maine Poetry & Story Exchange. In 2000 a chapbook of his poetry, titled FOUND IN A RED HAT, hit the scene and soon vanished. His work has appeared in other little magazines.

GREG JOLY is (depending on the weather and the season) a carpenter, mason, letterpress printer, editor, gardener, and sometime poet. He lives with his wife, Mary Diaz, on twenty vertical acres in Jamaica, Vermont, and has developed a covetous eye towards stones, cord wood and certain poems.

RAY KASS is an artist and the founder of The Mountain Lake Workshop, an ongoing series of collaborative and interrelated workshops centered in the environmental, cultural, and community resources of the Appalachian region of southwestern Virginia. An illustrated documentary catalogue, THE MOUNTAIN LAKE WORKSHOP: ARTISTS IN LOCALE (Virginia Commonwealth University, Richmond, 1983), by Dr. Howard Risatti, is available from the V.C.U.'s Anderson Gallery, or by contacting either the Mt. Lake Workshop or raykass.com. Kass' paintings are represented by A.V.C. Contemporary Arts in NYC and the Reynolds Gallery in Richmond, Virginia.

In the late 80s JIM KOLLER began wandering Europe as possible. Much of his recent work has appeared first in French and Italian translation.

MAXINE KUMIN is the author of thirteen books of poems, most recently THE LONG MARRIAGE, CONNECTING THE DOTS, and LOOKING FOR LUCK; a memoir titled INSIDE THE HALO AND BEYOND: ANATOMY OF A RECOVERY; three essay collections; a collection of short stories; four novels; and an animal-rights murder mystery. She has received numerous awards, including the Aiken Taylor Prize, the Poets' Prize, the Ruth E. Lilly Poetry Prize, and the Pulitzer Prize (in 1973) for UP COUNTRY, her fourth book of poems. She served as Consultant in Poetry to the Library of Congress before that post was renamed Poet Laureate of the United States, and as Poet Laureate of New

Hampshire from 1989 to 1994. BRINGING TOGETHER: UNCOLLECTED EARLY POEMS 1958-1988 will be released by Norton in June 2003.

DUDLEY LAUFMAN is 70 years old, was raised in the Boston area, has five children and four grandchildren. He went to agricultural school but has spent most of his time as a musician. He lives now with Jacqueline on the edge of the woods in Canterbury, New Hampshire, and earns his money by playing fiddles for dancing. He has published two trade editions of poems: AN ORCHARD & A GARDEN (William Bauhan Press, 1974) and MOUTH MUSIC (Wind in the Timothy Press, 2001), as well as numerous pamphlets, chapbooks and broadsides. His poems have appeared in *Hanging Loose, American Weave, Abraxas, Prairie Schooner, Red Owl, Lilabulero, Yankee, Wormwood Review* to name a few. He recently became a recipient of the Governor's Award in the Arts Lifetime Achievement Folk Heritage Award for 2001.

DANA LEVIN's first book, IN THE SURGICAL THEATRE, was awarded the 1999 American Poetry Review/Honickman First Book Prize and went on to receive five other prizes. A 1999 National Endowment for the Arts Fellow and 2001 Lannan Residency Fellow, Levin directs the Creative Writing program at The College of Santa Fe.

KRISTEN LINDQUIST is a native of Maine currently residing in Rockland. Her chapbook INVOCATION TO THE BIRDS was published by Oyster River Press in 2001 (in the Walking to Windward series, which also includes chapbooks by fellow contributors Betsy Sholl and Kate Barnes). She received her M.F.A. from The University of Oregon, and for many years was on the administrative staff of the Bread Loaf Writers' Conference.

WESLEY MCNAIR published two books in 2002, a new collection of poems, FIRE (Godine), and a volume of essays about poetry and place in northern New England, MAPPING THE HEART (Carnegie Mellon).

SAM MANHART is a recent graduate of The University of Maine's Master of Arts Program in English. He lives in Orono, Maine, with his wife Emilie and their dog Charlie. An instructor of composition and literature at The University of Maine, Sam has also taught at The University of Michigan's New England Literature Program. His poetry has appeared in *The Stolen Island Review.*

A native of Ruston, Louisiana, CLEOPATRA MATHIS has taught at Dartmouth College since 1982. The most recent of her five books of poems is WHAT TO TIP THE BOATMAN?, which won the Jane Kenyon Prize for Outstanding Book of Poems in 2001.

PETER MONEY's most recent book is FINDING IT: SELECTED POEMS (Mille Grazie Press). His poems have appeared in *The Sun, Talisman, The American Poetry Review, Berkeley Poetry Review, North Dakota Quarterly, The Wallace Stevens Journal, Lift, Compound Eye, Art/Life, Hummingbird, Solo,* on "The Writer's Almanac," and elsewhere. A former student of Allen Ginsberg, his interview with Ginsberg appeared in the 1992 edition of *Provincetown Arts.* "Plume & Clime" is from a long series, *The Mountain,* set in Vermont. "Teakettles, The Moon" first appeared in Peter's first book, THESE ARE MY SHOES. He teaches at the Community College of Vermont, lives with his wife and children at the northern base of Mt. Ascutney.

TERRY OSBORNE is a Senior Lecturer in the English Department and Environmental Studies Program at Dartmouth College. His work has appeared in the *North American Review, Chicago Tribune, Green Mountains Review, Vermont Life,* and *New England Monthly,* among others. His first book, SIGHTLINES: THE VIEW OF A VALLEY THROUGH THE VOICE OF DEPRESSION, from which "Roots of Air" is excerpted, was published in 2001 by Middlebury Press/University Press of New England.

JEAN PEDRICK is the author of WOLF MOON, PRIDE & SPLENDOR, GREENFELLOW, and several chapbooks. Her new book, CATGUT, is out from Salmon Publishing in Ireland. She lives from May to November at Skimmilk Farm in Brentwood, New Hampshire, where she holds a peer workshop, ongoing since 1975. She winters in Boston.

A former English teacher, for the past nineteen years CHARLES PRATT has with his wife owned and operated a small apple orchard in southeastern New Hampshire. His book of poetry, IN THE ORCHARD (Tidal Press), was selected as an American Library Association Notable Book of 1986.

ANINA ROBB is a writer living in the Shenandoah Valley of Virginia with her husband, Rob, and their cat, Little Scoop. She writes educational books and materials for both The Great Source and Scholastic, Inc. Her poems have appeared in a variety of literary journals and in the young adult collection,

Music and Drum. Her work has recently appeared in *Red River Review, Poetry Motel,* and *Milkweed.*

REBECCA RULE is the author of two collections of short fiction, including The Best Revenge (University Press of New England). She has co-authored two how-to books with Susan Wheeler: CREATING THE STORY and TRUE STORIES. Her audio tapes of Yankee humor are PERLEY GETS A DUMPSTICKER, FISHING WITH GEORGE, and MAVIS GOES TO YOGA. Her column on New Hampshire writers, Bookmarks, appears in the *Concord Monitor, Nashua Telegraph, Portsmouth Herald,* and sometimes the *Keene Sentinel.* THE BEST REVENGE was named outstanding work of fiction by the New Hampshire Writers Project.

JIM SCHLEY is an editor, teacher, and theater artist living on a land cooperative in Vermont. His poetry chapbook, ONE ANOTHER, was published in 1999 by Chapiteau Press (www.chapiteau.org). The piece "Firewood" appeared in an earlier version in the forestry magazine *Northern Woodlands.*

ELAINE SEXTON's first book of poems, SLEUTH, will be published by New Issues Press in 2003. Her poems have appeared in numerous journals inlcuding *American Poetry Review, The Christian Science Monitor, 5 AM, Prairie Schooner,* and *Rattapallax.* She lives in New York City and works in magazine publishing.

NEIL SHEPARD has published two books of poetry: SCAVENGING THE COUNTRY FOR A HEARTBEAT (1993) and I'M HERE BECAUSE I LOST MY WAY (1998), both from Mid-List Press. His recent poems appear in *The Paris Review, Ploughshares, Boulevard, Notre Dame Review, Triquarterly, New England Review, Ontario Review,* and elsewhere. He teaches in the B.F.A. Writing Program at Johnson State College and is the editor of *Green Mountains Review.*

JULIA SHIPLEY is interested in practically everything, but especially poetry and farming. She lives in Johnson, Vermont, with her cat and six chickens. "John Says" is an excerpt from a small chapbook of dispatches about dairy farming, funded by a grant from the Vermont Community Foundation.

BETSY SHOLL's most recent book is DON'T EXPLAIN, University of Wisconsin Press. She teaches in the M.F.A. Program of Vermont College and lives in Portland, Maine.

CHARLES SIMIC is a poet, essayist and translator. He teaches American Literature and creative writing at The University of New Hampshire. He has published sixteen collections of poetry, five books of essays, a memoir, and numerous books of translations. He has received many literary awards for his poems and translations, including the Mac Arthur Fellowship and the Pulitzer Prize. NIGHT PICNIC, his new book of poems, was published by Harcourt this year.

JAMES STURM is a cartoonist who lives in Vermont and is the author of THE GOLEM'S MIGHTY SWING.

SUSAN THOMAS has published work recently in *River Styx, Nimrod, Crab Orchard Review,* among others. New work is forthcoming in *Marlboro Review, Mudfish,* and *Cimarron Review.* She has won the Editor's Prize from *The Spoon River Poetry Review,* the *New York Stories* Annual Short Fiction Contest and the Tennessee Writer's Alliance Award for Creative Non-fiction. This year she was nominated for a Pushcart Prize in poetry.

ELIZABETH TIBBETS' manuscript, IN THE WELL, won the Bluestem Poetry Award (Bluestem Press, Emporia State University, Kansas) and will be published in 2003. Her chapbook, PERFECT SELVES, was published by Oyster River Press in 2001 as part of the Walking Windward series. Her poems have appeared, or will appear, in *The American Scholar, The Beloit Poetry Journal, Green Mountains Review, The Laurel Review, Prairie Schooner, The Spoon River Poetry Review,* and others. Her poems were nominated for a Pushcart Prize in 2000 and 2001. She lives in Maine where she works as a nurse.

CHARTER WEEKS is a native New Englander and has lived most of his life in New Hampshire. He has photographed in Europe, Asia, and South America as well as extensively in the U.S. He and his wife live in a 125-acre intentional community founded in the 1970s with thirteen other families. You may view his work at *www.isinglassmarketing.com.*

BARON WORMSER is Poet Laureate of Maine.

AUSABLE PRESS POETRY

C.K. Williams, *Love About Love*

Julianne Buchsbaum, *Slowly, Slowly, Horses*

Steve Orlen, *This Particular Eternity*

James Richardson, *Vectors: Aphorisms & Ten-Second Essays*

William Matthews, *The Satires of Horace* (translation)

Robert Boyers, *A Book of Common Praise* (essays)

Coming in 2003:
Eric Pankey, Adrian Blevins, Khaled Mattawa

SMALL PRESS DISTRIBUTION, 800-869-7553 / www.spdbooks.org
ALSO AVAILABLE AT amazon.com

Ausable Press welcomes unsolicited manuscripts. Before sending one, please visit our web site for our NEW guidelines: www.ausablepress.com, or send a self-addressed stamped envelope to: Ausable Press, 1026 Hurricane Road, Keene NY 12942, or e-mail editor@ausablepress.com.

Established the past 30 years in the backhills of southern Vermont, Longhouse Publishers & Booksellers specializes in all poetries, small press journals, fine first editions, fluffy ephemera, and carpentry, landscaping and dry stone building needs.

Some recent publications from our press include: Maurice Blanchot *The Instant of My Death*, Frank Samperi *The New Heaven Now*, edited by Bob Arnold *A Green Mountain Idyll for Hayden Carruth*, John Phillips *Path*, Cid Corman *Being Saigyo*, Alan Chong *Lau's Booklet* and *Joanne Kyger's Booklet*. Forthcoming: Theodore Enslin *A Folder for L.N.*

**website: www.LonghousePoetry.com
email: poetry@sover.net**

**Longhouse, Publishers & Booksellers
1604 River Road
Guilford, Vermont 05301**

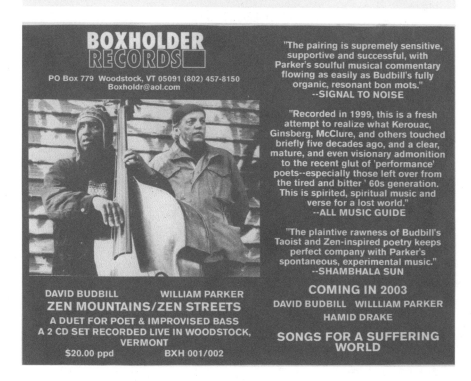

Bread Loaf

Writers' Conference

August 13-24, 2003

Michael Collier, Director
Devon Jersild, Associate Director

Faculty include: David Haward Bain,
Andrea Barrett, Charles Baxter, Linda Bierds,
Maxine Clair, Michael Collier, Cornelius Eady,
Lynn Freed, Linda Gregerson, Patricia Hampl,
Edward Hirsch, Randall Kenan, Margot Livesey,
Thomas Mallon, Cornelia Nixon, Sigrid Nunez,
Peter Turchi, Ellen Bryant Voigt, Dean Young

Special guest: Paula Fox

Financial Aid & Fellowship Deadline: March 1, 2003
General Application Deadline: April 19, 2003
Application materials must be postmarked by the dates above.

To request the 2003 brochure & application:
Bread Loaf Writers' Conference
Middlebury College, Middlebury, VT 05753
E-mail: blwc@middlebury.edu Phone: 802-443-5286
For more information visit www.middlebury.edu/blwc/

"I have sometimes imagined a library, *i.e.* a collection of the works of true poets, philosophers, naturalists, etc., deposited not in a brick and marble edifice in a crowded and dusty city. . . but rather far away in the depths of the primitive forest. . ."
-- Henry David Thoreau, 3 February 1852

The Thoreau Institute at Walden Woods
features the world's foremost collection of Thoreau-related materials,
a spacious reading room, and a variety of educational programs and resources.

Visitors are welcome by appointment to explore all that the Thoreau Institute at
Walden Woods has to offer. For more information, please contact:

Jeffrey S. Cramer, Curator of Collections
781-259-4730 or Jeff.Cramer@walden.org

Jayne Gordon, Education Programs Director
781-259-4712 or Jayne.Gordon@walden.org

www.walden.org

The Thoreau Institute at Walden Woods is a collaboration of
The Walden Woods Project and The Thoreau Society

VERMONT STUDIO CENTER

Four to Twelve Week Residencies
Fiction, Poetry, Nonfiction

VSC Residencies provide uninterrupted writing time within
an international creative community of 16 writers,
16 sculptors, and 32 painters per month.

Writing Residencies feature two Visiting Writers each month.
Visiting Writers give a reading and craft talk and are available
for individual conferences.

**25 Annual Writers' Full Fellowships,
VSC Grants and Work Exchange Aid.**

2003 VISITING WRITERS

Charles Baxter	Rikki Ducornet	Brigit Pegeen Kelly	Gerald Stern
Michelle Cliff	Stephen Dunn	E. Ethelbert Miller	Arthur Sze
Andrei Codrescu	Carol Frost	Carol Moldaw	Alexander Theroux
Robert Creeley	Jane Hamilton	Antonya Nelson	Rosanna Warren
Sharon Doubiago	Rodney Jones	Eric Pankey	Robert Wrigley
Norman Dubie	John Keeble	Michael Ryan	John Yau

VSC WRITERS ADVISORY BOARD:
Saul Bellow, Hayden Carruth, Robert Creeley, Mark Doty, Donald Hall,
Maxine Kumin, Philip Levine, Naomi Shihab Nye, Grace Paley

Next Full Fellowship Deadline: February 15, 2003

For complete information, contact:

**VERMONT STUDIO CENTER
Post Office Box 613, Johnson, Vermont 05656
ph: 802-635-2727 email: writing@vermontstudiocenter.org
fax: 802-635-2730 web: www.vermontstudiocenter.org**

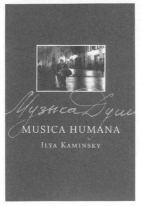

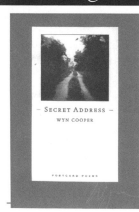

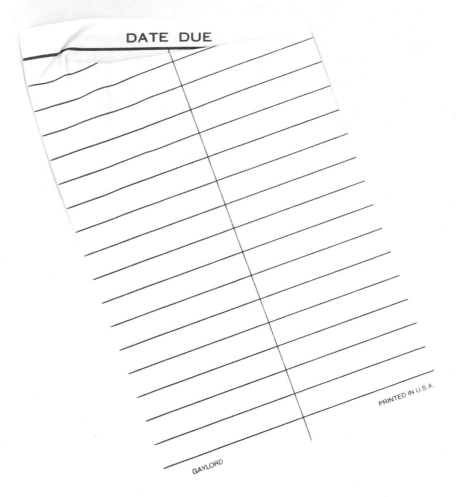

DATE DUE

PRINTED IN U.S.A.

GAYLORD

Acknowledgements

Dana Levin's poem "Quelquechose" first appeared in *Countermeasures*.

Dudley Laufman's pieces come out of Mouth Music (A Wind in the Timothy Book, 2001).

Geof Hewitt's "For Hayden" comes out of Only What's Imgained (The Kumquat Press, 2000).

Bill Holhouser's "Fireweed's Progress" was orignially published in Naked Bread (Every Other Thursday Press, 2001).

Donald Hall's "The Flies" appeared in a different form in Kicking the Leaves (Harper & Row, 1978).

Bob Arnold's Tiny Summer Book was originally published in a run of 100 copies (tel-let press, 1997). "A Line of Talk" appeared in *Coyote's Journal*, 1986.

The excerpt from John Elder's "Starting with the Pslams: A Reader's History" comes out of The Frog Run (Milkweed Editions, 2001).

Terry Osborne's "Root of Air" comes out of his book, Sightlines (University Press of New England, 2001).

The excerpt from Wesley McNair's "The Forest and the Trees" comes from Mapping the Heart (Wesleyan Press, 2002).

David Carroll's "Fishing Until Dark: 29 August" comes out of Trout Reflections (St. Martin's Griffin, 1993).

The quote in Julia Shipley's "Heron, Gnomon" comes from Lucy Lippard's Overlay: Contemporary Art and the Art of Prehistory, (The New Press, 1995).

photograph by Herman P. Bohlman

Coyote's Journal debuted in late 1964 with an issue containing works orginally accepted for publication in the *Northwest Review*, which had been shut down at The University of Oregon over censorship issues. Over the next thirty-plus years, *Coyote* published in periodical form the works of many of the authors who had appeared in *New American Poetry*, 1945-1960, and others who worked in the same vein, and later branched out to include ever-wider regions of the literary and physical world.

Jim Koller